Contemporary Lithic Analysis in the Southeast

A DAN JOSSELYN MEMORIAL PUBLICATION

Contemporary Lithic Analysis in the Southeast

Problems, Solutions, and Interpretations

EDITED BY
PHILIP J. CARR, ANDREW P. BRADBURY,
AND SARAH E. PRICE

The University of Alabama Press

Tuscaloosa

Manufactured in the United States of America

Typeface: Minion

∞

The paper on which this book is printed meets the minimum requirements of American National Standard for Information Sciences—Permanence of Paper for Printed Library Materials, ANSI Z39.48-1984.

Library of Congress Cataloging-in-Publication Data

Contemporary lithic analysis in the Southeast : problems, solutions, and interpretations / edited by Philip J. Carr, Andrew P. Bradbury, and Sarah E. Price.
p. cm.
Includes bibliographical references and index.
ISBN 978-0-8173-5699-6 (quality paper : alk. paper) — ISBN 978-0-8173-8607-8 (ebook)
1. Indians of North America—Implements—Southern States. 2. Indians of North America—Southern States—Antiquities. 3. Paleo-Indians—Southern States. 4. Tools, Prehistoric—Southern States—Analysis. 5. Stone implements—Southern States—Analysis. 6. Southern States—Antiquities. 7. Excavations (Archaeology)—Southern States. I. Carr, Philip J., 1966– II. Bradbury, Andrew P. III. Price, Sarah E.
E78.S65C67 2012
975′.01—dc23
2012000989

Cover image: Sarah Mattics, Staff Archaeologist, Center for Archaeological Studies, University of South Alabama, USA. Cover design: Erin Kirk New

Dedicated to the memory of George H. Odell, in recognition of his significant contributions to archaeology and lithic analysis.

To George—A tell-it-like-it-is lithic analyst with a great sense of humor! Thanks for taking us on the "morphological express" and explaining that "research problems r us."
We will miss our mentor, colleague, and friend.
—PJC and APB

Contents

Illustrations

Figures

Tables

Contemporary Lithic Analysis in the Southeast

1

Lithic Studies in the Southeast

Retrospective and Future Potential

Philip J. Carr, Andrew P. Bradbury, and Sarah E. Price

The southeastern United States, referred to in this volume as the Southeast, has a rich and varied natural landscape. The people who occupied this region for over 10,000 years before European contact were just as culturally rich and variable. One aspect of prehistoric research, often undervalued in the Southeast, is the study of lithic assemblages. More specifically, holistic integrated studies of lithic artifacts that contribute to our understanding of the past are accomplished only rarely. This is despite exemplars of the use of lithic data to provide insights into prehistoric lifeways (e.g., Anderson and Hanson 1988; Daniel 1998; Johnson 2000; Sassaman 1994) and early application of an organization of technology approach in the Southeast (e.g., Amick 1987; Claggett and Cable 1982; Goodyear 1979). Jay Johnson's (1993a:51–52) hopeful discussion concerning the future application of this approach as part of the processual paradigm in which "behavioral models could best be addressed through careful analysis of patterns in stone tool production, use, and discard" largely has remained unrealized.

A decade ago, Carr and Bradbury (2000) examined archaeological studies in the Southeast and found a general lack of lithic data usage. The arguments made for the application of an organization of technology approach 10 years ago remain valid today, as does their discussion of various methods of lithic analysis. There are still too few lithic specialists as practitioners in the region and too few specialized lithic studies (microwear analysis, refitting, minimum analytical nodule analysis), and there is too little concern with method and theory and a general lack of knowledge concerning advances and debates in lithic analysis. These shortcomings have resulted in a deficiency of contributions to lithic analysis in general from the southeastern perspective, a general stagnation of lithic analysis in the region, and a lack of understanding the potential contributions of lithic studies to the goals of archaeology.

With few exceptions, lithic analysis in the Southeast is approached with overly simplistic methods that lead to gross descriptions of assemblages by way of artifact counts and types from which few behavioral inferences can be made. Lithic analysis languished around the mid-twentieth century in the cultural historical paradigm and is too often mired there today. Such a tradition of emphasis on culture history to derive queries about prehistoric life and methods to answer them provides little consideration of cultural lifeways other than simplistic statements regarding stone tool manufacture. In an effort to not "point the finger" at one contemporary study, we refer the reader to the excellent discussion by Johnson (1993a:37–38) of how the typology employed for the Pickwick report resulted in the designation of a "workshop" but no discussion concerning biface production strategies. Similar contemporary statements, based on typologies or methods demonstrated to be flawed, show a lack of middle range theory and evaluation of low-level theory is rare. The use of flawed methods and lack of theory building have resulted in a failure to build accurate culture histories due to naïve definitions of artifact types that do not allow for a distinction between homologous and analogous traits.

Year after year we are discouraged by the number of reports, conference papers, and journal publications either not incorporating lithic data or employing outdated and flawed methods, especially regarding flake debris. For example, issues with the Primary, Secondary, Tertiary method (PST) of flake analysis have been recognized since the 1980s (Ingbar et al. 1989; Magne 1985; Sullivan and Rozen 1985). PST analysis generally involves the assignation of a flake to one of three types based on decreasing amounts of cortex. Inconsistency in its application was heavily criticized by Sullivan and Rozen (1985). Bradbury and Carr (1995) used an experimental data set to demonstrate that employing cortex as the only attribute for assigning a flake to a reduction stage is no better than a random guess.

Unfortunately, this typology is still used today and its use compels us to question the validity of the lithic data. As Sullivan and Rozen (1985) noted, researchers use different definitions of primary, secondary, and tertiary flakes (if definitions are included at all), which makes comparisons across data sets impossible. With no attention paid to such fundamental considerations, why should one think greater care is taken with other aspects of the analysis?

Flawed analytical methods go beyond the lack of a concrete, tested lithics lexicon. Inaccuracies result from the common practice of employing nonstandardized sieves for collecting size grade data and labeling univariate approaches using that data as "mass analysis" (Bradbury and Carr 2009; Carr and Bradbury 2004). Mass analysis, most closely associated with the work of Stan Ahler (1975, 1989a, 1989b), focuses on the size, shape, and cortex characteristics of flake debris aggregates. Flake debris is size graded by individual manipulation through a series of standard geologic sieves of varying mesh sizes. These data often are used in one of two ways: (1) a discriminant function analysis based on experimental data provides a baseline for determining the technological origin of archaeological materials, or (2) general mass analysis trends are used to assess the results of other analytical methods. Andrefsky (2007) strongly criticized the use of the method, and while Bradbury and Carr (2009) agree with some of this critique, they also find utility in the correct application of mass analysis.

Use of the Interpretation Free Method (IFM) is also prevalent due to its supposed simplicity of application, but resulting interpretations are questionable without the development of adequate middle range theory (see discussion in Amick and Mauldin 1989). IFM, originally developed by Sullivan and Rozen (1985), involves individually examining a piece of flake debris using a flow chart involving answering yes/no questions concerning the presence of certain attributes such as a single interior surface (ventral surface) and point of applied force (platform). Differing proportions of the resulting flake types were proposed to correspond to different types of reduction (i.e., core reduction, biface production). A number of researchers have conducted experiments that demonstrate the original propositions do not always hold (see papers in Amick and Mauldin 1989; Bradbury and Carr 1995). Lithic analysts often continue to record "flake portion" following this scheme and use this information in combination with other attributes.

Finally, Individual Flake Analysis (IFA) can be contrasted with aggregate techniques that focus on batches of flakes. Broadly, IFA could refer to any method in which attributes are recorded on individual flakes to categorize that flake, meaning that PST and IFM are forms of IFA. We most often associate IFA with the work of Magne (1985), who advocated using the number of platform facets for complete or platform remnant bearing flakes, or dorsal scars in the case of medial and distal flakes, to assign a flake to one of three reduction stages. While based on experimental work that demonstrates the method is better than a random guess, there is not perfect correspondence between facets/scars and reduction stage. For this reason, some researchers advocate the use of multiple lines of evidence for accurately understanding flake debris assemblages (Bradbury and Carr 1995; Carr and Bradbury 2000; Magne 2001).

Lithic studies in the Southeast focus on morphological descriptions of bifacial tools, with some attention paid to cores, unifaces, and "utilized flakes," which itself is a suspect category (e.g., McBrearty et al. 1998; Odell 1996a:24; Pevny this volume; Young and Bamforth 1990). The lithic assemblage rarely is considered as a whole; potential bias in recovery and classification is ignored; detailed studies of flake debris, such as IFA, are virtually nonexistent; and an overarching theoretical approach is lacking. This slapdash state of lithic analysis is difficult to reconcile with the regular employment of floral and faunal specialists on many projects, who bring the necessary experience to avoid such problems in their areas of interest.

There is certainly some excellent and innovative work conducted in the Southeast employing lithic data (e.g., Bruce 2001; Cobb 2000; Franklin and Simek 2008); however, the predominant state of lithic analysis in the region continues to frustrate us. It is this dissatisfaction with lithic analysis in the Southeast that led to a symposium at the 2009 Southeastern Archaeological Conference that culminated in this volume. The chapters in this volume use data from a wide temporal span (Paleoindian to Late Prehistoric) and a variety of southeastern sites to demonstrate how lithic analysis and integration of lithics into an interpretive framework leads to better archaeology. These chapters demonstrate the potential pitfalls and rewards of conducting lithic analysis. It is clear that traditional recovery and analytical methods are inadequate for attaining the goals of inferring past lifeways and investigating culture change. In equal evidence, a trained individual or team of analysts is best able to recognize the complexities of the natural and cultural formation processes that form a lithic assemblage, devise appropriate research designs, and make significant progress in attaining research goals.

While the case studies discussed in this volume derive from the Southeast and the intent of this volume is to demonstrate potential problems, solutions, and interpretations for archaeologists working in the region, these lessons are applicable on a broader scale. Work involving site formation processes, recovery and analyst bias, and experimentation often are viewed as simple cautionary tales. However, these instructive cases demonstrate the necessity of considerations beyond the bag of lithic material in front of you. Regarding those chapters aimed at specific aspects of prehistoric behavior, similar cases demonstrating the complexity of lithic assemblage formation could be derived from the American Southwest or southwest France. Taken together, the chapters in the volume consider many of the most critical issues in contemporary lithic analysis worldwide and demonstrate useful approaches from a southeastern perspective.

We do not intend to provide an overview of lithic studies (see Odell 2000, 2001 for a relatively recent discussion), rather, we work to place the current volume in the larger context of lithic research. This volume follows a recent trend in Americanist archaeology of an increased rate in publications related to lithic analysis and an increasingly narrow focus of these publications. For evidence, we arbitrarily start with the edited volume published 20 years ago entitled *Experiments in Lithic Technology* (Amick and Mauldin 1989), which was something of a watershed event because of its focus on flake debris. The roots of several of the chapters in the current volume (Bradbury and Carr; Cooper;

Franklin et al.; Potts; Price; Thacker et al.) are found there, and the focus on experimental research design and explicit discussion of that design (Amick et al. 1989) was critical for subsequent work. Next, we offer *Stone Tools: Theoretical Insights into Human Prehistory* (Odell, ed. 1996). While taken to task for not living up to its title (Clark 1999), this volume pushed and pulled at existing concepts prominent in lithic analysis such as tool design and curation, as well as providing case studies highlighting the utility of microwear analysis and refitting. Five years later, the publication of *Lithic Debitage: Context, Form, and Meaning* (Andrefsky, ed. 2001) was significant for bringing attention back to flake debris, an underappreciated and underutilized artifact class. Building on the success of a volume dedicated to lowly lithic debitage, the subsequent publication of *Aggregate Analysis in Chipped Stone* (Hall and Larson 2004) demonstrated further specialization by examining one approach to analyzing flake debris. There are many other edited volumes that could be mentioned and the publication of two "textbooks" to lithic analysis (Andrefsky 1998; Odell 2003) during this time period further illustrates the growing body of literature dedicated to lithics and lithic analysis.

The contributions to the current volume represent something of a mixed bag in terms of time periods, specific geography, artifacts examined, and methods. What holds these essays together is something of a pragmatic approach to lithic assemblages that characterizes much analysis in the Southeast, but they differ by recognizing potential problems and pitfalls with traditional methods and data, as well as offering solutions to problems through case studies that embrace trends in lithic analysis outside of the Southeast. We encourage such a "skeptical" movement (see general discussions by Sagan 1996; Shermer 1999, 2001, 2002, 2005) in Southeast archaeology generally and lithic analysis specifically. As Shermer (2002:16) suggests: "Modern skepticism is embodied in the scientific method, which involves gathering data to test natural explanations for natural phenomena. A claim becomes factual when it is confirmed to such an extent that it would be reasonable to offer temporary agreement. But all facts in science are provisional and subject to challenge, and therefore skepticism is a *method* leading to provisional conclusions" (emphasis in original). The complexity of human behavior, the ambiguities of the archaeological record, and our lack of knowledge demand that archaeologists recognize the provisional nature of their claims, continue to develop robust archaeological method and theory, and proceed in the spirit of skepticism.

We did not ask that the contributors subscribe to a single theoretical approach or that they adopt our specific conception of lithic analysis. However, we were pleased to see convergence in the majority of the contributions with a general approach we would label as the organization of technology, even if not explicitly recognized by each of the authors. We do not wish to put any of the contributors in a theoretical box and recognize some contributors are more closely aligned with other paradigms (see Edmonds this volume) or are actively exploring alternative, but potentially parallel, approaches (see Franklin et al. this volume). Because of the general importance of an organization of technology approach, either implicitly or explicitly, to contributions in this volume, we provide a general discussion of it here, as well as point out specific connections to certain chapters.

The Organization of Technology

The organization of technology is one approach for use in interpretation and integration of prehistoric lithic assemblages. Successes include providing insight into prehistoric human behavior based on the differential use of lithic raw materials, the design of tools from those materials, manufacture stages present/absent in an assemblage, use and reuse of tools, and, to a lesser extent, the discard of tools (e.g., Amick 1999; Andrefsky 1994a; Bleed 1986; Kelly 1988; Shott 1986; see chapters in Andrefsky, ed. 2008; Carr, ed. 1994; Hall and Larson 2004; Johnson and Morrow 1987; Odell, ed. 1996; Torrence 1989).

The organization of technology is rooted in processual archaeology and the work of Lewis Binford (e.g., 1977, 1978, 1979, 1980, 1982). Robert Kelly (1988: 717) offered an early influential definition of the organization of technology as "the spatial and temporal juxtapositions of the manufacture of different stone tools within a cultural system, their use, reuse, and discard, and their relation not only to tool function and raw material type and distribution, but also to behavioral variables which mediate the spatial and temporal relationships among activity, manufacturing, and raw material type loci." Margaret Nelson (1991) provided her own, similar, definition and made the organization of technology more explicit and easier to operationalize by outlining levels of analysis. In Figure 1.1, we offer a version of Nelson's (1991:fig. 2.1) framework modified so that it captures elements of both definitions and makes more explicit the relationships between levels.

As with the original, "environment" heads the framework as the context in which technology needs to be effective and responsive. It is important to note that there are more direct means of reconstructing past environments than lithic studies and this allows lithic analysts to focus on other levels. However, lithic analysts minimally must have an understanding of the raw material environment in order to apply this approach effectively, which is an important theme throughout the current volume. Distinguishing local and nonlocal raw materials and understanding the size, shape, and quality of specific materials (see Cooper; Edmonds; Franklin et al.; Potts; Thacker et al., this volume) are

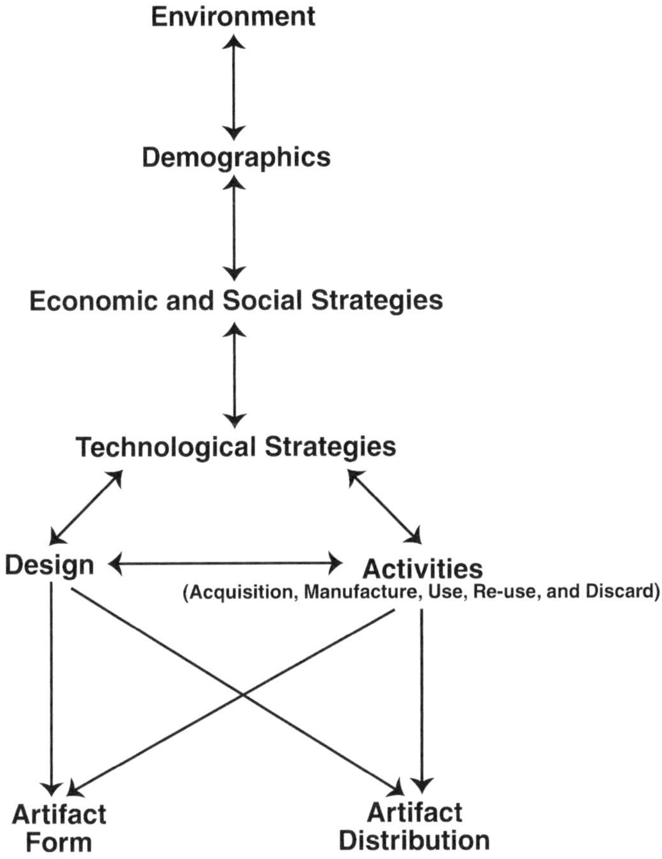

Figure 1.1. Expanded model of an organization of technology approach (after Nelson 1991:fig. 2.1).

all of critical importance for effectively using an organization of technology approach.

In our modified diagram, we have added "demographics" below "environment." The interaction of humans and the environment is a long-standing theme in anthropology. Population density is considered by some as a "prime mover" with regard to cultural change (e.g., Cohen 1985; Keeley 1988). Here, it is recognized that the number of stone tools found on the landscape and the forms of these tools are both impacted, if indirectly, by the number of people on that landscape. This is not to say that numbers of hafted bifaces or counts of flake debris are a direct indicator of population size. Through a complex web of other factors, demographics impact the formation of a lithic assemblage.

The next tier is "economic and social strategies"; prehistoric peoples employ these strategies within an environment such that their technology fulfills the demands of adaptation or they do not survive. As part of social and economic strategies, technology is responsive to kinship, politics, and religion, as well as the more regularly investigated subsistence and settlement patterns. In the modified version, the relationship between environment, demographics, and economic and social strategies is bidirectional in order to recognize that people not only adapt to an environment but also impact it and that population size dictates to some extent the strategies of adaptation employed. For example, the complete exhaustion of a quarry area is an impact to the environment by a population engaging in an intense exploitive strategy of a local area. Such two-way relationships are a key difference between Nelson's original framework and our revised version.

The fourth tier is "technological strategies," which again can affect, and be affected by, economic and social strategies. Technological strategies traditionally considered are curated and expedient. To these Nelson (1991:62) added opportunistic. The rationalization behind the bidirectional relationship with economic and social strategies is that new technologies, realized through diffusion or independent invention, will influence or revolutionize economic and social strategies (e.g., Price and Brown 1985:fig. 1.1). For example, the initial use of the bow and arrow certainly impacted subsistence/hunting methods and social strategies as evidenced by warfare (e.g., Blitz 1988; Bradbury 1997; Shott 1993, 1996c).

The fifth tier is composed of two separate, but related, aspects, "design" and "activities." Activities that pertain specifically to tool life history are included in our diagram to better aid in its operationalization for lithic analysis. Chapters in this volume by Miller and Smallwood, Pevny, and Sain and Goodyear closely relate to activities such as stone tool production and use. We recognize that many other categories of activities result from implementing economic and social strategies. Design includes considerations of whether tools are manufactured to be reliable or maintainable. In our framework, the relationship between design and activities is recognized. This is necessary because tool design is implemented through the specific aspects of activities outlined here, such as the manufacture of a reliable tool, which involves acquiring raw material of a certain quality, investing skill in its manufacture so parts are well fitted, and so on.

The bottom tier, made up of "artifact form" and "artifact distribution" as separate categories, derives from "design" and "activities," not simply from one or the other as originally indicated in Nelson's diagram. For example, the acquisition of raw materials impacts not only the distribution of artifacts but also the forms those artifacts can take. One cannot manufacture a classic Clovis using tiny quartz pebbles, which were heavily utilized in south Alabama for certain arrow points (see Potts this volume). Consider further how artifact form is responsive to activities because of the impact of use and reuse. Consider the final form of a stone tool broken during use, resharpened, and broken again. For example, Goodyear's (1974) classic study of various Dalton types demonstrated these types were the result of use and resharpening and not stylistic traditions. It is also easy to see how design impacts artifact form, as originally proposed by Nelson, and also distribution or, more generally, lithic assemblage composition. If expedient flake tools are preferred, the resultant flake debris and core forms would differ significantly from an assemblage resulting from the design and manufacture of a biface as a curated tool. Chapters in this volume by Edmonds and Price address the issue of artifact distribution in terms of what we often fail to recover in archaeological excavations.

We encourage lithic analysts in the Southeast to apply this model of the organization of technology in the analysis of lithic assemblages. In this way, the analysis of an assemblage is tied specifically to behavioral aspects of interest. Additionally, application will reveal strengths and weaknesses of the approach and encourage its continued expansion and revision. We have only begun the difficult, but rewarding, process of modeling lithic assemblage formation using an organization of technology approach, which involves developing theory broadly and at all levels (see Schiffer 1988 and discussion in Carr and Bradbury 2010). The goal of investigating prehistoric human behavior is difficult to achieve due to the complexity of that behavior and lithic assemblages being an imperfect reflection of those behaviors. In our view, application of the presented model allows us to best take advantage of lithic assemblages in understanding that complexity.

Contributions to This Volume

The chapters within this volume examine a number of important topics in lithic analysis but are not comprehensive in this respect. While we targeted several individuals and are pleased to include essays that together encompass all levels of archaeological theory and method, the list of participants grew somewhat organically as we networked to find lithic analysts with relevant research. The theme of demonstrating the potential of a quality lithic analysis for contributing to the larger goals of archaeology through case studies unites these essays.

Bias in classification is the subject of several chapters in this volume. Price examines how the size of screens used for field recovery affects the interpretation of lithic assemblages. She finds that the use of smaller screens increases not only the amount of flake debris from a site but also the amount of data for making behavioral inferences. Specifically, smaller screen size allows for the collection of late-stage tool production and tool maintenance debris, which is commonly missed using traditional methods, having important ramifications for site interpretation. Screen size is also a concern for Edmonds. In this case specifically, raw material data are lost by using larger screen sizes. Exotic materials at the Cork site were represented more highly in the smaller size grades and may not have been recovered had traditional 6.35-mm (.25-inch) screen been used for data recovery. Bias as related to taphonomic issues and microwear analysis are the subject of the chapter by Pevny. Traditionally, the bias has been to interpret any evidence of "wear" as human use. Several taphonomic processes can mimic culturally produced use wear and without this recognition traditional analyses are biased in identifying cultural agents as perpetrators, which leads to spurious inferences of prehistoric behavior. Distinguishing between taphonomic and cultural wear is critical for understanding stone tool use at any site.

Analyst bias and solutions continue as a major theme in several additional chapters. The concern addressed by Potts is the classification of quartz debris, which is common on many sites in the Southeast. Potts found discrepancies in the results of blind tests between several experienced analysts when examining quartz that were not apparent in these analysts' work with other raw material, such as chert. This finding guided the method she selected for the analysis of the archaeological assemblage in question. Bradbury and Carr attempt to reconcile differing conceptions of flake types through time by different analysts, specifically with regard to identifying blades and bipolar cores and flakes. Bradbury and Carr bemoan the various terms related to blades and bipolar cores/flakes and call for the strict use of specific definitions in lithic analysis. They suggest that a blade industry may not be present in Early Archaic assemblages and that the use of bipolar knapping during this time period likely is due to the small package size of raw materials. Toward this end, Sain and Goodyear provide a detailed study of blades from two Clovis components in South Carolina and sites in the surrounding area. With the development of a novel measure, blade score, to sort technological blades from blade-like flakes, their work demonstrates that blade manufacture was different at these sites from Clovis blade manufacture in the Southwest and Mid-South. Further, regional variation in the location of blade use is suggestive of a logistical mobility pattern.

A wide variety of case studies serve as exemplars for the organization of technology. The most common approach is to examine the lithic assemblage from a site or a number of sites in a region and make inferences regarding lithic assemblage formation based on a consideration of raw material distribution and patterning in the lithic assemblage. This approach is taken by several chapters in this volume. Miller and Smallwood examine bifaces from the Clovis component at the Topper site. They devise a biface thinning index and use this index to demonstrate that biface reduction is modeled better as a continuum than as stages. They find that different portions of this continuum are present in distinct areas of the Topper site. Cooper examines raw material distribution and differences between the Terminal Archaic and early Fort Ancient components at the Elk Fork site. He relates these differences to the mobility of the two groups. Thacker and colleagues examine lithic materials from a site in the Uwharrie Mountains of North Carolina. They conclude that differences in lithic assemblage composition between various components relate to how stone was being used at the site: during the Middle Archaic, individuals were being provisioned with stone, while later occupations were provisioning the place.

The chapter by Franklin and colleagues brings us back to a more general discussion of technological organization. There has been an ongoing debate between Old and New World archaeologists concerning the best approach to lithic analysis and whether significant differences exist between *chaîne opératoire* and the organization of technology. This conduct of New World archaeology by individuals with training on both sides of the Atlantic demonstrates the complementary nature of approaches, if not complete correspondence, and the fruitfulness of being aware of approaches and advances outside your geographic region of expertise. We hope to see lithic analysts in the Southeast who are as comfortable citing André Leroi-Gourhan and Jacques Tixier as they are Lewis Binford and Don Crabtree, as well as more recent researchers. This detailed study, employing multiple lines of evidence, demonstrates that a small rockshelter was not the traditionally inferred special-purpose activity site but rather a repeatedly occupied, residential base camp.

A coup perhaps recognized only by the session participants is the contributions of two well-respected voices in lithic analysis, William Andrefsky and George Odell. Though neither is from the Southeast or currently practices archaeology in the region, we felt their inclusion was vital. One intention of this volume is to show how approaches, methods, and ideas developed outside the Southeast are applicable here. The "outsider's perspective" of two people who have literally written the most recent textbooks on lithic analysis provides greater context for the case studies presented, as well as pointing to potential future trends in lithic analysis.

Conclusions

This volume provides a range of case studies that demonstrate that there are problems with gathering and using lithic data but, with attention to appropriate levels of theory and considerations of bias, that such problems are not insurmountable. The chapters here serve as exemplars of the kinds of research necessary for archaeologists to realize the potential of lithic data and provide a more complete view of the past. This is not an attempt to argue that lithic data are the most important data source available to archaeologists but simply to point out that in much current reporting of archaeological work the lithic assemblage is assumed to have little to no utility and the methods employed fulfill this expectation. In order to break out of this cycle, lithic analysis must be treated as a specialization alongside paleoethnobotany and zooarchaeology. The usefulness of such specialists is demonstrated well by the essays in this volume and we look forward to the findings of the next generation of lithic specialists.

Acknowledgments

We would like to thank each of the contributors to this volume for their participation and for allowing us to review their work here. It is fulfilling to expand our ideas concerning the use of an organization of technology approach. Conversations with Bob Kelly, Mike Shott, Peggy Nelson, Bill Andrefsky, and George Odell, and their published research over the years, have had a major impact on our thinking. Comments by Jay Johnson and an anonymous reviewer helped us frame our discussions. Any blunders, mistakes, or oversights are ours alone.

2

Omnipresent?

We Don't Recover the Half of It!

Sarah E. Price

A statement celebrating or proudly noting the ubiquity of lithic artifacts is the most common opening sentence to papers, books, and journal articles about this artifact class (e.g., Andrefsky 2009; Bradbury and Carr 2004a; Brown 2001; Cahen et al. 1979; Henry and Odell 1989; Larson and Kornfeld 1997; Odell, ed. 1996). These opening statements are misleading because the sheer size of many assemblages is daunting to many archaeologists. Interestingly, ubiquity creates a bias resulting in reduced recovery and employment of minimal analytical techniques. With regard to the latter, little more than handy measures of quantification are used, especially for debitage.

The conduct of lithic analysis, or botanical or faunal for that matter, is extremely time consuming and this is true for simply rough sorting and counting copious amounts of remains. Unfortunately (or fortunately) for paleobotanists and zooarchaeologists, rocks *are* more ubiquitous and better preserved in most cases. But what are we missing? What if lithics are more prolific than most site reports state? What could we learn from a more complete recovery and analysis of lithic artifacts? This chapter explores the actual ubiquity of lithic debitage and the research potential of these disenfranchised members of the lithic family for understanding the past.

Sifting Away the Evidence

Standard survey methods in the Southeast typically require the use of 6.35-mm (¼-inch) mesh for screening shovel test fill, and most Phase II testing standards require a minimum of 6.35-mm mesh as well. This is all well and good for determining the presence of most prehistoric activities and identifying a location for further investigation. Although recovery methods vary from state to state, there is not a standard requirement for the recovery of small artifact types at any phase of work. Oftentimes, small-mesh screens are used when artifacts such as historic trade beads are expected or when specific research questions are to be addressed, such as subsistence, which necessitates the use of fine screening or collection of special samples. This begs the question as to what lithics are missed due to the blanket use of standard recovery techniques. Here, several avenues of inquiry are employed to explore this question. First, archaeological data are reviewed to demonstrate the disparities in artifact recovery when utilizing different sampling and field methods. Next, experimental data are assessed to determine how much and what sizes of debitage are generated when making stone tools. The experimental data are then in turn used to demonstrate what is being left behind in the field. Finally, the potential of sampling strategies and research methods employed for efficient recovery and analysis of small lithic artifacts is explored.

The Real World—Ideal

It should come as no surprise to any archaeologist who has worked on a prehistoric site that flake debris routinely is lost when using 6.35-mm screen mesh. The following cases are used to provide quantification to this generalization. Three sites (1RU142, 22LI504, and 1CK56), varying greatly in terms of setting, assemblage composition, and type of occupation, provide examples of how small lithic artifacts augmented site interpretations. Depending on the assemblage, all or a sample of the debitage was subjected to any number of analytical techniques, but most often aggregate and individual flake analysis (following Bradbury and Carr 1995; Carr and Bradbury 2000). All lithic artifacts were size graded by hand manipulation through a series of nested, standard geological sieves graded in ⅛-inch increments: 25.4 mm (1 inch), 22.23 mm (⅞ inch), 19.05 mm (¾ inch), 15.87 mm (⅝ inch), 12.7 mm (½ inch), 9.52 mm (⅜ inch), 6.35 mm (¼ inch), 3.17 mm (⅛ inch), and 1.58 mm (1⁄16 inch).

Site 1RU142 is an example of how small lithic debris contributed to understanding site formation processes and prehistoric behavior (Price 2008). This site is located in sandy upland soils in eastern Alabama with no locally available knappable rock. The site was recommended for Phase II testing not because of high artifact counts or visible midden, but rather due to artifact recovery from at least 80 cm below the surface (based on one shovel test; Brooms 1992). The site was not delineated during the Phase I survey. Phase II testing began with close-interval (10-m) shovel testing using 6.35-mm mesh screen. Positive shovel tests yielded an average of 2.5 lithic artifacts, with a range of 1 to 7, for a total of 15 pottery sherds and 67 lithic artifacts.

Reflecting on these data and considering this site in the overall context of Phase I survey provides an interesting insight. If Phase I shovel testing had been conducted at 30-m intervals, there would have been only eight total tests, and only five positive, significantly reducing the artifact density. There were no diagnostics recovered in any of these shovel tests, and no visible midden. Would this site routinely receive a recommendation for Phase II testing? How many "lithic scatters" are determined ineligible for listing on the National Register of Historic Places (NRHP) during Phase I survey for these reasons? Like it or not, the number of recovered artifacts and artifact density play a critical role in site evaluation.

Phase II test units were screened with 3.17-mm mesh and artifact density rose to 57 lithic artifacts per square meter and a few diagnostics were recovered: still not particularly impressive. Despite a low artifact density, the site was determined eligible for listing on the NRHP and mitigation was recommended (Carr 2004). Fortunately, the potential of the lithic assemblage was recognized and 1.58-mm mesh was recommended in the Phase III research design. This resulted in a total of 27,334 lithic artifacts from Phase III units, 87 percent of which are smaller than 6.35 mm. Considering that charred wood and very fragmented calcined bone are the only subsistence remains, and 563 pottery sherds were recovered (or one sherd for every 49 lithic artifacts), you may be wondering what we were able to learn from this site and how the recovery of so many small lithic artifacts (<6.35 mm, n = 23,683) contributed to interpretations.

The smaller than 6.35-mm lithic assemblage significantly influenced interpretations regarding raw material acquisition and use, as well as how these changed through time at 1RU142. The lack of locally available knappable stone in this region meant that inhabitants discarded nonlocal materials over the course of several thousand years of occupation. Many of the materials were only recovered in the smaller than 6.35-mm size grades. We would not have been able to accurately document the range of raw materials exploited and how they were being reduced without the complete range of size grades. Because of the use of 1.58-mm mesh, we were able to determine that the use of some raw materials was consistent through time, while others increased and decreased across occupations. The small size grade data were informative about the types of activities taking place on site and about intensity of occupations. Little core and early reduction was occurring on site and a significant amount of final tool production and recycling was taking place through time, resulting in a large amount of debitage.

Since there was no visible midden and there were deeply buried deposits, how site 1RU142 formed was a central research question. The small lithic artifacts provided supplemental data to the soils analysis. Small lithic data showed that there was not a significant amount of vertical movement of artifacts, and that the vertical profile was more intact than previously thought. The greater than 6.35-mm flake proportions by levels indicated several occupations. Since small artifacts move vertically through a profile more often than large artifacts (Peacock and Fant 2002), a comparison of the small artifacts reinforced the distribution of the large artifacts, indicating that there was not a significant amount of vertical disturbance at the site.

The second example is a very different archaeological site, which also differs significantly in recovery methods. Site 22LI504 includes occupations from the Middle Archaic to Late Woodland and is located adjacent to dense gravel bars composed mainly of Citronelle formation chert (Peacock et al. 2010; Underwood et al. 2007). Phase II testing was conducted with 6.35-mm mesh and yielded 10,858 pieces of debitage, of which 13 percent (n = 1,379) are 3.17-mm incidental recovery. Incidental recovery refers to artifacts of a size that would normally pass through the screen employed in the field but are present due to any number of factors and represent unsystematic recovery. The total number of lithic artifacts other than debitage from Phase II units in the Archaic midden is 1,756, of which 28 percent (n = 493) are 3.17 mm. Phase III testing using 1.58-mm mesh screen excluded the Archaic midden, which was the densest deposit in terms of lithic artifacts. Phase III units in Midden B (Late Woodland midden) yielded 67,393 pieces of debitage, 87 percent of which are smaller than 6.35 mm.

If these numbers are any indicator, the Phase II assemblage could have been 72,915 just in debitage with the use of 1.58-mm mesh. Perhaps more important, the recovery of an Archaic stone-bead industry, which includes very small drill tips and bases, would have been exponentially larger. Twelve percent (n = 13 of 104) of the drill tips and bases incidentally recovered from the Phase II test units in the Archaic midden are smaller than 6.35 mm, a similar proportion to the debitage recovery. Johnson (2000:table 3) provides metric attributes for drill bits from Watson Break, all of which (n = 154) are smaller than 6.35 mm.

While the recovery of the small flakes did not alter the conclusions about raw material use, it was critical for accurately assessing the amount of final tool production and rejuvenation taking place at this site. It was not simply a quarry site, a stopover to acquire new material, but a location where people acquired raw material, manufactured, and used stone tools and beads.

A third example is 1CK56, a Late Woodland site with local but limited types of raw materials available in the general vicinity (Price 2010). All Phase III units were screened through 1.58-mm mesh, but as of this writing the 1.58-mm debitage has not been analyzed. Even so, 3.17-mm artifacts account for 68 percent of the analyzed assemblage, and the inclusion of the 1.58-mm debitage will no doubt increase the assemblage exponentially. Significantly, almost 20 percent of the bifacial tool fragments are smaller than 6.35 mm, and these fragments contributed extensively to the interpretation of use and discard behavior at the site. Almost all of the hafted bifaces exhibiting impact failures are smaller than 6.35 mm. Since this type of artifact is an indicator of on-site hunting and processing, it is important to note that the evidence was recovered because small-mesh screens were used.

A Minimum Analytical Nodule Analysis (MANA) of an isolated midden deposit at 1CK56 was completed. Using Tallahatta sandstone bifaces as a starting point, nine individual raw material nodules were identified. Of the 359 Tallahatta sandstone flakes recovered from the provenience, 244 were attributed to one of nine nodules, of which 59 percent are 3.17 mm, clearly demonstrating the importance of this size grade in the analysis and interpretation of the reduction activities that took place in this area. The four biface fragments recovered were early-stage production failures. The recovery and analysis of the 3.17-mm debitage from other nodules was the only indicator of successful bifacial tool production from Tallahatta sandstone.

These three sites demonstrate that using smaller than 6.35-mm screen results in a significant increase of lithic assemblages and better interpretations. Rightly or wrongly, artifact density plays a role in arguments of significance particularly when making a case for Phase II testing. Not only are more artifacts recovered, but more information is obtained regarding raw material choice (see Edmonds this volume), production, use, and discard.

The Real World—Actual

High numbers of incidentally recovered flakes, as with 22LI504, are present in several assemblages from sites screened with 6.35-mm mesh during Phase II fieldwork. This is not necessarily surprising considering that Carr and Bradbury (2004:28) found that 6.35-mm (¼-inch) hardware cloth typically has openings smaller than ¼ inch. The amount of less than 6.35-mm recovery appears to vary by field technician with some more thoroughly working unit fill through the screen than others.

Site 1MG910, a rockshelter with knappable materials nearby, had an artifact density of 146 per square meter. The incidentally recovered less than 6.35-mm artifacts account for 34 percent of the assemblage. If we use previously discussed values as estimates, the recovered assemblage accounts for only 13 percent of the total potential assemblage. Expected activities, such as core reduction and early tool production, are overrepresented when the incidental artifacts are excluded from the analysis. Raw materials not available in the immediate vicinity are underrepresented or not present when incidentally recovered artifacts are excluded. Undoubtedly, systematic recovery of lithics less than 6.35 mm would have significantly altered interpretations. At present, only informed speculation is possible as to what debitage types are missing, as well as which more rare artifacts such as biface tips from impact fractures and drill tips.

In another case, Phase II testing of 20 sites in Florida, all at varying distances from raw material sources, was carried out mainly with 6.35-mm screen. The exceptions are three sites at which 1.58-mm mesh was employed due to the anticipated presence of historic trade beads. At these sites, units were not systematically screened with 1.58-mm screen, making it impossible to estimate the total assemblage size. The average incidental 3.17-mm lithics recovered from all 20 sites account for 34 percent of the total recovered lithics, with a range of 14 to 69 percent. Perhaps most surprising was that the third-highest percentage of small lithics recovered (50 percent of the total assemblage) was not from one of the sites selected for screening with 1.58-mm mesh. A significant number of biface fragments, representing impact fractures, was incidentally recovered (n = 74), of which 9 percent are smaller than 6.35 mm.

One of the Florida sites, 8TA452, is interpreted as a quarry, due to exposed chert at the surface and a lithic artifact assemblage composed of 74-percent early-stage reduction debris. This lithic assemblage includes 30-percent incidentally recovered 3.17-mm debitage. Individual Flake Analysis (IFA) indicates that the 3.17-mm material is from tool not core reduction, demonstrating that there were other activities taking place on the site in addition to raw material acquisition. This is important as no tools were recovered from test units. The smaller size grade flakes allowed insights beyond the typical site type label of quarry.

These examples illustrate interpretations of site function are greatly enhanced if smaller lithic artifacts are recovered. Regardless of site function or proximity to raw materials, small lithic artifacts are present. Whether a quarry or logistical campsite, types of activities are reflected in the lithic artifact assemblage. An important facet in the investigation of lithic technologies is how and where particular segments of reduction took place. If people were acquiring raw materials as well as fashioning complete tools at a raw material source, then our understanding of land use is enhanced. Lithic analysts will not be successful at achieving lofty goals of investigating social and economic strategies (Carr et al. this volume) if they cannot make accurate statements concerning activities conducted in the past.

Experimental Excess

Experimental data can add perspective and aid in identifying patterning in lithic assemblages. Experiments provide a means of linking observed patterns in an archaeological assemblage to prehistoric behavior. All of the experiments discussed here were conducted for a variety of projects with different research questions. For the experiments in which I was involved, knapping was conducted over a dropcloth and all flakes were collected from each reduction episode and bagged in sequence as they were removed. The type of percussor used and the goal of the removal were recorded for each flake removal. After each change in percussor, a mass collection of the lithic "dust" from the dropcloth was made.

In the first set of experiments, 18 bifaces were manufactured from small, fist-size Citronelle gravels by Andrew Bradbury. The assemblage included 563 3.17-mm flakes, or 42 percent of the analyzed experimental assemblage (the 1.58-mm material was only quantified by weight due to the goals of the original project). Without the smaller than 6.35-mm material, or if an assemblage lacked finished tools (i.e., lithic scatter), the amount of final tool reduction and retouch would be underrepresented.

Similarly, two stone bead blank manufacturing experiments using Citronelle gravel cobbles (out of 20, only two attempts were successfully completed) produced totals of 391 and 402 flakes, respectively. Of these, an average of 72 percent of the debitage was 1.58 mm, and 21 percent was 3.17 mm. Bead production would most likely be spatially segregated and using standard 6.35-mm recovery methods, 93 percent of the lithic debitage produced from this activity would be left behind. While we are unsure at this time whether flake debris from bead manufacture is in fact distinctive compared to that of tool manufacture, limited recovery surely makes this more difficult, or impossible, to ascertain.

In another set of experiments, six Bangor chert flake blanks were reduced to finished bifaces and yielded a total flake assemblage of 6,475 flakes. All of the flakes designated as late tool production debris are smaller than 6.35 mm. Further, only 13 percent (n = 851) of this assemblage would be recovered using 6.35-mm screen. The 6.35-mm and larger debris does not indicate a focus on tool production, but rather early-stage reduction. If those finished bifaces were transported off the site after completion, the significant amount of tool finishing that took place on site would be missed.

Finally, a number of core and biface reductions were conducted using Coastal Plain chert from Alabama. Core reduction experiments resulted in a total of 2,036 flakes, 94 percent (n = 1,194) of which were smaller than 6.35 mm. Two biface reductions from resultant flake blanks produced 1,162 flakes, of which 97 percent (3.17 mm = 210; 1.58 mm = 916) were smaller than 6.35 mm. Just the two biface reductions alone resulted in an assemblage larger than many site's entire lithic assemblage, but only when the smaller than 6.35-mm lithics are included.

These experiments confirm the tremendous amount of small-sized flake debris produced from minimal knapping episodes. Clearly all reduction types can produce small flake debris and late-stage tool production results in copious amounts. Percentages of core reduction versus tool production are standard in the "Results" section of a lithic analysis report. The trustworthiness of such data is questionable if 6.35-mm mesh was used in the field. If we are interested in the range and intensity of production activities at a site, then standardized collection of small flake debris is necessary to recover this portion of the reduction sequence.

Experimental data in the archaeological literature that include 3.17-mm or smaller debitage are rare, although those available studies lend support to the ubiquity and potential of small flake debris. Thirty "medium sized dart points" were produced in a set of experiments that started with "preforms" that were then used and rejuvenated, resulting in an experimental assemblage of 4,221 flakes (Towner and Warburton 1990:318). Of those, 98 percent of production and 99 percent of rejuvenation flakes were smaller than 6.35 mm. Stahle and Dunn (1982) reported that 70 percent of the debitage from 12 biface experiments was smaller than 3.17 mm. Ahler (1989b:92–93) provided data for both core and biface experiments in which an average of 81 percent of size-graded flakes were 3.17 mm; unfortunately he did not report 1.58-mm debitage. Baumler and Downum's (1989:table 1) experiments showed that out of 22 scraper production experiments seven exclusively yielded smaller than 6.35-mm debitage, and for the remaining 15 experiments 97 percent of the debitage was smaller than 6.35 mm.

Essentially, we are missing minimally 60 percent and potentially 99 percent of most lithic assemblages due to the prevalent use of 6.35-mm screens for field recovery. The need to use small-mesh screens to obtain accurate faunal samples was recognized by at least 1969, as it dramatically affects interpretations of subsistence strategies (Thomas 1969). The same is true for interpretations generated from lithic artifacts.

Ubiquity Redux

To further the case for recovery of small lithics, and delving even smaller, there is the issue of microdebitage. There is not a clear definition of what constitutes microdebitage. Surprisingly, some researchers consider flake debris smaller than a quarter inch as microdebitage. Nadel (2001) is even more extreme and defines microdebitage as flakes smaller than 1 cm. At the other extreme, Hull (1987:772) defines microartifacts as those smaller than 1 mm and Sherwood et al. (1995:429) as "sand-sized particles less than 2 mm." While defining microartifact ranges based on project goals is appropriate, a standard definition would aid in comparability, especially between experimental and archaeological data. Regardless of definition, there are numerous studies on the usefulness of microdebitage in interpreting occupations of sites (e.g., Hull 1987; Nadel 2001; Peacock and Fant 2002; Sherwood et al. 1995), although there are few published experimental data. The value of microdebitage stems from its relative immunity to reuse, curation, cleaning activities, biased collection techniques or analysis, and postdepositional processes.

Fladmark (1982:207) reported from six bifacial experiments that 99.5 percent of the debitage produced (no total provided) was between .063 and 1 mm, 1 mm being the maximum size of his microdebitage. Nadel (2001) did not perform experiments, but in his recovered assemblage the 16,500 macroartifacts contrasted with the 34,000 microartifacts indicates that potential microassemblages following a 2-mm or less size grade are enormous. Fladmark (1982:207) states, "It is bothersome to note that over 99 percent numerically of all particles produced by lithic reduction have routinely been missed by standard archaeological recovery techniques." Not only is this "bothersome," but it undermines the science of archaeology.

Microdebitage sampling and analysis demonstrates that very small samples are sufficient for obtaining data necessary to test a range of questions. Nadel (2001) used 5-g samples from different areas of the site investigated and obtained results comparable with those of more comprehensive samples. The argument against sampling for microartifacts is most often the processing time. Microdebitage sampling and analysis clearly is appropriate when questions concerning site formation processes or site activities are to be addressed. It is simple to collect the samples while in the field and then make a determination of subsequent disposition. The fact that this is not common procedure or required in state fieldwork standards demonstrates a lack of awareness of the contribution of microartifacts for making interpretations of the past.

Bias, Bias Everywhere

Too often, archaeologists excavate a site that will be completely destroyed. Rarely is there an opportunity to preserve even a portion of a site for future work. The data and samples collected at the time of excavation are all we will have in perpetuity. While a particular project may not have the funds for analyzing small-sized flake debris and a particular researcher may not have the inclination, the lack of recovery hampers future work and interpretations.

There are two issues that should be addressed at all stages of an archaeological project: sampling bias and observer bias. Unsystematic, subjective sampling leads to questionable conclusions. It should be emphasized that unsystematic sampling using 3.17-mm or 1.58-mm screens is of limited utility. By not collecting samples from every unit excavated on a site, collection bias is introduced as many lithic activities are spatially segregated. If screening all unit and/or feature fill through smaller mesh is not feasible, then systematic column samples or some method of standardized collections should be made from stratigraphically meaningful units from all areas excavated.

In the event of small-screen recovery, appropriate sampling strategies in the lab are of even greater importance since a complete analysis is typically not feasible. It is erroneous to simply analyze lithics from feature contexts and ignore midden deposits, or vice versa. Since lithic analysis is based on understanding the amount of variability within an assemblage, it is important to recognize and mitigate variation introduced by sampling and observer bias.

As an example, Roth (2009) examined laboratory sampling and its effect on site interpretations in addition to interobserver bias. An initial sample of 20 percent (n = 487) of a site's debitage was analyzed, and later it became possible to analyze the entire (n = 2,306) lithic assemblage (Roth 2009:17). The final conclusions and interpretations did not vary significantly from the initial sample results, which Roth attributes to recorder bias rather than sampling bias. Roth conducted the initial analysis, but then used students to analyze the entire assemblage under her supervision. She argues that certain flake attributes were more subject to erroneous classification and therefore affected the interpretations between the sample and the full analysis. This raises a host of issues but certainly points to the importance of adequate sampling and reliable, valid methods of analysis because conclusions in this case are based on potentially spurious data.

Another interesting case study concerning bias was conducted by Dibble et al. (2005) in which the effects of excavator bias, collections management, and analyst bias on interpretations were examined by comparing newly excavated and analyzed data to those from original 1970s investigations. They found that although there were major inconsistencies between collectors in the field, and gaps in the documentation, they were able to recognize and overcome (in many cases) these biases and make use of most of the 1970s data sets. They did find that because of inconsistencies between observers that site interpretations were skewed. It is interesting to note that when they rescreened the backfill from the previous excavations they found that although the original excavators did not use screens there was very little bias introduced. Only "31 pieces larger than 2.5 cm in maximum size" were found in the screened backfill and the backfill "mostly contained objects less than 5 mm in size" (¼ inch or smaller) and they concluded the lack of screening did not bias the collection in the field (Dibble et al. 2005:322). After the previously presented experimental and archaeological data, it would seem that this was indeed a source of bias introduced in the field collection both in the original and more recent excavations.

In yet another case, Milne (2009:58) found that a 20-percent sample was not representative of the entire lithic assemblage, even though the entire assemblage exhibited a low level of variability. Artifact attributes that were statistically different included size grades, dorsal scar counts, cortex, and stages of reduction, which all significantly affected the site interpretations. Milne provides a useful method for determining adequate sample sizes based on the individual assemblage that also generates data for aggregate analysis. His sampling technique creates a situation in which multiple lines of data are generated and a statistically viable sample is analyzed.

The use of appropriate sampling strategies is just as important as recovery methods when conducting lithic analysis, and maybe even more so when recovery includes small artifacts. If you are increasing the amount of material recovered, sampling becomes even more important. A 20-percent sample is often the "rule of thumb," but Milne (2009) makes an excellent case for sampling based on the individual assemblage.

Interpretative Powers of the Very Small

As discussed here and by Edmonds (this volume), nonlocal raw materials are often more numerous in small size grades than local materials. Phase III mitigations at two coastal Alabama sites, where the nearest knappable stone is over 200 km away, would have had negligible counts of lithic artifacts with the exception of the 3.17-mm and 1.58-mm data (Price 2008, 2009). These size grades demonstrated that the inhabitants obtained raw materials from a number of sources, not just "local" sources.

The same is true for the previously discussed 1RU142 assemblage, in which over 90 percent of all the raw material types were present only in the smaller than 6.35-mm size grades. The presence/absence of raw materials affects interpretations concerning movement of people across the landscape and prehistoric exchange. As an example, the difference between the presence of 38 Knox chert flakes (9.52 mm and 6.35 mm) and 236 (smaller than 6.35 mm) is of importance. Considering that no chipped stone tools of Knox chert were recovered, the debitage was the only line of evidence for the presence and use of Knox chert at the site, and the presence of the small-sized pieces indicated that there was a significant amount of reworking of Knox tools on site.

There are difficulties in assigning small-sized flake debris to a specific raw material type. However, in some cases certain raw materials are distinctive at the 1.58-mm size grade, such as Tallahatta sandstone common to southern Alabama and Mississippi. In other cases, the specific raw material may not be distinctive to type, but to a region. The geological origins of many Ridge and Valley cherts likely preclude assignment to specific types such as Bangor and Tuscumbia cherts at the 3.17-mm and 1.58-mm size, but quantification of general geological origin might be as informative. Raw material identification in all cases is best guided by overall familiarity, an extensive type collection, and access to a knowledgeable geologist or other regional expert (see Carr and Stewart 2004). In analyzing lithic data, it has been repeatedly demonstrated that some raw materials, especially extralocal materials, are most abundant in small size grades, so being able to say that there are nonlocal materials present in the small lithics that are not in the macroassemblage is just as important as being able to identify them to a specific outcrop or formation.

Although size grade is not necessarily a direct correlation between debitage and the type of activity that produced it, it is relatively accurate to say that most pressure flakes are smaller than 6.35 mm. Patterson (1990:553) examined this exact relationship but did not include flakes smaller than 10 mm^2 because "recovery of flakes of sizes less than 10 mm^2 is usually poor in archaeological investigations, especially because 6-mm (¼-inch) mesh screens are commonly used." This exclusion seems to be completely contradictory to all experiments and data available at that time! Along this line, Carr and Bradbury (2004) excluded debitage smaller than 6.35 mm from their discussion of mass analysis since standard field recovery methods do not systematically recover this size grade. However, they do recognize that the exclusion "potentially provide[s] skewed data" since "eight of the 20 small tool experiments did not produce any flakes greater than ¼ inch in size" (Carr and Bradbury 2004:27). If we do not develop data sets that include counts for small size grades, we cannot know the information potential. These authors do advocate the recovery and study of smaller than 6.35-mm mesh material in regard to identifying and understanding late-stage reduction (Carr and Bradbury 2004:42) and this is supported by Towner and Warburton's (1990) data, as well as the experiments discussed here.

Finally, Ahler's (1989b) summary data indicate that 3.17-mm flakes account for 94 percent of all debitage produced during pressure flaking. Since these flakes are typically indicative of late-stage tool reduction and rejuvenation, one can only begin to imagine the implications for assemblage and site interpretations. All of the so-called lithic scatters might tell a different story if those sites were investigated using small-mesh screens.

The integration of smaller than 6.35-mm debitage in interpretations is perhaps most relevant in the various forms of aggregate or mass analysis, one of the most widely employed debitage analytical techniques (Hall and Larson 2004). The technological inferences made using aggregate analysis will be conditioned by the smaller size grade data when available and utilized. The statement "all lithic manufacture produces large quantities of small-sized debitage, but not all lithic reduction produces large debitage" (Baumler and Davis 2004:54) is well supported by the data presented and reviewed here.

Regardless of theoretical orientation method(s) used for flake debris analysis, small size grade data can be very informative. Individual Flake Analysis might not be particularly useful since the attributes used to assign flakes to a reduction stage (i.e., facet or dorsal scar count) might be difficult to accurately record on small flake debris. Further, the same patterning may not hold; you can only have so many flake scars on a 3.17-mm piece of debitage. In fact, Magne (1985) used 5 mm as his minimum flake size cutoff when counting facets and dorsal scars. Although not a method I regularly employ, a flake morphology classification might be more appropriate for these size grades. The amount of shatter in small size grades versus other types of flakes can be informative as to the type of reduction taking place on site (e.g., the quarry site example previously discussed). Flake type analysis should be informed by experimental data since material type can affect the proportions of shatter to flakes regardless of reduction technique.

Another analytical technique that is underutilized in the Southeast in general that can be greatly enhanced by the recovery and analysis of small debitage is MANA. As demonstrated by the example from 1CK56 discussed here as well as in work by Baumler and Davis (2004) and Bruce (2001), 3.17-mm debitage contributed significantly to MANA studies. Baumler and Davis' (2004:table 3.1) inclusion of small size grade debitage increased the data set for their MANA 900 percent. The key to these analyses was the selection of appropriate contexts. The same could be said for refitting, also woefully underutilized in the Southeast (see Franklin and Simek 2008 for a discussion). There are insufficient data on refitting involving small size grade data to discuss here, but their inclusion should be explored if refitting is undertaken.

Importantly, it is not only flake debris that is missed. Based on data reviewed here, an average of 10 percent of bifacial tool fragments are smaller than 6.35 mm, and these mainly represent use-related failures such as impact fractures and haft snaps. Small tools and tool fragments are just as important in inferring the types of activities that took place at a particular location in prehistory as complete and large tool fragments. These tool fragments are almost always missed by lab technicians completing an initial sort and are only recognized during detailed flake debris analysis.

Finally, small-sized lithics contribute more broadly than explicating technology and lithic-related activities. Site integrity is a cornerstone of significance and small lithics have the potential to contribute extensively to understanding site formation processes and the effects of cultural and postdepositional processes. Relative proportions of size-graded artifacts must include smaller than 6.35-mm data to examine vertical artifact movement (e.g., Peacock and Fant 2002). As demonstrated by many, microdebitage is less susceptible to movement due to human actions, recycling, and any number of other forces that render other artifact classes of little use in assessing integrity (Behm 1983;

Healdan 1995). Researchers have demonstrated success in using simple calculations of small debitage to determine areas of primary (i.e., flintknapping) and secondary (i.e., refuse disposal) deposition and site organization (Baumler and Davis 2004; Sherwood et al. 1995).

Implications

With this wide-ranging and expansive presentation of archaeological and experimental data and discussion of small-sized lithics, I am not advocating that every Phase I survey be conducted with 1.58-mm mesh screen. Rather, each survey tract and site should be evaluated with this information in mind and appropriate strategies developed. For many situations, use of 3.17-mm screen for survey may not significantly add to field time. With so much emphasis on density and diagnostics, it is no wonder that the "lithic scatter" has been relegated to the insignificant column in state site file databases. Although this bias has been recognized and the research potential of lithic scatters has been documented by Austin (2001) and various papers in Rieth (2008), not a single researcher calls for revising recovery methods to include small size grade debitage. Further, not all sites need to include microdebitage sampling, but rather appropriate sampled contexts might reveal information about spatial patterning of activities at a site (sensu Sherwood et al. 1995).

On the other hand, I do advocate Phase II testing be conducted with 3.17-mm screens: at this point in an archaeological investigation it is "do or die" for a site, and all possible information should be systematically collected. Casting a "smaller" net provides the necessary information to make informed decisions. In Phase III mitigations, all attempts should be made to collect appropriate data for realizing the significance of the site. If lithics contribute to answering questions of significance, then 1.58-mm mesh should be employed and standardized microartifact samples collected.

As culture resource managers, our job is to excavate, process, analyze, and curate information about the past within the constraints of (often inadequate) budgets and deadlines. We are constantly making judgments about the value of artifacts and their information potential in the field and lab. There is a bias in general against debitage and smaller lithics specifically that stems from the belief that they are not worth the time, effort, and money for recovery and analysis. A conversation with an archaeologist at the Poverty Point site revealed that visiting researchers complained if asked to use small mesh sizes, even if to simply recover small artifacts, not analyze them (Greenlee, personal communication 2009). It would seem that we should recognize that a site that is considered a national treasure deserves the best recovery techniques, regardless of research interests.

The bias against small lithics is perpetuated by not generating and including experimental data to demonstrate their utility. When these sizes are recovered, the abundance ensures they are not included in any significant way to further interpretations. This bias could be mediated by awareness of data potential, appropriate research designs, and sampling strategies. Bias can be introduced at any level of an archaeological investigation, but if you begin with biased field data it will persist throughout the subsequent stages of analysis and interpretation. Inferences about prehistoric activities and behavior are only as good as the information that is collected and analyzed. If we continue on the current path of recovery, the evidence for many aspects of prehistoric lifeways will continue to reside in the backfill.

Acknowledgments

I would like to thank Phil Carr and Andrew Bradbury for allowing me to be a part of a valuable learning experience. Much gratitude to Phil, Andrew, George Odell, William Andrefsky, Jay Johnson, and the anonymous reviewer for comments, advice, and edits to this chapter. Any errors are my sole responsibility.

3

Beyond Stages

Modeling Clovis Biface Production at the Topper Site, South Carolina

D. Shane Miller and Ashley M. Smallwood

In the late eighteenth century, William Henry Holmes (1894) introduced the concept of "stages of production" in the manufacture of stone tools. While the theoretical landscape has changed drastically in the past century, lithic analysts have continued to use this methodological construct (Bleed 2001, 2002), particularly in the southeastern United States (Carr and Bradbury 2000:125–126). Specifically, many studies of lithic technology, especially those geared toward the analysis of Paleoindian biface technology, have a tendency to view the lithic reduction process as occurring as a series of sequential stages proceeding toward an ideal form, a fluted point ready to be hafted (Callahan 1979; Morrow 1996; Sanders 1990; Whittaker 1994). However, in recent years many have argued for an alternative approach that views stone tool production as a continuous process (Amick 1985; Bleed 2002; Bradbury and Carr 1999; Carr and Bradbury 2000; Ingbar et al. 1989; Johnson 1989; Shott 1996a; Wilson and Andrefsky 2008). In this chapter, we attempt to identify evidence for discrete stages in the production of Paleoindian Clovis type bifaces from the Topper site (38AL23), a prehistoric chert quarry in Allendale County, South Carolina. We argue, as have others, that sequential stages may be arbitrary stops in what might otherwise be modeled as a continuous process. To illustrate this point, we conduct both technological and spatial analyses of a sample of Clovis bifaces, bifacial fragments, and overshot flakes. Our results indicate that biface production was technologically a continuous process consisting of multiple reduction trajectories. However, the result of our spatial analysis indicates that biface production was segmented across space, such that it may have been a staged process, which is different from previous models of Clovis biface manufacture. Finally, we discuss how analyses of biface production based on continuous variables, as opposed to stages, can be integrated with studies of cultural transmission and the organization of technology.

Stage Approaches to Analyzing Eastern Fluted Points

Callahan's (1979, 1991) model for reconstructing stages in the production of Clovis points remains one of the most regularly applied constructs for analyzing eastern Paleoindian fluted points. Based on extensive experimental reproduction and analysis of bifaces from the Williamson and Flint Run sites in Virginia, Callahan (1979:30) identified nine stages of biface reduction beginning with initial procurement of raw material to the production of a finished biface (Stage 1, Obtaining the Blank; Stage 2, Initial Edging; Stage 3, Primary Thinning; Stage 4, Secondary Thinning; Stage 5, Shaping; Stage 6, Fluting the First Face; Stage 7, Preparing the Second Flute; Stage 8, Fluting the Second Face; Stage 9, Retouching). He utilized both continuous metric variables (e.g., width-to-thickness ratio, edge angles) and nominal attributes (e.g., nature of the cross section). He also incorporated a series of continuous, yet subjective, classifications that he subdivided categorically. Some of these attributes are "nature of flake scars," "degree of regularity of outline," and "degree of trim." This approach has been widely utilized (and modified) in the 30 years since its inception, perhaps most notably in Sanders' (1990) analysis of the Adams site in western Kentucky and Morrow's (1995, 1996) examination of biface technology at the Ready-Lincoln Hills site in Illinois. However, both Sanders and Morrow noted variation in the production trajectories that could not be adequately described using a strict interpretation of Callahan's stage classifications. In order to examine variation both between and within assemblages, they were forced to create additional stage categories to account for nuances in production. This methodological technique is similar to Bleed's (2002) use of an "event tree" method for distinguishing differences in prismatic blade technology. In other words, these studies illustrate that the only way to address variation using a categorical framework is to create more categories.

As an alternative perspective, some studies have suggested that the initial stages of fluted biface manufacture proceeded in a nonlinear fashion, wherein edging, thinning, and shaping co-occur (Bradley 1974; Frison and Bradley 1980). Moreover, other analysts have attempted to define stages by analyzing debitage from both archaeological and experimental contexts (Bradbury and Carr 1999; Ingbar et al. 1989; Shott 1996a) and have argued that lithic reduction is better modeled as a continuum. In particular, Shott (1996a) analyzed the debitage from the reproduction of a Gainey type Paleoindian biface and found no evidence for discrete stages. Instead, Shott argued that the variables he examined (i.e., platform width, flake weight, and dorsal scar density) predicted the order of flake removal. More recently, Wilson and Andrefsky (2008) examined retouch from both the production and the subsequent use of three experimentally made bifaces and found these modes of reduction could be modeled using continuous variables. Furthermore, they argue that the transition from hard-hammer to soft-hammer percussion may also be apparent from their experimental reproductions. However, this represents one of the only visible transition points that can be derived from their experiments, although they do not describe these as stages.

In this chapter, we adopt the analytical position that Shott (1996a:6) advocates: "There is no doubt that qualitative changes may occur in reduction (e.g., with a change in hammer or a shift from core to flake reduction), or that stages may exist; they probably do in some cases. But we should evaluate this view, not assume it *a priori.* As the starting point in any reduction analysis, we should entertain the null hypothesis that reduction can be modeled as a continuous process." In other words, we seek to determine whether there is evidence for the kind of reduction stages previously described for Clovis biface production in the eastern United States (i.e., Callahan 1979; Morrow 1996; Sanders 1990) in the biface assemblage from the Topper site. Additionally, following Bleed (2001), we attempt to discern whether the process of making bifaces at the Topper site is teleological or evolutionary; that is, does it appear that there was an adherence to a uniform design or is there evidence for multiple reduction trajectories in the process of making Clovis bifaces.

The Topper Site (38AL23)

The Topper site is a prehistoric chert quarry that was discovered as part of a survey of property belonging to the Clariant (formerly Sandos) Corporation (Goodyear and Charles 1984). The site has been extensively excavated in the past decade and has a known area of 578 m^2. Buried, intact Clovis deposits have been excavated from three distinct areas of the site. The first is a Pleistocene age alluvial terrace adjacent to a chute-channel of the Savannah River, where the artifacts have been buried by a combination of both alluvial and colluvial processes (Goodyear and Steffy 2003; Waters et al. 2009). The second area, known as the Hillside, is a gradual escarpment where the majority of the tertiary-aged chert source outcrops. The most recent excavations have been conducted (Goodyear et al. 2007) in a portion of the Coastal Plain uplands.

While the artifacts located on the Hillside and in the uplands are buried at depths over 70 cm in most places, the process responsible for their burial is currently unknown. Miller (2007) analyzed a 64-m^2 block excavation from the Hillside to examine the effects of postdepositional processes. He found a vertically discrete deposit of artifacts containing diagnostic Clovis artifacts including fluted preforms, prismatic blades, and blade cores. All temporally diagnostic artifacts dating to later time periods were found stratigraphically superior to this deposit, and 97 percent of the pottery assemblage is found in the plow zone levels or the levels immediately below it. These findings, in conjunction with an analysis of the refitted artifacts, indicate only minimal vertical displacement of artifacts and the presence of a stratigraphically discrete Clovis component.

The sample of bifaces (n = 147) used in the technological analysis comes from proveniences designated as part of the Clovis component (Goodyear et al. 2007; Goodyear and Steffy 2003; Miller 2007) and displays attributes consistent with Clovis technology (Callahan 1979; Howard 1990). In particular, the samples used in this analysis come from 64-m^2 (Block A) and 32-m^2 (Block B) excavation blocks removed during the 2004–2008 field seasons. Both blocks were removed in 5-cm excavation levels and screened through 3.17-mm (.125-inch) mesh. Additionally, artifacts larger than 5 cm were piece-plotted, either manually or using a total station transit.

Methods

In addition to nominal attributes, traditional staging models utilize metric ratios such as maximum width to maximum thickness to model the reduction process (Callahan 1979:30–31). With this in mind, we measured length, width, and thickness, and calculated maximum width to thickness ratios for our sample of 147 bifaces. However, over 70 percent of the original sample was too fragmented to ascertain maximum length, width, and thickness. As a result, the use of stage designations relied heavily on the lithic analyst's subjective assessment of variables such as edge sinuosity, plan view outline, and the flake removal technique.

As an alternative to using width to thickness ratios, we derived a simple measurement that is a continuous quantification of Callahan's (1979:30) "nature of flake scar interval" variable. We calculate this flaking index (FI) as $\Sigma S/\Sigma L$, where *S* represents a flake scar (larger than 2 mm) that intersects with a bifacial edge and *L* is the length of a bifacial edge. In other words, we count all of the flake scars that intersect with a bifacial edge and divide this number by the total length of the bifacial edge (Figure 3.1). This yields an average number of flake scars per the length of the bifacial edge. A biface at an early stage of reduction is expected to have larger, more widely spaced flake scars, while a finished biface is expected to have smaller, more closely spaced flake scars at the bifacial edge (Figure 3.2). Whereas Callahan's (1979) width-to-thickness ratio can only be used on complete bifaces, the flaking index can be calculated for complete bifaces, biface fragments, and overshot flakes and therefore has more practical utility for examining quarry-related production discards. This measurement also can be viewed as a derivation of Johnson's (1984, 1989) "thinning index" and Wilson and Andrefsky's (2008:96–99) "ridge count retouch index."

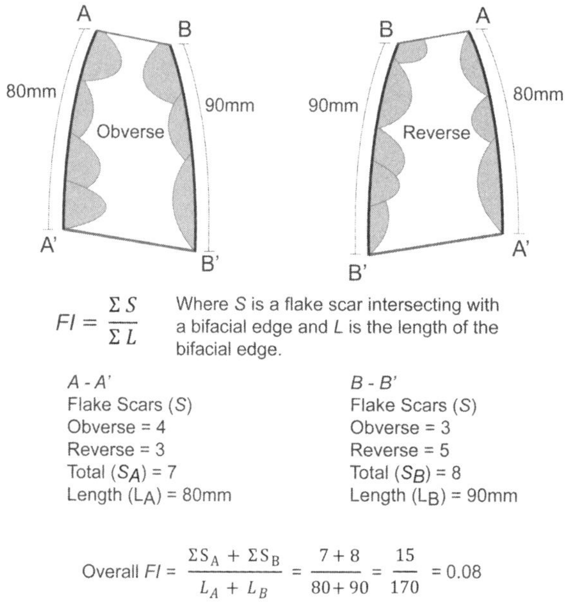

Figure 3.1. Calculation of the flaking index.

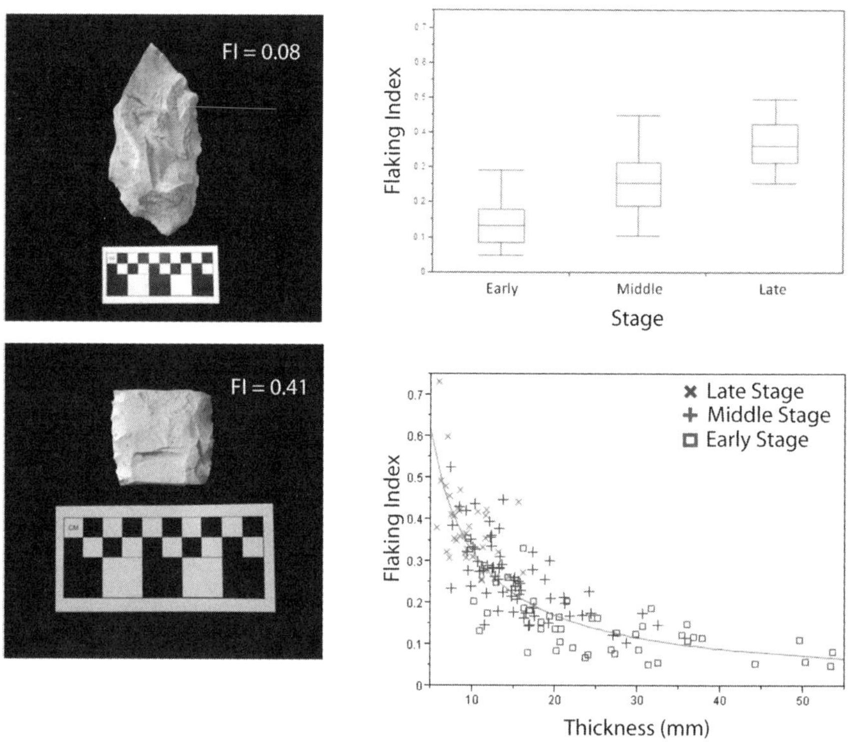

Figure 3.2. Flaking index values for two examples and graphs of flaking index plotted for reduction stages and thickness.

Results—Technological Analysis

When we began analyzing the biface assemblage, we relied on preexisting stage models (i.e., Callahan 1979; Morrow 1996; Sanders 1990) as the standard analytical framework in both Paleoindian and southeastern archaeology. Since the majority of our sample consisted of incomplete specimens, we had difficulty separating the Topper biface assemblage based on Callahan's nine stages. We then opted to assign the bifaces to three successive reduction stages based on the presence or absence of cortex, edge shape and sinuosity, and type of flake removal technique. In order to control for interobserver variation (i.e., Beck and Jones 1989), all stage designations were assigned by Smallwood. We next compared the flaking index values for the three groups using a nonparametric Kruskal-Wallis test (Kruskal and Wallis 1952) and found that the medians of our three subdivisions are statistically different ($\chi^2 = 74.4$; $df = 2$; $p < .0001$). However, we noticed that there is considerable overlap in the distributions of the flaking index in these three subdivisions and decided to compare two continuous variables (flaking index and thickness) to further test the validity of our subdivisions (Figure 3.3). The results indicate that these subdivisions are not discrete and instead conform to a continuous, log-linear trend ($R^2 = .70$; $F = 336.69$; $df = 1$; $p < .0001$).

Rather than observing a single, standard trajectory proceeding from an unmodified spall to a hafted fluted point, we found morphological variation in the assemblage that crosscuts reduction stages. These bifaces represent diverse production strategies and distinct manufacturing trajectories. We classified this variation into several categories: early-stage bifaces, point preforms, fluted points, and what we preliminarily term oval-shaped bifacial tools (Figure 3.4). Early-stage bifaces and preforms at Topper fall generally within the reduction continuum described by Callahan's (1979) stages and have typical Clovis technological elements (Bradley 1982, 1991; Collins 2002; Huckell 2007). Early-stage bifaces from Topper are thick bifaces with shapes that range from irregular to crudely shaped rowboat forms. They have sharp and sinuous edges, they often retain cortex, and they have large, widely spaced percussion flake scars.

We classified point preforms as percussion-flaked lanceolates with a rowboat-shaped outline. They have marginal and overshot flaking and multistage end thinning (Collins 2007; Collins and Hemmings 2005). Moreover, they appear to have been broken or discarded during manufacture and do not exhibit any evidence of use as tools. Topper flintknappers produced preforms with lengths greater than 100 mm, similar to those recovered at other Clovis quarries (e.g., the Gault site; Collins 2007), but they also manufactured small preforms. Large preforms (Figure 3.4a) would allow for use cycles that involve episodes of reworking and reshaping, but the ability to do the same with the smaller preforms

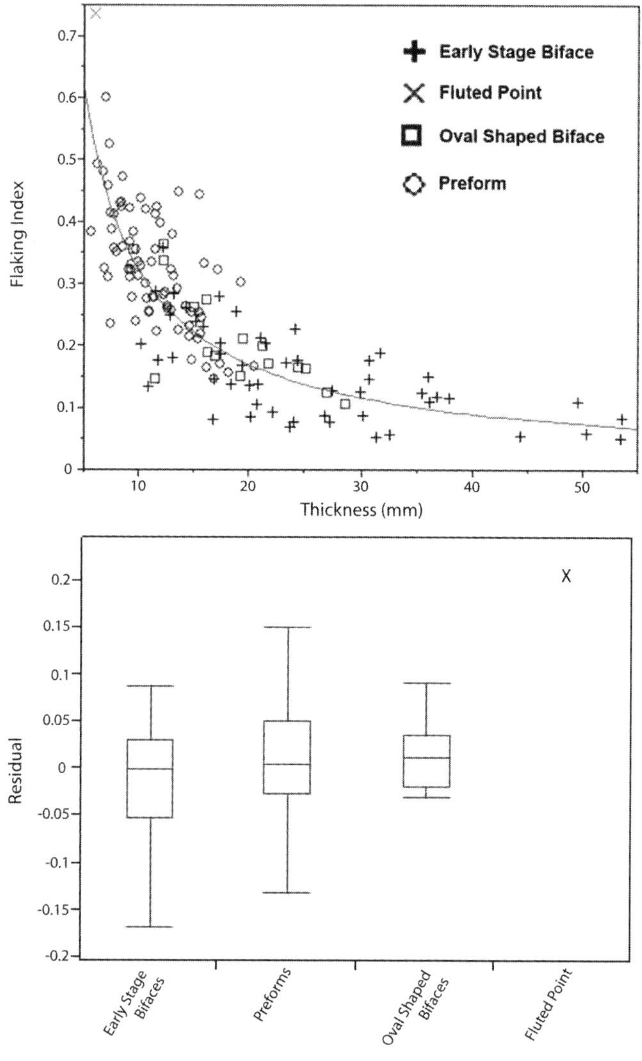

Figure 3.3. Flaking index and thickness by morphological category and box plots of the residuals by morphological category.

would have been much more limited (Figure 3.4b). Many of these smaller preforms have evidence of the original spall, such as a distinguishable ventral flake surface and plano-convex cross sections, suggesting they were made from flakes. They have sharp lateral edges and have not yet been abraded at the base. The small preforms actually fall within the size range of extensively used and reworked Clovis points from the Gault site Area 8 (Waters et al. 2011). In fact, the mean length of the small Topper preforms (59.9 mm) is shorter than that

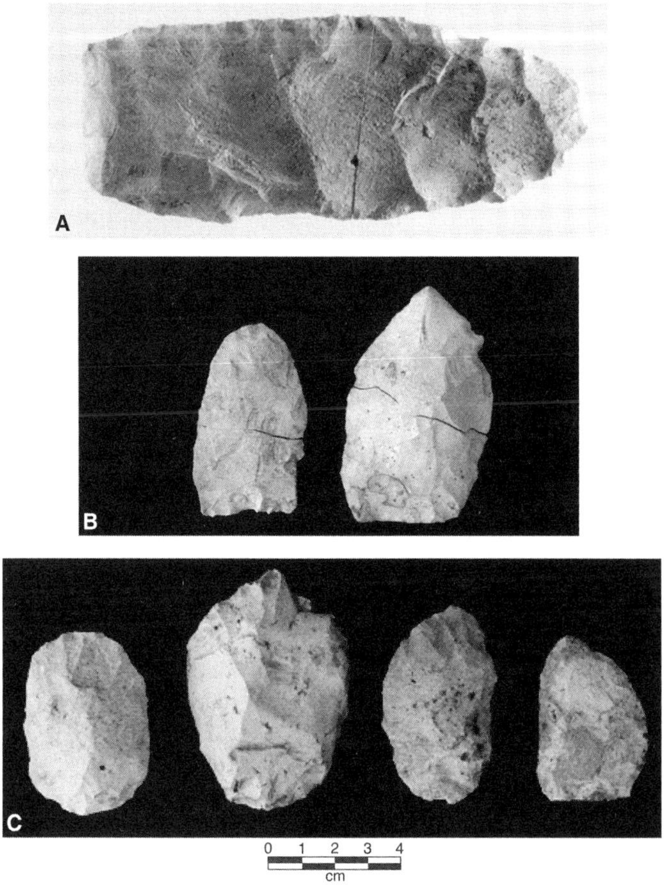

Figure 3.4. Preforms and bifacial tools from the Topper site: a) large preform; b) small preforms; and c) possible bifacial tools.

of the extensively used, finished points from Gault (60.6 mm). General explanations for the production of smaller preforms include a transition in subsistence economy in which hunters began to target smaller game animals (Anderson 2004); a functional difference between points crafted for spearing and those crafted for throwing (Ellis et al. 1998); and, despite traces of pressure flaking, overshots, and end thinning, evidence of novice knapping (see Bamforth and Hicks 2008). At this point, the variation might best be explained by the differences in spalls obtained from the Coastal Plain chert nodules. While variation in spall size does not yet explain *why* Clovis knappers were willing to continue working material of limited size, it does help explain *how* variation was introduced in the biface production process.

The biface assemblage also includes discoidal cores and possible bifacial tools that represent variability from a preform production trajectory and may be evidence of other on-site activities (Figure 3.4c) (Collins and Hemmings 2005:17–18). These bifaces have plano-convex cross sections similar to adzes, backed lateral margins, and excurvate blade edges typical of knives. The exact role of these bifacial tools awaits further investigation. Thus, the presence of bifaces that may have been produced for functions other than those of fluted points, when considered along with the dichotomy in preform size discussed previously, further underscores the potential for multiple production trajectories within the biface assemblage. As a result, we found that traditional stage models are ill equipped for describing the variability within the biface assemblage because of an intrinsic assumption that fluted points of standard size ratios were the intended finished product.

Results—Spatial Analysis

A spatial analysis was conducted on two excavation blocks in the Hillside area of the site near a visible outcrop of chert (Figure 3.5). These two excavation blocks encompass 96 m^2 and contained 59 bifaces and 12 overshot flakes. Of these, 27 bifaces were found in Block A, which yields a biface density measurement of .42 bifaces per square meter. The remaining 32 were found in Block B, with a biface density of one biface per square meter; more than twice the density of Block A. The opposite pattern was observed in the distribution of overshot flakes, whereby nine were found in Block A and only three were recovered from Block B.

We next compared the flaking index values of bifaces and overshot flakes between the two blocks and found that they had different distributions. The distribution for Block A was skewed toward lower flaking index values, while the flaking index values for Block B were normally distributed with a higher mean value. Using the nonparametric Mann-Whitney *U* test (Mann and Whitney 1947), we found that the median values for the two blocks are significantly different ($z = 2.38$; $p = .017$). The skewed distribution of the flaking index for Block A indicates that this block has more bifaces, biface fragments, and overshots belonging to the initial part of the reduction continuum. In Block B, the normally distributed values represent a wider range of the reduction continuum, but with a higher overall mean flaking index.

To augment our analysis of the flaking index distributions, we next examined the distribution of our early-, middle-, and late-stage subdivisions to account for potential spatial variation in nominal attributes, such as the presence of cortex and flaking technique. We utilized Pearson's chi-square test (Plackett 1983) to determine whether there is a particular group that is overrepresented or underrepresented. Our expected distribution was that the bifaces should be

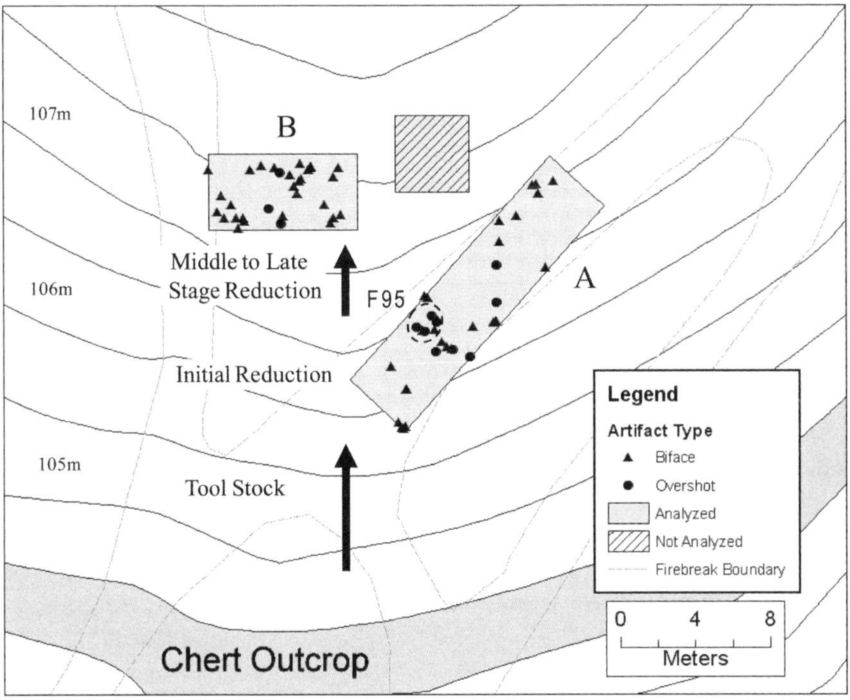

Figure 3.5. Spatial model of biface production at the Topper site.

equally divided among the three subdivisions. When the chi-square value was calculated for the entire assemblage, we found bifaces in later stages are generally underrepresented on the Hillside ($\chi^2 = 8.63$; $df = 2$; $p = .013$). However, the chi-square test for the Block B sample indicated no significant biases in the distribution of reduction stages ($\chi^2 = 2$; $df = 2$; $p = .37$). In the Block A sample, the number of late-stage bifaces is significantly underrepresented ($\chi^2 = 7.96$; $df = 2$; $p = .018$). The near absence of late-stage bifaces in Block A also appears to be driving the significant chi-square value found for the total sample. These results mirror our findings using the distribution of flaking index values between the two excavation blocks.

There are several additional lines of evidence that could prove useful for understanding biface production in this part of the site. For example, we examined the percentage of complete bifaces and found that only 14 percent of the bifaces in Block B were complete, while the percentage more than doubles to 36 percent in Block A. Additionally, a dense concentration of large spalls and roughly flaked cores was excavated in Block A, which also included several large battered quartz cobbles in the immediate vicinity. In fact, seven of the eight battered quartz cobbles weighing more than 100 g are located in Block A.

On the other hand, Block B is the only area on the Hillside that produced an expended fluted point.

Based on this spatial analysis, we propose a preliminary model to explain the spatial variation in biface production observed in these two excavation blocks (see Figure 3.5). We suggest that Clovis knappers amassed large quantities of tool stock from the outcrop in the area of Block A. In this area, multiple lines of evidence indicate a locus for producing bifaces early in the reduction continuum. The majority of bifaces in this sample have less refined flaking, later stages are underrepresented, and there is a higher discard rate for complete early- and middle-stage bifaces. In Block B, we find the opposite pattern, which we interpret as evidence for biface production that has progressed further into the reduction continuum. The lines of evidence include bifaces with more refined flaking, a representation of bifaces that could be classified as belonging to a "late stage" of production, and a lower discard rate for complete bifaces.

Assuming that all the artifacts found in these Clovis deposits are contemporaneous, it appears as if the production of bifaces may be segregated across space in relation to the chert outcrop. In other words, tool stock was acquired from the outcrop, initially reduced in the area around Block A, and further reduced around Block B. An alternative hypothesis is that these two loci represent different occupations. In that case, the spatial variation in biface reduction may indicate two separate quarrying events with different production goals.

Discussion

Our goal in this analysis was to determine whether there is evidence that biface production occurred as a staged process at the Topper quarry and to evaluate whether it proceeded in a unilinear fashion from spalls to complete fluted points. Our results find that when modeled using a flaking index and thickness, there were no "breaks" or "clusters" indicating differential reduction or discard consistent with staged models of biface reduction (i.e., Callahan 1979). Furthermore, the results of our technological analysis indicate that, while there is evidence for manufacture representing the entire fluted-point production continuum, there is also evidence for morphological variation that suggests use of other tool types. These bifaces lack the rowboat-shaped outline characteristic of Clovis biface production and may have been intended for use as choppers, adzes, or discoidal cores. Moreover, even in the category we classified as preforms, there is variation in size distribution that alludes to the possibility of multiple trajectories for producing fluted points and other bifacial implements.

While our technological analysis finds little support for a staged, unilinear process, our spatial analysis may point to several interruption points. First, raw material was acquired and transported to a higher elevation away from the chert outcrop. Next, bifaces were initially reduced and most likely rejected due to breakage, the presence of a flaw, or a failure to thin. Finally, bifaces were most likely transported to a higher elevation yet again, where reduction progressed to where the discard pattern includes bifaces representing the later parts of the reduction continuum. One possible explanation for the spatial variation observed in the assemblage is that it may signal a transition from direct percussion to pressure flaking, a hypothesis supported by the presence of large, battered quartz cobbles found in the area containing bifaces skewed toward the early part of the reduction continuum. Consequently, instead of biface production proceeding in a unilinear, steplike fashion from one ideal shape to the next, the "stages" observed in the spatial patterning may be much more general in nature and reflect transitions from hard to soft hammer/pressure flaking techniques.

Conclusion

When we began analyzing the biface assemblage from the Topper site, our first step was to choose an orthodox method for explaining biface reduction (i.e., Callahan 1979) in the hope that we could gather data comparable to those of other assemblages and address broader research questions. For example, variation in the production of Clovis bifaces could provide the foundation for a research design based on cultural transmission theory (Boyd and Richerson 1985; Shennan 2008), which could then be used to evaluate Early Paleoindian settlement models such as Kelly and Todd's (1988) "high technology forager" or Anderson's (1990, 1996) "staging area" model. Additionally, comparing the biface assemblage from the Topper site with those of other sites in the Savannah River valley, as well as with isolated finds recovered in Georgia and South Carolina, would be beneficial for generating and testing models concerning landscape use, lithic provisioning, and technological organization.

However, like others (Bradbury and Carr 1999; Ingbar et al. 1989; Shott 1996a), we encountered a series of practical and theoretical limitations when attempting to apply an approach based on identifying production stages. First, one of the few objective, continuous measurements used in stage approaches is the ratio of width to thickness. Because of the fragmentary nature of quarry assemblages, we were unable to determine the maximum width and thickness for a large percentage of the Topper biface assemblage. As an alternative, we developed a flaking index, which failed to parse out discrete stages. Second, stage models uncritically collapse variation into broad categories and assume a progression to a uniform end product, usually a hafted biface. Our analysis of the Topper assemblage finds that while some bifaces were most likely intended for use as fluted points, others may have been used as tools or cores. Finally, relying solely on stages as an analytical unit constrains comparisons of lithic production and provisioning strategies with subsequent hunter-gatherer groups. In particular, Beck et al. (2002) adapted a field processing and transport model proposed by Metcalfe and Barlow (1992) to examine lithic raw material movement in a series of sites in the Great Basin. However, they use proportion of bifaces by reduction stage as their unit of analysis. By using continuous measurements, as opposed to aggregate categories, it would be more straightforward to compare Clovis lithic provisioning strategies to those of hunter-gatherer groups that did not make Clovis points. In other words, is a "Stage 3" Clovis biface comparable to a "Stage 3" Early Archaic corner-notched biface? The use of continuous measurements may be one way to sidestep this issue.

On the other hand, we would also caution against throwing the proverbial baby out with the bathwater when it comes to using approaches based on identifying reduction stages. Despite our inability to identify stages using continuous variables, we did find evidence for spatial segregation of the biface assemblage, albeit one that was different from the stages represented in traditional models. This would seem to imply that biface production did not always consist of a single, uninterrupted event. Moreover, these apparent stages may be more related to a shift in reduction technique (i.e., direct percussion versus pressure flaking) than to steps in a standardized procedure for making a biface. However, we would like to point out that this conclusion is not based on an a priori assumption about how biface production should occur, but instead is based on a post hoc interpretation of archaeological data. This finding is in large part due to the buried, intact nature of the Clovis component, which is a rare occurrence in the southeastern United States (Anderson 2005; Goodyear 1999) and alludes to the importance of other Paleoindian quarry sites with buried components, such as Gault (Collins 2002, 2007; Waters et al. 2011) and Carson-Conn-Short (Broster and Norton 1993, 1996), where technological and spatial analyses can be combined to help discern the various strategies and trajectories used to make stone tools.

Acknowledgments

We would like to thank Phil Carr, Andrew Bradbury, and Sarah Price for inviting us to participate in this volume as well as William Andrefsky and George Odell for their insightful comments. We would also like to thank Al Goodyear for facilitating our addiction to Paleoindian archaeology and studies of lithic technology. He has provided both of us with some truly unique research opportunities at the Topper site for which we are both very grateful. We would also like to thank the Clariant Corporation, the Southeastern Paleoamerican Survey, Inc., and the South Carolina Institute for Archaeology and Anthropology for logistical support. David Anderson, Boyce Driskell, Ted Goebel, Steve Kuhn, and Tom Pertierra all influenced our approach to analyzing stone tools. Finally, we would like to express our gratitude to the many volunteers who brave the heat, snakes, mosquitoes, and testy graduate students to make the excavations at the Topper site possible. However, we alone are responsible for any and all errors in this chapter.

4

A Comparison of Clovis Blade Technologies at the Topper and Big Pine Tree Sites, Allendale County, South Carolina

Douglas Sain and Albert C. Goodyear III

Prehistoric people made design choices in the manufacture of stone tools in response to social and economic strategies employed, as well as the raw material environment in which they operated. Some, including Clovis people, manufactured a distinctive flake type, blades, for use in a variety of tasks or for modification into specialized tool forms. The variable occurrence of blades in the archaeological record (e.g., Bar-Yosef and Kuhn 1999; Parry 1994) indicates that certain social and economic strategies and/or cultural historical trajectories conditioned the manufacture of this distinctive artifact form. However, more data concerning the distribution and character of Clovis blades are needed in order to address the broader anthropological implications of their occurrence in the archaeological record. Blades, as such a distinctive form, can serve as an exemplar for lithic analysts interested in broader questions of tool design and technological strategies. Moreover, the role of blades in the organization of Clovis lithic technology as related to prehistoric settlement strategies deserves further consideration.

A number of factors influence the final form and distribution of stone tools (Carr et al. this volume; Nelson 1991). These include, but are not limited to, settlement strategies, the function of the tool, the availability and material properties of suitable stone, and specific manufacture techniques employed in response to such properties. For example, a nodule chosen to serve as a core for the production of flakes requires an alternative reduction strategy than one intended to become a projectile-point preform. Likewise, the size, shape, and quality of the selected raw material affect morphological attributes of lithic detachments. Last, use of certain striking implements and core types during the manufacturing process influences technological attributes. As a result, variation in specific attributes of stone tools and differential distribution of these tools across geographic regions are useful for making inferences regarding settlement-subsistence strategies and other aspects of prehistoric lifeways.

Clovis Blades

Blades are a specific tool form infrequently recovered from lithic assemblages. A blade is an elongated flake detached from a specifically designed core (Collins 1999). Blades have long fascinated archaeologists due to their specialized nature. A combination of attributes, including long, sharp, lateral margins, provides for a flexible and versatile tool sufficient for various tasks (Boldurian and Hoffman 2009). Functions that blades may have served include slicing, cutting, and scraping, related to working organic media such as hide, meat, wood, and bone. If original cutting edges became dull through use, simple maintenance by way of retouching the blade margin extended the use life for such tools.

In North America, blades have been reported from a number of site types spanning multiple cultural periods (Parry 1994). Blades are recovered frequently at quarries where they were produced, at kill/camp sites where food was processed, and at habitation sites where they were employed for use in various tasks. Moreover, such tools are considered to have served in the "preparation for ritual activities" in some cultures (Odell 2003:155).

Early evidence for blades in the New World derives from presumed pre-Clovis contexts such as Cactus Hill in Virginia (McAvoy 1992) and Topper in South Carolina (Goodyear 2005). These assemblages typically are dominated by small blade and bladelet production, as opposed to the larger blades frequently found in Clovis contexts. With a few notable exceptions, blades have not been well documented from Archaic lithic assemblages (see Bradbury and Carr, this volume, for a discussion of Early Archaic blades), though such items are recovered from many later Woodland, Mississippian, and Mayan sites (Parry 1994).

Clovis blade technology has increasingly drawn the attention of lithic analysts (e.g., Collins 1999; Dickens 2005). The earliest description of a Clovis blade assemblage was that of a cache of 17 blades recovered from Blackwater Draw Locality No. 1 in 1962 (Green 1963). Subsequent research at other nearby sites yielded additional blade assemblages. These blades are often recovered in stratified context, as caches, or are found in association with the remains of proboscideans and other Pleistocene age animals (Collins 1999). To these western examples can be added Clovis quarry and quarry-related sites in the Southeast. Blades and blade cores are found consistently in the Mid-South at sites such as Wells Creek Crater (Dragoo 1973) and Carson-Conn-Short in Tennessee (Broster and Norton 1996) and the Little River Clovis complex in Kentucky (Sanders 1990).

In a comprehensive study devoted to Clovis blade technology, Michael Collins (1999) examined blades recovered from more than 20 assemblages from the Southern Plains and Mid-South. This study was undertaken to identify the diagnostic characteristics of Clovis blade technology versus blades recovered from non-Clovis contexts. Collins recorded metric and technological attributes of blades from each assemblage and documented the extent of similarity between each site. He (Collins 1999:9) found that Clovis blades share a number of attributes in common, including flat bulbs of force, small platform remnants, and curved, longitudinal cross sections. Typically, these large blades, measuring 75 mm or longer, are associated with cores that are conical or wedge shaped.

Since Collins' influential study, additional analyses have been undertaken in an attempt to refine our understanding of Clovis blade technology (e.g., Boldurian and Hoffman 2009; Meltzer and Cooper 2006). However, many blade studies tend to emphasize tool function, as opposed to how variation in blades and blade core reduction strategies may relate to issues regarding raw material preferences and technological organization (Rasic and Andrefsky 2001:62).

The recent discovery of blades in stratified context with Clovis projectile points at the Big Pine Tree and Topper sites has extended the geographic range of such tools to the southern South Atlantic Slope (Goodyear 1999; Goodyear and Steffy 2003). This study summarizes blade research at these two sites. A method is presented for documenting variation in blade technology, which in turn enables comparison to other Clovis blade assemblages. Most important, results can address broader issues such as technological organization and settlement subsistence systems.

The Allendale-Brier-Creek Clovis Complex

The Topper and Big Pine Tree sites are two stratified quarry-related lithic reduction sites located within 2 km of each other along the Savannah River in Allendale County, South Carolina. At Topper, excavations conducted through the Southeastern Paleoamerican Survey totaling 596 m^2 have yielded an abundance of lithic artifacts spanning the entirety of cultural history (13,500 years) in the area. The discovery of fluted points and preforms in various stages of production indicates a Clovis component at the site. The presence of blades, blade cores, and blade production debitage also suggests blades were a significant component of Clovis tool manufacture at the site. One source of raw material at Topper is Allendale chert, available as nodules eroding from a hillside slope. This material is a key source of high-quality chert in the region. However, large nodules may not have been available in abundance at Topper, which placed restrictions on the capability of prehistoric knappers to produce lithic tools of certain sizes and shapes.

The Big Pine Tree site is a prehistoric, multicomponent quarry and lithic-processing site situated on Smith Lake Creek, an active floodplain tributary of the Savannah River (Goodyear and Foss 1993). High-quality Allendale chert, locally available as river cobbles from the bottom of Smith Lake Creek, provided Paleoindians with lithic resources from which to produce stone tools (Goodyear 1997, 1999). As of 2009, a total of 80 m^2 had been excavated at Big Pine Tree. The diversity and density of artifacts found at Big Pine Tree, including utilization observed on blades, suggest that the site may have served a number of activities apart from chert processing and stone tool manufacture (Goodyear 1999).

Research Design and Methods of Analysis

There are various definitions of blades, and the use of terms such as *blade-like flake* causes confusion when attempting to make comparisons between sites (Bar-Yosef and Kuhn 1999; Bradbury and Carr this volume; Parry 1994). According to Johnson (1983:50), a blade is defined as a long, thin flake with a "prepared broad angle platform, parallel lateral edges, and dorsal flake scars that parallel the longitudinal axis of the blade and originate from the same platform." While many definitions use technological attributes as criteria for defining a blade, few provide a method allowing such attributes to be quantified. The present analysis operates under the assumption that blade manufacture may be differentiated from strategies that produce blade-like flakes based on six technological attributes. In this procedure, each attribute is weighted with a value ranging from 1 to 3, where 1 is the least diagnostic and 3 is the most diagnostic, as indicative of its importance in discriminating between blades and blade-like flakes (Table 4.1). The attributes were selected based upon an assessment of previous research and what attributes are considered most diagnostic in identifying blades. Attributes, with weighted values in parentheses, include the following: presence and directionality of two or more prior removal scars (3), cross section (3), lateral margins (2), platform angle (2), characteristics of the bulb of force (1), and distal termination characteristics (1).

As no single attribute defines a blade, the method developed here considers a suite of attributes and allows results to be quantified for comparative purposes. By computing a technological blade score based on the aforementioned six characteristics, an individual flake can be more consistently assigned as a blade or not. Technological blades have two or more parallel flake scars on the exterior surface that emanate from the same plane or margin. These blades also

Table 4.1. Blade attribute values

Attribute	Value	Blade	Blade-Like Flake
Flake scar direction	3	Unidirectional	Multidirectional
Cross section	3	Triangular/trapezoidal	Lenticular
Lateral margin	2	Parallel	Irregular
Platform angle	2	> 60	< 60
Bulb prominence	1	Diffuse	Salient
Distal thickness	1	Distal > proximal	Proximal > distal

have "relatively even, parallel lateral margins" (Collins 1999:9). When multiple scars are present, they are either unidirectional or bidirectional, but typically not multidirectional. Additional attributes of blades include cross sections that are triangular to trapezoidal in form, platform angles of 60 degrees or higher, diffuse flat bulbs of force, and distal terminations that are thicker than proximal ends.

In order to choose the sample of blades for this analysis, the assemblage was initially sorted according to cultural provenience. Only those blades recovered from stratigraphically discrete deposits containing diagnostic Clovis bifaces were chosen for analysis. Next, the blades and blade-like flakes were identified and pulled out. Blade-like flakes are defined as artifacts that are morphologically similar to blades, yet do not share all of the technological attributes of blades. Blade-like flakes can occur as a byproduct of biface or core/flake production, and they are sometimes used as expedient tools. Blade-like flakes are large, twice as long as their width, and have at least one dorsal ridge. These attributes are used to distinguish blade-like flakes or "possible blades" from all other flakes. Unlike technological blades, blade-like flakes usually exhibit three or more of the following attributes: multidirectional scars of previous flake detachments on the exterior surface, cross sections that are lenticular in form, irregular lateral margins, and platform angles of 60 degrees or less.

A blade score was determined for each specimen in the sample. The maximum value a specimen can obtain is 12, which is indicative of an "ideal blade." For this analysis, specimens receiving a blade score of 7 or higher were regarded as technological blades. Those with a value less than 7 were considered blade-like flakes.

Once identified, the blade and blade-like assemblages from Topper and Big Pine Tree were sorted by completeness, and a number of additional attributes were recorded: condition of the platform remnant, exterior and interior surfaces, maximum blade length and width (in millimeters), weight (in grams), dimensions of the platform remnant (in millimeters), and an index of curvature.

The index of curvature is a ratio of two measurements: (1) blade length and (2) the distance between the interior surface of the blade and a perpendicular flat plane that extends between the proximal and distal ends (Collins 1999:86). Measurements of blades and blade-like flakes were taken only on complete specimens or items that exhibited a specific observable attribute.

Blades were subsequently classified as to the presence or absence of post-detachment modification. Where modification was observed, the location and nature of modification on each specimen was recorded. Categories of modification include chips, breaks, striae, and polish. Breaks can occur as a result of the manufacturing process or as a product of postdepositional alteration. Furthermore, breaks can also be the result of trowel or shovel damage incurred during excavation. A limitation of this analysis is the differentiation of breaks as a cultural occurrence from those caused by postdepositional and/or natural processes. Cultural modification includes retouch and applies to any type of trimming (unifacial or bifacial), at any angle, that is restricted to any margin or edge of an artifact (White et al. 1963). This may be accomplished through production, use, or rejuvenation of a tool during its life span. The presence of modification was identified macroscopically, assisted with the aid of a hand-held lens (10×).

During manufacture, a range of types may be produced. Blade types are classified based upon the presence or absence of exterior surface cortex and the number of previous blade removal scars. The presumption is that as core reduction progresses, decreasing amounts of cortex should exist on the exterior surface of blade detachments, while the number of prior removal scars increases. Blade types considered in this analysis include (1) primary decortication blades, or those with the dorsal surface nearly to completely covered in cortex; (2) secondary reduction blades that exhibit an exterior surface partially, but not completely, covered in cortex and that have two or more prior blade removal scars; and (3) interior blades having no dorsal cortex and three or more scars of prior removals. It should be noted, however, that these measures of cortex are imperfect. Blade reduction may not follow a specific pattern around the core, and as such, some interior blades may be detached prior to complete cortex removal.

In addition to the blade types listed above, two subclasses, corner blades and crested blades, were also identified. Corner blades are defined as blades removed from the corners, sides, or ends of cores, and these reflect episodes of core preparation or rejuvenation. Crested blades have a central ridge, created as part of the core preparation process. If a natural, straight ridge is not present on the core, one is created through the removal of multiple unifacial or bifacial flakes taken perpendicular to the longitudinal axis of the core. This process allows for the detachment of straight, parallel blades.

In order to gain additional insights into blade production technology, all blade cores were examined. Each core was initially classified based on morphology as well as the technological attributes of the platform and core faces. Attributes recorded for each core consist of the number and direction of removal scars; platform type; and presence or absence of rejuvenation. Core types identified in these assemblages were wedge shaped, cylindrical, and conical.

Results of Analysis: Topper Site

Based on the results of the attribute analysis, a total of 257 blades and blade fragments from Topper were identified from a sample of 333 flakes identified as potential blades (Figure 4.1). Most blades (n = 135; 52.5 percent) have a score of 8 or 9, while 108 have a blade score of 10 or more. The majority of the 76 blade-like flakes (93.4 percent) have a score of 3 to 6 (Figure 4.2b).

When complete blades (n = 139) were examined according to attribute condition, a number of patterns emerged. Most have parallel, unidirectional scars on the dorsal surface, as opposed to bidirectional scars. Scar counts range from 2 to 15, with higher counts occurring on interior blades and on crested blades. When the sample was separated according to cross section, most complete blades were triangular in shape, which also holds true for most of the proximal and distal blade fragments. However, most medial segments exhibit trapezoidal cross sections.

Topper blades are as long as 150 mm, but most (n = 102) range from 50 to 75 mm in length, with an average of 63.8 mm. When considering curvature, Topper blades have a mean index of curvature of 3.98 mm. Platform remnant size was recorded for each complete blade. Platform remnants are relatively large, with a mean width of 12.26 mm and a mean depth of 6.18 mm. Most blades (n = 236), complete or broken, at Topper are interior or secondary.

Eight blades (2 percent) from Topper exhibit evidence of postdetachment modification. Blade modification consists of retouch resulting from the systematic detachment of flakes from either lateral margin or end or is a result of use wear, detected macroscopically. Modified blades consisted of six complete blades, one crested blade, and one distal fragment.

A total of 22 cores from Topper were classified as formal blade cores. These include a single cylindrical core, two that are conical, and 12 wedge-shaped cores. The remaining seven cores are fragments and remain unclassified.

The single cylindrical core has two opposing platforms. One served as the primary platform from which blades were detached. The opposite platform appears only to have been used for core maintenance: to rejuvenate the core; straighten the core face; or correct errors. There is flaking along the distal end of the core that may be related to straightening, yet there is no evidence for attempted blade removals from this surface.

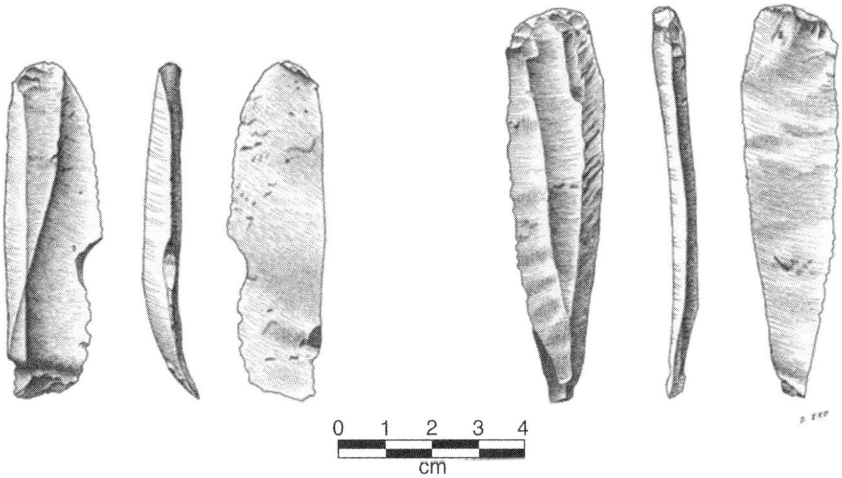

Figure 4.1. Examples of Clovis blades from the Topper site.

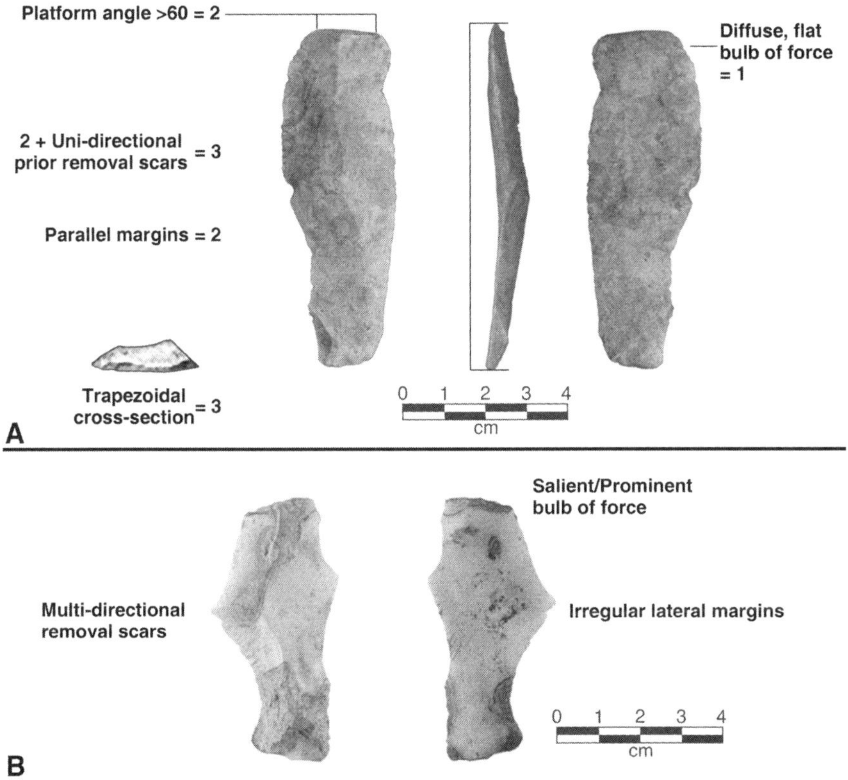

Figure 4.2. Examples of blade score determinations: a) Big Pine Tree site blade with a blade score of 11; b) Topper blade-like flake with a blade score of 6.

Conical cores (n = 2) have a single platform from which multiple, unidirectional removals were struck at approximate right angles to the plane of the platform. One of the conical cores has blade scars around the entire circumference of the platform. The second conical core exhibits flaking on three of its four sides.

The wedge-shaped cores were produced by the initial removal of a series of blades from a single platform. This manufacturing trajectory results in cores whose morphology may be described as "hoof shaped" (Goodyear 2005). When blades of the desired form could no longer successfully be removed, the core was rotated, most often 90 degrees, but occasionally 180 degrees, on its axis and a second series of blades was detached. This series of blades was usually removed at an angle perpendicular to, and sometimes diagonal to, the initial striking platform, using the remnant scars from the first set of blades as a new platform. This pattern of rotation could have been repeated a number of times, utilizing as many as four core platform surfaces.

Big Pine Tree Blade Technology

A total of 474 blades and blade fragments were identified from the Clovis strata at the Big Pine Tree site. Blades from Big Pine Tree are technologically comparable to those found at Topper, though they exhibit a much higher incidence of modification in the form of retouch.

A blade score analysis was conducted using a sample of 127 of the previously identified blades and blade fragments. The results of this analysis identified 114 technological blades (see Figure 4.2) and 13 blade-like flakes. As with Topper, most blades at Big Pine Tree have scores of 8 or 9 (n = 72; 63.2 percent), and only eight have a score of 7. The remaining scores are 10 or more (n = 34). All but two blade-like flakes have attribute values that range from 3 to 6.

When these blades were examined according to attribute condition, most (n = 90) were found to have parallel, unidirectional scars of prior blade detachments. Exterior scar counts range from 2 to 11. Cross sections are predominantly triangular, occurring on 95 blades. Finally, most blades at Big Pine Tree are interior (n = 85), with no evidence of exterior surface cortex.

All complete blades were measured with digital calipers. Results found that most (n = 325) are shorter than 50 mm, and a frequency distribution of the complete blades found two peaks, with the majority ranging in size from 20 to 25 mm and the remainder from 35 to 40 mm. Only 71 (21.8 percent) blades were longer than 50 mm. All blades and blade fragments at Big Pine Tree were examined for the presence of modification or utilization. It was found that 39 (12 percent) of the complete blades and 36 blade fragments exhibit some form of modification. Interestingly, the incidence of modification occurs most often on blades longer than 60 mm.

A total of 13 blade cores were identified at Big Pine Tree. Of these, eight are complete and five are fragments. Seven complete cores are classified as wedge shaped and a single core is conical. Not surprisingly considering the blade data, a high percentage of cores at Big Pine Tree are small, averaging less than 60 mm in length.

Discussion

This analysis examined a sample of blades recovered from Clovis strata at the Topper and Big Pine Tree sites. To identify technological blades, we developed an attribute value analysis or blade score to exclude blade-like flakes. While we see this as an effective measure, the discovery of so few blades at Topper having values of 12, indicating "perfect blades," is intriguing. A potential explanation is that blades recovered at quarry sites more often represent failed detachments or those lacking characteristics deemed worthy of curation. As such, one should expect greater variation in blade attributes at quarry reduction sites. Blades recovered at greater distances from raw material sources should exhibit attributes reflecting those most desired to serve intended tasks.

A comparison of the two blade assemblages found that the two are similar, although some variation exists in blade morphology, specifically size. The blades from Big Pine Tree are of interest because small blades are generally not thought to be part of a Clovis lithic toolkit (Collins 1999), and this may represent regional variation in strategies of blade production. While this discovery may be interpreted as an alternative reduction strategy that complements macro-blade production, an alternative possibility is that morphological discrepancies in the raw material package influenced selection preferences and core form. For example, Big Pine Tree is located along a tributary of the Savannah River, and a primary source of raw material included chert cobbles extracted from the creek bottom. At Topper, a significant source of raw material was the upland chert outcropping. Nodules available from the upland outcrop at Topper are larger than the river cobbles available at Big Pine Tree. As a result, the production of large blades at Big Pine Tree may have been constrained by available raw material.

At Topper and Big Pine Tree, results demonstrate that variation does exist in Clovis blades when compared to assemblages from other regions. For example, in the West and Mid-South, Collins (1999) found that Clovis blades are strongly curved, have small platform remnants, and have lengths often exceeding 100 mm, attributes not commonly found on blades at Topper and Big Pine Tree. At Topper and Big Pine Tree, blades frequently have wide, thick platform remnants, exhibit slight to no curvature, have diffuse bulbs of force, and have high platform angles.

The most intriguing discovery from this study is the relative absence of modification observed on Topper blades when compared to the abundance of modified blades from Big Pine Tree. Importantly, the present analysis only examined blades macroscopically, and future microscopic analyses may yield alternative results. The present findings would seem to imply that the Clovis inhabitants at Big Pine Tree put greater emphasis on the use of blades on site than did those at Topper. This discovery is compelling when one considers that the sample of artifacts examined for these analyses was taken from 80 m^2 at Big Pine Tree, compared to 543 m^2 at Topper. Moreover, and more importantly, this discovery raises questions concerning technological organization and involves the relationship(s) between Clovis blade production, mobility, and technological organization in the greater region.

The pattern of Clovis blade production, transport, and discard found at Topper suggests that (1) on-site technological blade manufacture was geared toward specific tool production and blade use away from the quarry; (2) cores primarily served for production of blades on site; (3) the blades present on site represent discards during manufacture; and (4) groups in the region were tethered to some extent to sources of raw material for purposes of tool replenishment. Based on the low quantity of formalized cores from Topper, it is possible that some were retained to serve as portable sources of tool stock, to be reduced as the need arose. However, if such strategies were in place, these cores have yet to be recovered from off-site locales.

At Big Pine Tree, the presence of blade modification as well as of other unifacial tools indicates that other activities, apart from quarrying, were taking place. Whereas Topper was exploited as a quarry and short-term base camp, Big Pine Tree may have served as a longer-term base camp where craft activities may have occurred. Moreover, the site setting may have influenced decisions in daily subsistence practices. The location of Big Pine Tree on an active floodplain provided easy access to the river, a place of plentiful riverine resources. As such, one may expect higher numbers of tools, such as blades, in areas where activities such as scraping and cutting for hide, bone, and woodworking were conducted.

Modified blades and tools on blades have been reported from other sites in the Mid-South including the Nuckolls, Wells Creek Crater, and Carson-Conn-Short sites in Tennessee, as well as Adams in Kentucky. A microscopic examination of a sample of 15 blades from the Nuckolls site found all exhibited evidence of use (Ellerbusch 2004).

In an effort to better understand the role of blades in the organization of Clovis technology in the Savannah River valley, a sample of blades recovered from a number of locations off-site and at distances from Topper and Big Pine Tree was examined. These blades were recovered as surface finds by various collectors, and all exhibit evidence of modification. In addition, all are manufactured from Allendale chert. We recorded technological and morphological attributes for each blade and results show that blades recovered from the outlying region are technologically similar to those at Topper and Big Pine Tree. Morphologically, however, such blades are longer and a number are multifunctional, having been modified to serve multiple purposes. Such attributes may be expected on blades recovered where raw material is scarce and at distances from quarries. That is, long blades would be selected at source locations for curation and use elsewhere, and these tools would have served multiple functions. Moreover, the technological attributes (wide platform, diffuse bulbs, straight in profile) often found on modified blades recovered afield are considered here to represent those attributes best suited for use by Clovis people.

Conclusions

An analysis of a sample of blades from the Topper and Big Pine Tree site assemblages was undertaken to separate technological blades from blade-like flakes, to examine variation in tool design across space, and to identify factors that conditioned the manufacture of blades. A result is the production of a blade score method, which enables quantification of blade attributes. Data derived from this method can serve to make comparisons with other blade assemblages and ultimately address broader issues of technological organization.

The Topper and Big Pine Tree blade assemblages were found to be technologically similar, with variation occurring only in blade size. It appears that strategies of blade production in the area differ from those documented in other regions, notably the Southwest and Mid-South. It is inferred that the variation in blade size between these assemblages is based on the package size of available raw materials.

A most intriguing finding of this study is the role of blades in the organization of technology in the region. Unmodified blades recovered at Topper are interpreted as discards of the manufacturing process. In contrast, the higher incidence of blade modification at Big Pine Tree strongly suggests that other activities apart from lithic production were also taking place there. The discovery of isolated multifunctional blade tools from the outlying region alludes to the significance of quarries as sources of raw material for purposes of tool replenishment. As there are limited chert sources in the Savannah River valley, such findings imply tools were designed to complement a logistical strategy carried out by prehistoric people in the region.

Future studies should examine the potential for variation in other tool forms, across different regions, and in locales of varying raw material availability. More comprehensive studies of the organization of Clovis technology will provide additional insight into their lifeways.

Acknowledgments

A number of individuals provided us with support through this research. We thank Kenn Steffy, Shane Miller, Ashley Smallwood, Tom Pertierra, Clariant Corporation, and members of the Allendale Paleoamerican Expedition. We thank William Andrefsky and George Odell for their comments on earlier drafts of this chapter. Jessica Beltman provided assistance with the figures. We would like to thank Jay Johnson and an anonymous reviewer for their insightful comments. Finally, we thank the editors, Philip Carr, Andrew Bradbury, and Sarah Price, for their observations and helpful remarks.

5

Distinguishing Taphonomic Processes from Stone Tool Use at the Gault Site, Texas

Charlotte D. Pevny

Artifact context is particularly important when conducting lithic microwear research. An assessment of artifact context must include consideration of what happens to an artifact after it enters the archaeological record (Schiffer 1996; Schnurrenberger and Bryan 1985). Taphonomic processes alter this record and complicate interpretations of artifact and site function (Levi-Sala 1986). Whether these processes occurred at the time the artifact was discarded, while in situ, during excavation, or in a laboratory setting, understanding the life history of an artifact is critical to any functional study because lithic artifacts—particularly debitage—are subject to a variety of postdepositional processes that alter flake surfaces and fracture thin, acute edges. Sometimes this damage mimics patterns of cultural use observed on tools. Distinguishing postdepositional modification, both macroscopically and microscopically, from modification related to tool use can be challenging. The extensive Clovis debitage assemblage recovered from Excavation Area 8 at the Gault site (41BL323), Texas, provided an opportunity to study patterns created by both tool use and postdepositional processes.

Site Background and Context of the Lithic Assemblage

The Gault site, located at the headwaters of Buttermilk Creek, was visited by hunter-gatherer groups for at least 13,000 years and contains evidence of Paleoindian, Archaic, and more recent prehistoric occupations. Freshwater seep springs, a diverse array of floral and faunal resources, and an outcrop of high-quality Edwards chert provided an ideal environment for hunter-gatherers. For the Clovis inhabitants, the Gault site served as a quarry for the acquisition of tool stone and a camp where Clovis groups resided and conducted daily activities. Excavation Area 8 functioned as a workshop where old tools, such as extremely resharpened projectile points and endscrapers, were discarded and new tools, such as blades and projectile points, were manufactured (Waters et al. 2011). In Excavation Area 8, two separate Clovis components, geological Units 3a and 3b, were identified. Approximately 67,000 lithic artifacts were recovered from these stratigraphic units within a 20-m^2 excavation block. A total of 66,685 pieces of this material were debitage.

In total, 113,521 pieces of debitage from 42 m^2 were analyzed from Early Archaic, Late Clovis, and Clovis deposits. This includes 6,377 flakes, flake fragments, and pieces of angular debris approximately 2.5 cm or larger examined at the attribute level and 107,144 pieces smaller than 2.5 cm subjected to aggregate analysis. The microwear study only incorporates Clovis debitage larger than 2.5 cm recovered from the 2000 field season (n = 3,375).

The lower Clovis component at Excavation Area 8, Unit 3a, immediately overlies a gravel deposit of limestone and chert cobbles. Unit 3a represents a ponding episode in which clay quickly accumulated within a shallow depression. This dark yellowish-brown clay underwent pedogenic alteration and developed wedge-shaped peds with readily identifiable slickensides (Waters et al. 2011). A one-gravel-thick colluvial lag separates Unit 3a from Unit 3b, which is the upper Clovis component. The gravels in this lag deposit are the densest and largest in the south end of the excavation block. Geologic Unit 3b was deposited above this lag during overbank flooding episodes from Buttermilk Creek. The fluctuating watertable created alternating wet and dry conditions that affected the preservation of organic materials such as bone (Luchsinger 2002).

Although the Clovis artifacts from Excavation Area 8 occur in primary contexts within undisturbed late Quaternary deposits, site formation processes affected the lithic artifact assemblage and, in turn, affected microwear analysis of the debitage assemblage.

Factors That Affect Microwear Analysis

Unlike other forms of lithic analysis, microwear research offers a means of addressing the functional aspects of stone tool use. When used conservatively with knowledge concerning site context and formation processes, raw material type, and manufacturing techniques, microwear analysis can identify tools and patterns of tool use. Viewed in conjunction with knowledge about other portions of the lithic toolkit and reduction strategies used to outfit that toolkit, interpretation of how those tools were used allows lithic analysts to construct and test hypotheses of human behavior as they relate to stone tool technology (see Carr et al. this volume).

In reference to use wear, the problematic nature of debitage and edge-modified assemblages—tools that are "expedient" or "less formal"—has been addressed by other researchers (Bamforth 1986; Keeley 1982; Odell and Odell-Vereecken

1980; Shea 1987; Shen 1999; Young and Bamforth 1990). Microwear traces do not have time to accrue on tools utilized for brief periods and any wear that may develop can be removed during subsequent use and resharpening. If culturally produced polish is, in fact, present, it may not have developed enough to assess worked material. Further complicating the situation, both mechanical and chemical taphonomic processes can create damage that mimics wear or can even produce pseudo-tools (sensu McBrearty et al. 1998).

Although difficulties exist, a number of Paleoindian researchers have successfully applied the methods of lithic microwear analysis to functional studies of chipped stone tools (Bamforth and Becker 2006; Hudler 2003; Kay 1999; Marshall 1985; Minchak 2007; Shoberg 2007; Smallwood 2006; Smith and Toth 1990; Tomenchuk and Stork 1997; Wiederhold 2004). For example, Kay (1998) found that 52.5 percent of the Edwards chert edge-modified specimens from the Wilson Leonard site in central Texas had evidence of use even though this assemblage was subject to several postdepositional processes. Further, 28.8 percent of the unmodified flakes were identified as tools or tool fragments.

Several studies exist that typologically or morphologically categorize Clovis edge-modified assemblages (Eren 2005; Ferring 2001; Huckell 2007; Irwin and Wormington 1970; Rule and Evans 1985; Wilmsen 1970), but few have incorporated microwear analysis (see Kay 1999; MacDonald 1968; Marshall 1985 as notable exceptions), and this is broadly applicable to lithic studies in the Southeast for all time periods (see Franklin et al. this volume). The new millennium has witnessed an increase in Clovis microwear research mainly generated by investigations at the Gault site (Minchak 2007; Shoberg 2007; Smallwood 2006; Wiederhold 2004), as well as the Pavo Real site (Hudler 2003), also located in Texas. While technological analyses of Clovis edge-modified assemblages have generally taken a back seat to the infamous fluted projectile point, microwear research is not biased toward bifacial implements. Only three studies have attempted to identify wear on Clovis projectile points or bifaces (Hudler 2003; Kay 1996; Smallwood 2006).

Though few would question the function of Clovis bifaces in relation to game acquisition, research suggests that some artifacts, generally considered "projectiles," actually served a variety of purposes (Ahler 1971; Kay 1998; Odell 1996b; Smallwood 2006). If the use-life history of such a seemingly straightforward component of the hunter-gatherer venatic assemblage is more complex than originally considered, then what functional applications have been incorrectly assigned—or overlooked—for other items in the Clovis toolkit, especially those considered expedient? The field of lithic microwear research provides the possibility to address this issue using low- and high-magnification microscopic analysis. Under the right circumstances, these strategies allow detection of use damage and determination of the dominant tool motion; therefore, the inferred activity in which a tool was engaged can be identified (Hayden 1979; Odell 2003).

It has been demonstrated that the macroscopic approach to discern tool use is insufficient (Young and Bamforth 1990), nor is it a strictly reliable means of separating tools from pseudo-tools (Levi-Sala 1986; McBrearty et al. 1998). Experimental replication, and microscopic study of the resulting data set, can help identify or discern patterns of postdepositional damage, though these data should be applied cautiously. Clearly stated, without identification of naturally produced damage and the forces that cause damage, we run the risk of introducing erroneous data. However, every portion of an archaeological assemblage—even the more problematic ones—can potentially contribute to the description and understanding of both cultural and site formation processes (Donahue 1994).

Interpretations of tool use must be based on reliable data resulting from microwear analysis. Postdepositional processes can interfere with analysis and prevent valid interpretations of stone tool use (Levi-Sala 1986, 1996). To avoid misidentifying fractures not related to use as indicating intentional human use, microwear analysts must understand (1) how stone fractures; (2) how stone interacts with other bodies in motion; (3) how stone is affected by postdepositional processes; and (4) how stone is affected by intentional human modification and use. Microwear can result from either cultural or natural processes acting upon the surface of a lithic artifact. Experimental archaeology provides a way to differentiate between the two alternatives. This is especially relevant for debitage assemblages because it can be difficult to recognize the combined effects of multiple postdepositional processes, to explain how these processes alter individual flakes, and to interpret what this means for assemblage-scale patterning (Rasic 2004).

How Stone Fractures

Fracture mechanics provide the basis for describing how stone breaks and flake formation occurs (e.g., Cotterell and Kamminga 1979, 1987). The basic principle behind the study of past reductive strategies is that fracture is both controllable and predictable. For the lithic analyst, this allows the identification of patterns of tool manufacture. For the lithic microwear analyst, this allows the identification of patterned tool use. Simply put, fractures caused by tool manufacture and tool use are observable on archaeological materials. The combination of fractures forms a consistent, characteristic arrangement or pattern that in most cases is distinct from fracture caused by natural processes.

Bending and cone initiations are two types of fracture central to microwear analysis because they occur under different loading conditions, provide information on the amount of force applied to a tool edge, and provide information on the hardness of the worked, or contact, material (Hayden and Kamminga

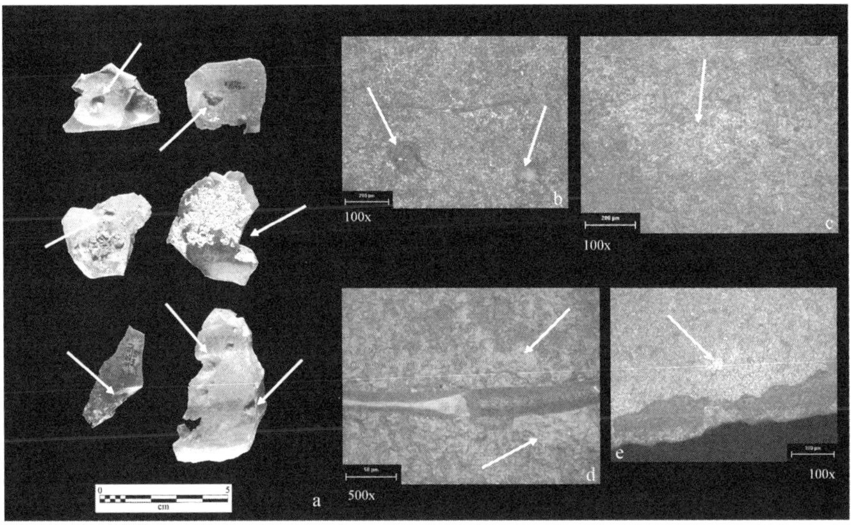

Figure 5.1. Mechanical processes that altered debitage from Excavation Area 8: a) macroscopically visible thermal stress indicators including potlids and spalled edges; b) microscopically visible potlids—note patina forming in potlid on right side of image; c) and d) soil sheen or soil polish showing textural change of artifact surface; e, soil sheen and a bright spot near damaged flake edge.

1979). Related to fracture mechanics, contact mechanics deal with the stress-strain mechanisms at the juncture of two surfaces. In reference to microwear, this means soft materials afford a broader contact area between the tool and the contact material and generally result in bending fractures on a tool edge. With hard materials, a smaller area of the tool surface is in contact with the worked material and the result is cone initiation removals and edge crushing (Lawrence 1979). The problem for microwear analysts is that postdepositional processes can sometimes produce similar types of fracture.

On debitage from Excavation Area 8, flake removals were small, generally conchoidal in shape, and represented by short, broad removals with the negative bulb of force clearly visible. In most cases, these cone-initiated removals (Figure 5.1a) were not as invasive as intentional retouch or use, and their location was discontinuous and unpatterned.

How Stone Interacts with Other Bodies in Motion

Tribology is the science of interacting or contacting surfaces in relative motion and the related phenomena of friction, lubrication, and wear (Goryacheva 1998). Although friction and lubrication are integral components of tool use, wear—the loss of material from one or both contacting surfaces or any form of surface damage caused by rubbing one surface against another (Mate 2008)—

is the ultimate concern of lithic microwear analysts. The tribological literature lists up to 80 different terms for wear and its related mechanisms; however, the four principal wear processes are adhesion, abrasion, surface fatigue, and corrosion (Rabinowicz 1995). These wear mechanisms can occur during tool use or as a result of postdepositional processes.

Adhesive wear transpires when two surfaces contact each other and adhere at localized sites. Wear transpires as the two surfaces move relative to each other and one surface removes material from the other surface at these junctions. Abrasive wear occurs when two uneven surfaces press together and material is displaced. Surfaces are uneven because of topographic projections, called asperities, which make a material surface feel rough (Mate 2008). The displaced material or debris acts as an abrasive and accelerates wear. Surface fatigue addresses the repeated sliding or rolling of two bodies in relation to each other. Repetitive action induces the formation of surface or subsurface fractures, which eventually results in fragmentation. Corrosive wear occurs within a chemically reactive environment. Oxygen and water vapor are common corrosives that adsorb into flake or tool surfaces.

In sum, these processes result in the physical expression of what microwear analysts refer to as use indicators, including linear indicators, striations, polish, rounding, and abrasion. Grossly simplified, when two surfaces are pressed together contact is made first at asperities, which become flattened through adhesion or abrasion and create plateaus referred to as polish (Levi-Sala 1996). Asperities and fragmented debris create surficial grooves or striations. Linear indicators are thin streaks of polish; both indicate direction of motion. Fatigue and fatigue-like mechanisms become more significant in later stages of wear associated with long-term tool use and failure. Corrosive wear may contribute to the formation of patination and mask or eradicate microwear indicators.

In terms of the debitage from Excavation Area 8, adhesive wear was visible in the form of material residues, such as metal streaks left on artifacts from excavation tools and screening procedures. Paraloid B-72 acrylic resin, which was used to label artifacts, interfered with microscopic analysis as well, particularly if the label was removed and reapplied. Abrasion was microscopically visible in the form of random striations and bright spots of polish in various locations on flake surfaces. Much of the debitage assemblage exhibited some degree of microfracture (fractures 2 mm or less from the flake edge).

How Stone Is Affected by Postdepositional Processes

Determining whether use indicators were caused by intentional human modification or postdepositional factors can be a formidable task, especially for a novice analyst. Many types of postdepositional processes can damage stone tools and debitage. These include mechanical processes, such as trampling, that fragment lithic artifacts, and chemical processes that patinate stone surfaces. Microwear analysts must demonstrate that patterns observed on lithic artifacts do not result from natural causes before these patterns are used to determine whether a specimen is actually a tool, tool use is inferred, and these data are used to draw conclusions about past human behavior.

Not limited to functional applications, microwear analysis is employed in other archaeological arenas to understand how postdepositional agents, both mechanical and chemical, affect archaeological materials and site formation processes (Burroni et al. 2002; Donahue and Burroni 2004). Levi-Sala (1986) demonstrated through experiments that natural processes modify lithic artifacts in ways that mimic culturally produced use wear. She designed experiments to replicate conditions causing soil sheen, to monitor the appearance of random bright spots of polish, to observe the effect of sediment on existing microwear polish, and to document resulting edge damage. During experimentation, Levi-Sala found that existing polishes were removed from artifact surfaces and the orientation of cultural-use indicators, such as linear indicators and striations, changed in alignment.

Soil sheen, also referred to as X-polish (Driskell 1998) or mild particulate polishing (Donahue and Burroni 2004), is considered for the current study as an abrasive mechanism resulting from the contact of a lithic artifact's surface with particulate matter in the soil or silicates from the stone itself. The development of polish during sedimentation and site formation is a mechanical process that is poorly understood. In addition, it is incompletely known how the properties of different sediments, such as sand or clay, affect lithic surfaces. In Excavation Area 8, soil sheen was present on all the macrodebitage examined (debitage larger than 2.5 cm [1 inch]; n = 3,375). Soil sheen varied in intensity and was distributed differentially across flake surfaces. This soil polish sometimes was identified as a narrow band concentrated along flake edges (see Figure 5.1c–e). The texture of lithic artifact surfaces was abrasively changed; asperities were flattened in the same way seen with tool use. The shrink-swell clays within Unit 3a could have contributed to the formation of soil sheen. The result of wetting and drying processes was clearly visible in field observation and in thin section (Luchsinger 2002).

Another form of mechanical damage not often considered in microwear studies is thermal alteration. There are no published studies directed toward understanding the potential effects of thermal alteration to lithic surfaces and the implications for microwear analysis. In an archaeological setting, thermal alteration or thermal stress may result from insolation, wildfire, or human-controlled fire features (Rasic 2004). Lithic raw material can be intentionally altered or "heat treated"; it also can be unintentionally thermally altered if debitage is discarded near a hearth.

On the debitage from Excavation Area 8, evidence of thermal alteration, such as potlid or crenated fractures and crazing (Flenniken and Garrison 1975; Mandeville 1973; Purdy 1975; Purdy and Brooks 1971), was distinguishable from intentional human modification (see Figure 5.1a). Approximately 11 percent (370 of 3,362) of the macrodebitage from Units 3a and 3b was characterized as thermally altered. However, microscopic examination of flakes revealed thermal fractures on flake surfaces that were not observable macroscopically (see Figure 5.1b). It is possible that thermal alteration adversely affected more of the debitage assemblage from Excavation Area 8 than could be macroscopically identified. In addition, thermal alteration reduces the tensile strength of stone (Purdy 1974, 1975), therefore increasing chances of postdepositional fracture (Bleed and Meier 1980; Towner 1984).

Trampling, as a postdepositional form of mechanical damage, was suggested long ago by Bordes (1961) and for over 40 years research has attempted to identify diagnostic traits associated with trampling (Flenniken and Haggerty 1979; Gifford-Gonzalez et al. 1985; Keeley 1980; Knudson 1979; Lopinot and Ray 2007; McBrearty et al. 1998; Nielsen 1991; Pryor 1988; Rasic 2004; Shea and Klenck 1993; Tringham et al. 1974). The modification associated with the trampling of artifacts, particularly debitage, by humans or animals has been studied repeatedly through experimental replication with contradictory results. Raw material type, substrate, and artifact density contribute to the amount of edge damage that occurs on experimental assemblages of debitage subjected to trampling. Trampling, particularly in dense clusters of knapping debris, produces pseudo-notches on flakes (McBrearty et al. 1998; Vallin et al. 2001) and on other types of material such as bone (Blasco et al. 2008). The dense Clovis deposits at Excavation Area 8 and the ubiquitous fractures observed on flake edges, particularly small cone-initiated removals (Figure 5.2), suggest a mechanism that could affect the collection at the assemblage level. Trampling by humans and animals, particularly large game, could cause this kind of assemblage-wide damage.

Not limited to mechanical actions, postdepositional processes affecting archaeological assemblages include chemical agents that alter, or patinate, the surface of stone. Experimental studies have demonstrated that chemical factors modify microwear traces (Levi-Sala 1986; Plisson and Mauger 1988; Winton 2004). At Excavation Area 8, water is perhaps the most aggressive chemical agent because it acts as the medium for other constituents in solution including calcium carbonate, iron, manganese, and other dissolved ions (Figure 5.3a). Calcium carbonate adhered to approximately 98 percent of the debitage assemblage from Excavation Area 8 and often prevented microscopic examination of flake surfaces (Figure 5.3b–c). It is not completely understood how calcium carbonate affected the microwear analysis of the debitage assemblage from Ex-

Figure 5.2. Examples of damaged flakes eliminated during debitage and use-wear analysis. The upper set depicts dorsal flake surfaces and the bottom set shows ventral surfaces. Note the jagged, notched edges and L- and V-shaped fractures.

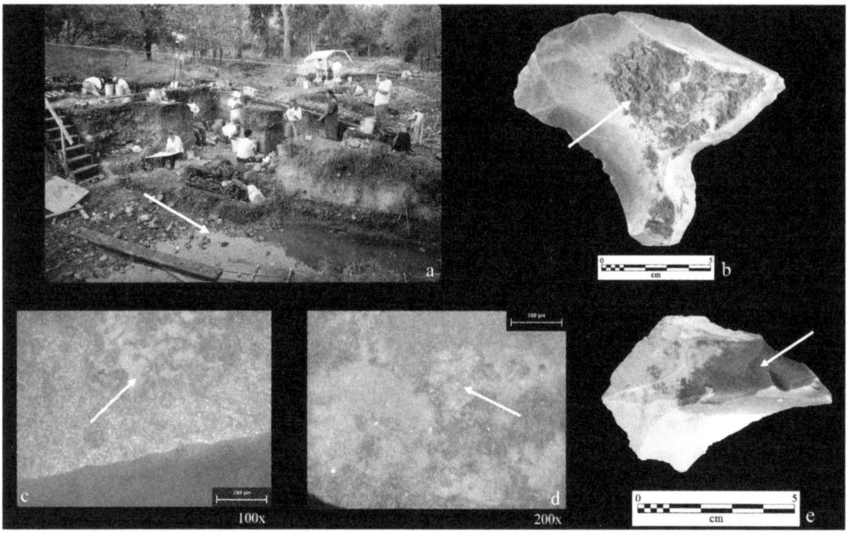

Figure 5.3. Chemical agents that affected debitage: a) standing water within Excavation Area 8, spring 2000; b) calcium carbonate encrusted on surface of flake AM438-174; c) calcium carbonate forming on the edge of flake AM291-N2-1204; d) white patina over polish; e) differentially patinated surface of flake AM214.

cavation Area 8, besides preventing examination of flake surfaces. In some areas where calcium carbonate was detached from flake surfaces, no soil sheen was present, only a matte surface. This was not quantified but bears further investigation in relation to the preservation of microwear indicators.

Studies of patination or varnish formation on archaeological specimens have centered on the identification of the processes involved in the formation of patination (Rottländer 1975; Stapert 1976), understanding the way the process of patination affects artifacts (Ackerman 1964; Pineda et al. 1997; Schmalz 1960; Sheppard and Pavlish 1992; Winton 2004), and the way patination affects microwear analyses (Keeley 1980). Formation of patina, which microscopically appears as a white haze or fog (Figure 5.3d), is attributed to several factors. These include exposure to sunlight and wind (Clark and Kurashina 1981; Shea 1999), the chemical composition of soils, and site hydrology. Certain types of weathering round arrises and edges of lithic tools (Deller and Ellis 2001). While some of the Clovis debitage from Excavation Area 8 was patinated, nearly all of it had a yellow or ocher-colored stain (Figure 5.3e). Rottländer (1975:109) suggests that ocher or brown patinas result from iron oxides and hydroxides. Orange-colored redoximorphic concentrations, related to the reduction, translocation, and oxidation of iron and manganese oxides, were located throughout Unit 3a and Unit 3b matrices and carbonate nodules from both units were stained by iron and possibly manganese as well (Luchsinger 2002). Scanning electron microscopy/energy-dispersive x-ray spectroscopy analysis of brown to black residues, identified on blades from Excavation Area 8, showed elevated levels of iron and manganese (Minchak 2007:63–66, appendix F). This residue was also noted on flakes within the debitage assemblage. Ocher staining and white patinas have been observed at other Clovis sites in Texas such as Aubrey (Ferring 2001:139) and Pavo Real (Hudler 2003:255).

Intentional Human Modification and Use

Microwear analysis began with the realization that stone tools acquire modification through use (Curwen 1930). The functional information derived from this use went beyond the existing static typological approaches to tool classification (e.g., Bordes 1961) and provided researchers with a dynamic means to identify patterned activity, and therefore behavior, within the archaeological record. Semenov's (1964) traceology and kinematics laid the foundation for the development of microwear research and a number of researchers in the 1970s and 1980s (e.g., Grace 1989; Hayden 1979; Keeley 1974, 1980; Keeley and Newcomer 1977; Odell 1975; Odell and Odell-Vereecken 1980; Tringham et al. 1974; Vaughan 1985) worked toward the standardization of analytical methods with an emphasis on the use of experimentally produced replicates, or analogues, to compare to archaeological materials. In the infancy of microwear analysis, a series of blind tests—and related debates (Keeley and Newcomer 1977; Odell and Odell-Vereecken 1980)—cast doubt on its reliability. The issue was complicated further by confounding ideas concerning the development of polish (e.g., Anderson-Gerfaud 1981; Del Bene 1979; Diamond 1979; Unger-Hamilton 1984; Witthoft 1967) and the role played by postdepositional processes (Levi-Sala 1986, 1996) in microwear analysis.

The use of low and high magnifications, in conjunction with experimental analogues to compare to the archaeological assemblage, is a practical means of identifying tool use. The low-magnification approach uses magnifications up to 100× and classifies the shape and size of flake scars, as well as the extent and distribution of those scars along a modified edge, to determine whether an edge was used and to assess whether the tool was used on hard or soft materials (Odell 1975). Identification of use indicators, such as polish and the rounding of tool edges and projections, potentially allows recognition of utilized edges (Odell 1981, 2003; Odell and Odell-Vereecken 1980; Tringham et al. 1974). The high-magnification approach (Keeley 1980) incorporates magnifications from 100× to 500×. Microfracture, polishes, striations, and micro-rounding are used to infer worked material through differentiation of polish types. The two methods of analysis are complementary and aid in identification of culturally modified artifacts, the detection of use wear, and the determination of the dominant tool motion. Inferences can then be drawn about the activity in which a tool was engaged and the worked material. Experimental replicates provide a way to explore the actions or processes involved in tool use, as well as postdepositional damage.

When describing microwear on flaked stone tools, analysts often refer to "patterned" flaking (Odell 1981; Schnurrenberger and Bryan 1985; Tringham et al. 1974; Vaughan 1985). In terms of intentional human modification and use, this pattern consists of regularly spaced flake removals along a tool edge, which generally are continuous, overlapping, and similar in size (Odell 2003). Experimentation has demonstrated that different patterns of flaking occur during various types of tool use and these patterns can be correlated to the actions (e.g., cutting, scraping, or boring) that produced the flaking (Odell 1981, 2003; Odell and Odell-Vereecken 1980; Shea 1987; Tringham et al. 1974).

Trampling Experiments

The postdepositional factors discussed above affected the debitage assemblage from Excavation Area 8 to various degrees. However, it was suspected early in the project that trampling of the dense lithic deposits in Units 3a and 3b—flakes and other lithic artifacts were layered one on top of the other with no separation—caused the damage to flake edges observed during excavation and analysis. To explore this possibility, a series of experiments was undertaken to study the effects of trampling on debitage. These experiments provided analogues for comparison to the debitage from Excavation Area 8. The analogues allowed characterization of the type of edge damage produced on flakes by human trampling and provided a data set to analyze for discernable patterns of trampling damage.

To differentiate trampling damage from wear produced during tool use, experimental analogues also were used as tools. Experiments involved a variety of handheld or simply hafted unifacial tools manufactured from tabular pieces of Edwards chert and focused on the identification of microwear resulting from longitudinal, transverse, and rotational motions on a diverse assortment of worked materials. To date, I have butchered bison; scraped wet and dry bison hide; cut wet horsehide; and cut, scraped, drilled, and scored a variety of hard and soft materials including wood (seasoned oak, green oak, green bois d'arc/osage, river cane, bamboo), bone (elk, deer, cow), antler (elk and deer), turtle shell, grasses, and gourds. This research generated an assemblage that formed the analogues I used for comparison with Clovis artifacts.

Experimental Methods and Results

For the trampling experiment, a total of 276 flakes were produced using Edwards chert collected from the vicinity of the Gault site. These flakes included replicate biface thinning flakes and Clovis-like blades produced by Bill Dickens. Normal (Frison and Bradley 1980:24; Masson 1998:685–686) or core reduction (Hemmings 1987:438) flakes, produced during initial reduction, primary thinning, and core preparation, also were used in the experiment. These three types of flakes were identified in the Clovis debitage assemblage from Excavation Area 8 (Dickens 2005; Pevny 2009). Each flake used in the experiment was numbered and flake edges were scanned using a 10× hand lens to identify and record any existing fractures; a sample of the experimental flakes was examined with low and high magnifications. Two 50-cm^2 areas were marked off on a clay substrate and flakes were placed on the ground with the number facing up. In the first square, flakes (n = 90) were positioned in a single layer on the ground (Experiment T1 = low density). In the second square, flakes (n = 186) were placed in two layers with flake surfaces and edges in contact with other flakes (Experiment T2 = high density). With 15 students, each area was trampled for approximately 10 minutes.

The flakes, and any flake fragments, were collected and washed. All of the flakes were analyzed from Experiment T1. A sample of 93 flakes was analyzed from Experiment T2. Each flake was partitioned into four quadrants. Four "damage" attributes were recorded for each quadrant (Table 5.1). The length of flake removals along the flake edge was measured and classified as either abrupt (2 mm or less) or invasive (larger than 2 mm). The amount of damage was categorized as none (0 percent), light (1 to 33 percent), moderate (34 to 66 percent), or heavy (67 percent or greater). The pattern of edge damage was either uneven (irregularly sized removals resulting in a jagged edge) or even (similarly sized removals). Bifacial damage was noted (presence/absence). The presence or absence of several types of flake removals was recorded: bending and cone initiations, crescentic fractures (90-degree snap fractures), and crushed or abraded edges. A sample of flakes (n = 5) from each experimental group was analyzed on the stereo and compound microscopes to determine whether microscopic damage occurred during trampling. The presence or absence of bright spots, striations, and linear indicators was noted.

At the assemblage scale, few differences were observed between the two experimental trampling data sets (Table 5.1). In most instances, flake removals were abrupt (2 mm or less from the edge), damage was moderate to heavy, flake edges were jagged and uneven in appearance, and damage to flake edges was often bifacial. The percentages of each attribute for each flake quadrant were roughly the same, implying that damage in one quadrant is a good pre-

Table 5.1. Results of trampling experiments

Attribute	Experiment	Quadrant 1	Quadrant 2	Quadrant 3	Quadrant 4
% abrupt flake removals	T1 (n = 90)	75.6	68.9	66.7	73.3
	T2 (n = 93)	78.5	79.6	77.4	73.1
% moderate to heavy damage	T1 (n = 90)	64.4	67.8	66.7	76.7
	T2 (n = 93)	48.4	53.8	55.9	46.2
% irregular damage	T1 (n = 90)	63.3	56.7	54.4	51.1
	T2 (n = 93)	74.2	74.2	68.8	69.9
% bifacial damage	T1 (n = 90)	67.8	70	73.3	74.4
	T2 (n = 93)	51.6	55.8	54.8	50.5

dictor of damage in the other three quadrants. Other than classic bending and cone initiations, fracture types included 90-degree crescentic or snap fractures, L- and V-shaped fractures, and crushed or abraded edges. Microwear analysis revealed bright spots and multidirectional striations in random locations away from flake edges. Two of the five sampled flakes from Experiment T1 had bright spots and striations; one flake had only bright spots. Four of the five flakes from Experiment T2 had both bright spots and striations. All 10 flakes were microfractured or crushed in random locations around the edge and flake arrises sometimes were abraded or rounded. In only one instance did a flake edge show patterned, continuous flaking that might be misinterpreted as retouch or use.

Discussion of Experiments

In some circumstances it can be difficult to discern the effects of postdepositional damage; even breakage related to fairly aggressive mechanical processes such as plowing have been confused with microwear, as in the initial analysis of the Clovis blades from the Keven Davis cache, Texas (Kay 1999:139–140). However, postdepositional damage can be distinguished from intentional use if the whole assemblage is taken into account and the types of edge damage are identified. Mallouf (1981) operationalized terminology for plow damage as observed on the Brookeen Creek cache, Texas. This is a possible Clovis blade cache; 82 percent of the specimens were manufactured from Edwards chert. Several types of mechanical damage on the blades impacted by plowing implements are very similar to the damage observed on the experimental trampled data set. This is not surprising; bounded by its inherent physical proper-

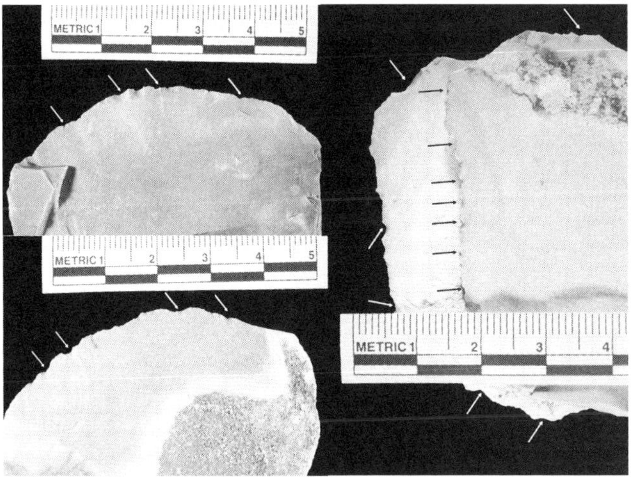

Figure 5.4. Examples of flakes damaged during trampling experimentation. Note the unpatterned placement of flake removals along the jagged edges and the crescentic L- and V-shaped fractures.

ties or structure, lithic material is limited in the ways it can fracture no matter the causal conditions. V-shaped and L-shaped fractures seem to be particularly associated with high-impact damage situations.

The types of fracture observed on flakes in the trampled data set provided the best comparative analogues to the Excavation Area 8 debitage assemblage. Bending and cone initiations were evident, but they were erratically and discontinuously located on the edges of flakes (Figures 5.4 and 5.5). L- and V-shaped fractures occasionally were developed enough to form pseudo-notches along flake edges (see Figure 5.5). Cracks sometimes are associated with this fracture type and are located at the juncture of the edges of the L or V shape. Crescentic fractures, often termed "snaps" (Grace 1989), frequently were identified on flakes as well. This type of semicircular fracture occurs at approximately 90 degrees to the edge of the flake. Flake edges raking against each other produced a type of "trampling retouch" similar to Mallouf's (1981) plow retouch.

Microwear Analysis of the Clovis Debitage Assemblage from Excavation Area 8

Microwear analysis was employed to investigate the patterns of fracture observed on flakes and flake fragments from Excavation Area 8 and to determine whether fractures resulted from natural processes or intentional human modi-

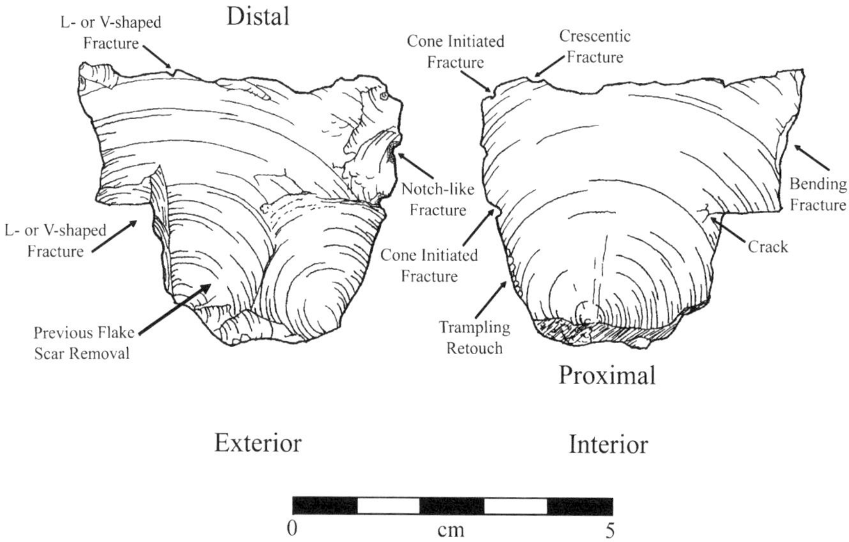

Figure 5.5. Fracture types observed on trampled flakes. Note the predominantly jagged, notched edges resulting from cone-initiated, bending, crescentic, and L- and V-shaped fractures.

fication. The fracture patterns observed on the archaeological specimens were compared to those in the trampling data set.

Individual Attribute Analysis (IAA) was conducted on 3,375 pieces of Clovis debitage (Unit 3a = 2,384; Unit 3b = 991) larger than 2.54 cm (Pevny 2009). A number of nominal and ordinal traits (Andrefsky 1998:85–108) were chosen for the debitage assemblage and each piece was analyzed and then grouped into technological categories based on a suite of attributes. During IAA, it was noted that many flakes and flake fragments showed evidence of macroscopic fracture on edges. Because of the novice status of the microwear analyst, a fairly conservative approach was taken during selection of the initial sample. Of the 3,375 pieces of debitage, 258 (7.6 percent) were culled for further analysis. Some of these flakes showed modification that related to tool use, some likely were damaged by postdepositional processes, and some displayed damage that was equivocal. These flakes were chosen because they had at least one edge with some continuous flaking, even if it was a small amount. Low-magnification analysis was conducted with a Leica Z12.5 stereo microscope to scan edges and describe fracture patterns with magnifications ranging from 10× to 100×. The locations and types of flake removals, the directions of flake removals, and the types of flake terminations were noted.

From this sample, 212 pieces were eliminated (82 percent) based on observation of unpatterned flake removals, including numerous cone-initiated, L-shaped, and V-shaped fractures, crescentic breaks, and crushed or abraded edges (see Figures 5.1e and 5.2). The fracture patterns observed on these 212 pieces were similar to the damage seen on flakes from the trampling data set. Broken, unpatterned edges do not necessarily result from postdepositional processes alone (Grace 1989); it is possible that some of the pieces rejected at this stage of analysis included unretouched flakes that were used, discarded, and then postdepositionally damaged.

The remaining 46 flakes or flake fragments (Unit 3a = 31; Unit 3b = 15) were selected for additional analysis based on the location of patterned flake removals, extending onto the surface of the flake more than 2 mm from the edge. These patterns included invasive to moderately invasive flake removals that were similar in size and shape, contiguous, and located on flake edges that could be used as tools. Because use indicators (polish, striations, linear indicators) are harder to identify with low magnifications, these 46 pieces were analyzed at high magnifications using a Leica DMLA compound microscope with magnifications of 100×, 200×, and 500×. Careful attention was given to arrises close to the contact zone (the area of the flake or flake fragment likely to be in contact with the worked material). Both the exterior and interior flake surfaces were analyzed. If an edge was particularly microfractured, the surface adjacent to, and above, the uppermost row or tier of flake removals was examined. This unfractured surface was the area most likely to retain microwear indicators. Intensity of polish was characterized using the system developed by Grace (1989). Polish ranged in intensity from Type A to Type D, with the former showing very little flattening of asperities or linkage between polished areas and the latter showing well-developed polish wherein asperities are leveled and isolated areas of polish are linked. The location of linear indicators, striations, edge rounding, and arris rounding also was noted.

After analysis using the compound microscope, 20 additional flakes were eliminated from the sample. The flaking on these 20 pieces of debitage was patterned, but not invasive, and microwear indicators were not identified on these flaked edges (Figure 5.6). Instead, rounding, polish, and striations were noted on areas of the flake not typically associated with tool use. Therefore, these 20 flakes are considered equivocal.

The 26 remaining flakes and flake fragments are considered tools. Inferences related to how the tool was used and on what type of material could only be made confidently in nine instances. These artifacts produced reliable indicators suggestive of kinematic motion (Figure 5.7). Of these nine tools, five were used on hard or medium-hard materials in a transverse or scraping motion, three were cutting tools, and one was hafted and used as a projectile (Pevny 2009).

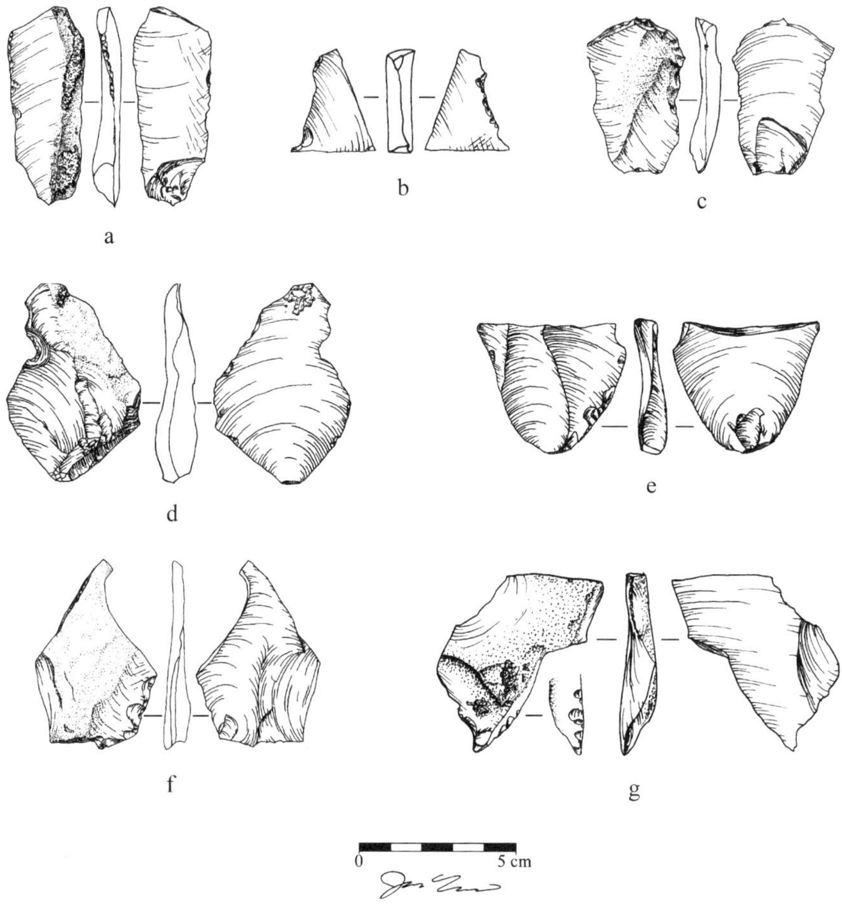

Figure 5.6. Possible tools with patterned, less invasive flaking: a) AM196-F-1430; b) AM268-K-1182; c) AM244-1007; d) AM397-P-1195; e) AM277-K2-1110; f) AM383-F-1192; g) AM397-G-1193.

Discussion

Twenty-six unequivocal tools were identified from the Clovis deposits at Excavation Area 8 at the Gault site. This is less than 1 percent of the original sample (n = 3,375). Flaking patterns contributed the most to inferences of tool use in conjunction with microwear indicators, but only after the elimination of the "background noise" or damage caused by postdepositional processes. Use of the stereo microscope helped define patterns of edge fracture, while use of the compound microscope identified polish, linear indicators, and striations. These microwear indicators were not present in significant quantities;

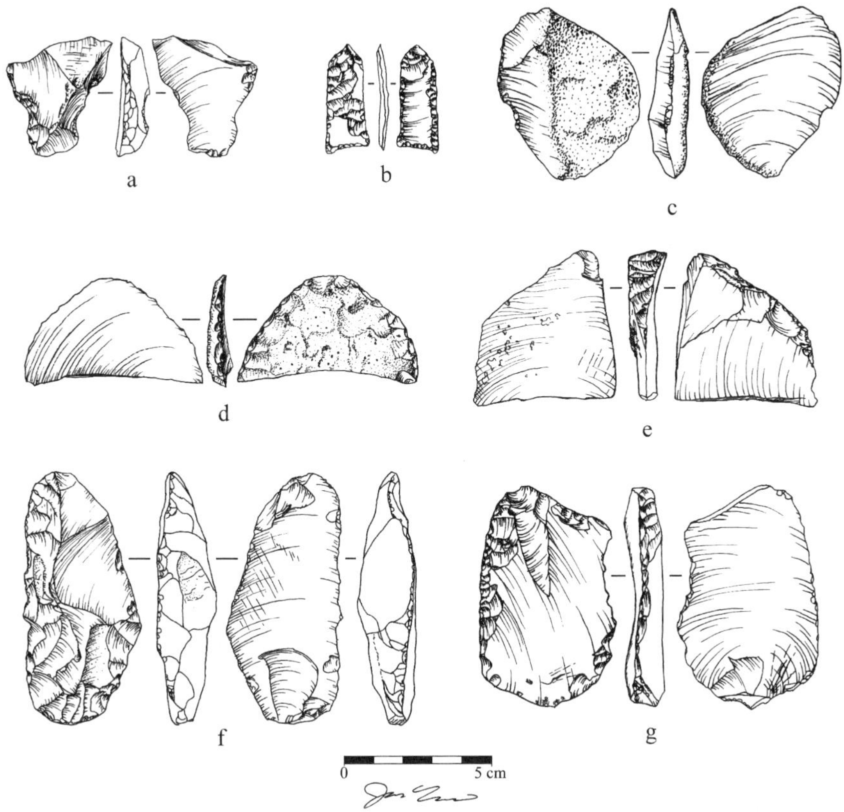

Figure 5.7. Tools with evidence of kinematic motion: a) AM4-1091; b) AM239-B-1573; c) AM347-L108-1126; d) AM303-E-1108; e) AM291-N2-1204; f) AM423-I2-1158; g) AM319-S-1138-L100..

they served to reinforce interpretations of whether or not a flake was actually a tool and in only nine instances did their presence and location on tool edges allow inferences related to kinematic motion.

Over 20 years ago, Grace (1989) called attention to the difficulties involved in distinguishing between fractures due to use and those related to postdepositional processes and provided several criteria for making such determinations. These guidelines suggest that indications of use wear are present when

1. a definite pattern of consecutive fractures occurs along a potentially used edge;
2. fractures are associated with an edge that has the functional capability consistent with such fractures;

3. fractures occur on one edge only and this edge has potential for use;
4. corroborative evidence is present in the form of polish, striations, linear features, or rounding;
5. only fractures on an unretouched surface are considered.

Based on these criteria, and on the patterns observed on flakes from trampling experiments, it seems probable that postdepositional processes are at least partially responsible for the macroscopic damage observed on the debitage recovered from Excavation Area 8. The effects of mechanical agents, most likely trampling, were evident in the form of L-shaped and V-shaped removals. Bright spots, multidirectional striations, or crushed and abraded edges also related to mechanical damage. Differentially patinated flake surfaces (microflake removals occurring at different times) support this conclusion. Differential patination of microflake scars on materials from Excavation Area 8 suggests that, in some instances, debitage was damaged more than once. A flake would not have to move very far, if at all, for recurrent damage to occur. Trampling scatters and flips flakes, a phenomenon witnessed during experimentation reported here, and this type of horizontal displacement was documented in other trampling experiments (Pryor 1988; Villa and Courtin 1983:277–278), particularly those conducted on hard substrates (McBrearty et al. 1998:122; Nielsen 1991:500). New fractures could happen each time an area of debitage is traversed.

Determining the percussor in this situation is challenging; it could be an object underneath the flake that acts as the fulcrum (e.g., the uneven surface of the ground, gravels, or another flake) or an object above (e.g., colluvium, another flake, or a foot, paw, or hoof). Fractures on many broken flakes were often bidirectional, indicating that two breaks occurred with stress from different directions at the same or different times. Although the archaeological materials from Excavation Area 8 were subjected to relatively low-energy environmental factors, the Unit 2 gravels at the base of Clovis Unit 3a and the colluvium deposited between Units 3a and 3b probably contributed to postdepositional damage. If these breaks occurred during Clovis times and were subsequently patinated or discolored, they would resemble tools. Lack of striations or polish would not be cause to discount these pieces because high-magnification use indicators are not necessarily expected in an "expedient" assemblage.

The paucity of microwear indicators identified in the Excavation Area 8 tool assemblage likely relates to the nature of the assemblage—edge-modified tools. Edge-modified tools, generally referred to as utilized, unretouched, expedient, informal, or flake tools, require little or no effort in their production. Considered unstandardized or casual with regard to form, they are manufactured, used, and discarded over a relatively short period. Tools that are ephemerally used retain few use indicators. If used on harder worked materials, microwear traces may be removed during reuse and resharpening. Tools used on softer worked materials may not produce wear indicators even when extensively used, a conclusion reached through experiments conducted for the microwear study related to the Excavation Area 8 blade assemblage (Minchak 2007). Minchak used an experimental blade 500 times to cut grass and no polish or other types of wear formed. On the other hand, Smallwood (2006) demonstrated that a single use event can produce evidence of utilization. Replicate Clovis points were used to penetrate large mammal carcasses; one projectile point came into immediate contact with bone, which caused both an impact fracture and microscopic use-wear indicators. Logically, more intensively used tools (e.g., projectiles and endscrapers) will have more pronounced evidence of use than expediently used blade and flake tools.

Finally, the lack of edge-modified tools and microwear indicators relates to how Excavation Area 8 was used during Clovis times and the primary activity conducted at this locale. Excavation Area 8 served as a workshop where projectile points and blades were manufactured by Clovis inhabitants (Waters et al. 2011). As with the edge-modified assemblage, few utilized blades were identified (Minchak 2007) at Excavation Area 8. The only tools that did show evidence of extensive use were the highly reworked Clovis projectile points (Smallwood 2006) and the worn endscrapers (Wiederhold 2004) discarded in this portion of the Gault site.

Conclusions

It was evident early in the investigation of the Gault site Excavation Area 8 that identification of postdepositional processes—environmental and cultural, ancient and modern—was critical to accurately identifying tools. The identification of agents contributing to mechanical damage of debitage from Excavation Area 8 included scrutiny of excavation and laboratory procedures, soil movement, thermal alteration, and trampling. Chemical modification of artifact surfaces resulted from a complex combination of agents identifiable through microscopic study, but the intricacy of their relationship is not fully understood at this time. The complex interaction that occurs between various postdepositional forces may be fully appreciated in microwear studies, but perhaps not fully addressed (although see Evans and Donahue 2005).

Although lithic material is extremely enduring, it is still subject to chemical and mechanical alteration. The interplay between postdepositional mechanisms becomes complicated when more than one is at work, either simultaneously or successively, at an archaeological site. The causal sequence of one or more of these forces in conjunction can be more difficult to discern. Despite these limitations, identification of tools and tool use was possible. Experimentation and study of the experimental analogues allowed me to distinguish postdepositionally damaged debitage from edge-modified tools. This study concludes that postdepositional damage affected most of the debitage collection and there was minimal use wear—or minimal observable use—on flakes. Taphonomic processes greatly interfered with drawing firm inferences on both tool use and the identification of tools. What use is observable seems to relate to working harder materials in a transverse motion.

Of the 66,502 artifacts left behind at Excavation Area 8, over 99 percent (n = 66,364) were debris from the manufacture of new tools. This debris consisted of expended cores and flakes, as well as manufacturing rejects such as blades and bifaces. Only 76 blades are considered the desired products of blade production. Worn-out and discarded tools such as projectile points (n = 5), endscrapers (n = 10), and a knife were left behind. Debris was occasionally used on site; 20 blades and 26 flakes were expediently used at Excavation Area 8. All of the debitage greater than 2.54 cm, as well as all of the blades and bifaces recovered from Excavation Area 8, underwent use-wear analysis. Over 99 percent of this material is locally available Edwards chert.

Lack of microwear in the biface assemblage (e.g., manufacturing rejects) indicates this portion of the lithic assemblage comprised unsuccessful attempts to manufacture Clovis projectile points. Use-wear analysis of the five complete and broken points determined they were used for multiple functions (Smallwood 2006). All of the points have linear indicators and a patterned distribution of polish indicative of their use as projectile points. Two specimens acquired evidence of use as knives. Use-wear indicators also show these points were hafted during their use life. Use of these points as both projectiles and knives suggests that at least two were hafted on short, detachable foreshafts. Also abandoned at Excavation Area 8 was the radially broken midsection of an ultrathin-like bifacial knife (Smallwood 2006). Use-wear studies have suggested that Folsom ultrathin bifaces were used as knives (Jodry 1998) and were sometimes purposefully broken to produce radial break tools (Root et al. 1999). The ultrathin-like biface recovered from Excavation Area 8 was located in the lower Clovis stratum (Unit 3a). The biface exhibited right-angle breaks and use wear along the broken edges (Waters et al. 2011), suggesting it was used as a cutting tool when it was a biface and continued to be used as a cutting tool after it broke. This knife, like the projectile points, was part of a mobile toolkit discarded at the end of its use life.

Ten extremely worn endscrapers were discarded at Excavation Area 8 (Wiederhold 2004). These scrapers are morphologically similar, with the characteristic bit, hafting notches, and spurs observed on many Paleoindian endscrapers. Use-wear analysis of the endscrapers from Excavation Area 8 identified minimal polish and rounding on the bits, the type of wear usually associated with hide scraping. In their present condition, the endscrapers from Excavation Area 8 are not suitable for scraping hides. The bits are heavily damaged with step fractures and crushed edges. The crushed and step-fractured bit edges suggest these scrapers were used on a drier, more rigid material—at least at the end of their use life (Wiederhold 2004).

Only 15 blades from Excavation Area 8 were used (Minchak 2007); use wear is minimal, indicating these blades were used ephemerally. Six blades were retouched intentionally and four of these have evidence of use. Nine blades have edge wear from use alone. Use-wear analysis suggests they were used on soft and hard materials.

Twenty-six flakes show evidence of use (Pevny 2009). Twenty-three of these edge-modified tools were retouched and three were used without any additional modification. Eleven of these tools show microscopic evidence of expedient use. Five of the 26 flakes probably were used to scrape hard or medium-hard materials such as bone or wood. Two tools were used to cut and three tools probably were used to scrape and cut. A small projectile point, made from a thin flake, is the only tool in this assemblage that shows extensive use. The production of this point does not follow the biface reduction trajectory employed during the production of other points at Excavation Area 8. The lateral edges and base are highly abraded, implying this artifact was hafted during use, and the distal end was reworked after it was broken through impact.

In conjunction, the results of the analyses of the lithic assemblage suggest that during Clovis times Excavation Area 8 served as a workshop primarily dedicated to the manufacture of blades and projectile points. New tools were produced for use on site, for hunting and gathering expeditions away from Gault, and possibly for off-site transport and caching. It is highly likely that the provisional, edge-modified tools were used at Excavation Area 8 during the manufacture of new tools and other domestic activities, such as food preparation.

Acknowledgments

I thank Michael R. Waters, Harry J. Shafer, and David L. Carlson, who provided continuous support and guidance throughout the process of analyses and writing. I am especially indebted to the Center for Study of the First Americans, where I served as a research associate and a post-doctoral fellow. Many thanks go to Philip J. Carr, Andrew P. Bradbury, and Sarah E. Price for inviting me to participate in the symposium and for their insightful comments, which greatly improved this chapter. I am so grateful for the encouragement of, and sometimes laborious discussions with, my friends and colleagues; Thomas A. Jennings, Shane Miller, and Ashley M. Smallwood played key roles in getting this chapter completed. The talented Joshua L. Keene drafted the artifact illustrations. Finally, Jay Johnson and an anonymous reviewer provided extremely constructive comments on this chapter. That being said, any mistakes found herein are completely my own.

6

Evaluating Early Archaic Blade and Bipolar Technologies

Andrew P. Bradbury and Philip J. Carr

Nearly 20 years of debate and discussion have taken place concerning the use of an organization of lithic technology approach for making inferences of past human behavior (e.g., Kelly 1994; Simek 1994; Torrence 1994). Importantly, significant efforts have been made to apply and expand this approach (e.g., Andrefsky 2008a; Bradbury et al. 2008; Carr 2008; Carr and Bradbury 2001; Cobb 2000; Odell 2003; Shott and Nelson 2008). We present our current conception of the organization of technology in Carr and colleagues (this volume), which guides the analysis presented here.

One method of examining how prehistoric people organized their technology is the study of a specific technology with a consideration of the different contexts in which it is utilized. Examples include Kelly's (1988) now classic "Three Sides of a Biface" article and Parry's (1994) examination of prismatic blade technologies in North America. The latter has specific relevance to this study. Parry examined nine different examples of blade production in North America across space and time and assessed the relationship with subsistence, mobility, and hereditary ranking. While he points to craft specialization as an important factor leading to adoption of blade technology, he suggests no single factor explains all occurrences (Parry 1994:94). Torrence (1994) cited this approach as an exemplar for lithic analysts due to the focus on technological choices and change across space and time.

Here, we propose an examination of two technologies, blade and bipolar, in the Southeast during the Early Archaic with context provided by a discussion of Paleoindian use of these technologies. While employing a narrower focus, this potentially allows for a clearer understanding of cultural historical connectedness or lifeway discontinuity and culture change. The Early Archaic in the Southeast was not discussed in Parry's (1994) overview. However, there is general acceptance by archaeologists in the region of the occurrence of blades in Early Archaic assemblages as well as bipolar cores and flakes. The work presented here is a first attempt to broadly examine bipolar and blade data for the Early Archaic in the Southeast.

Early Blade and Bipolar Use in the Southeast

Traditional cultural historical frameworks suggest a relatively homogenous Paleoindian period with a clear distinction between it and the Early Archaic. Yet, the reported use of blade and bipolar technologies in the Early Archaic, among other aspects, is evidence for some form of "continuity" between these time periods. In addition, *pièces esquillées* are noted from some Early Archaic sites in the region. The relationship between bipolar technology and *pièces esquillées* is unclear.

For this study, Early Archaic assemblages are those with side-notched (e.g., Kessel, Early Side Notched, Big Sandy I), corner-notched (e.g., Thebes, Lost Lake, Kirk Corner Notched, Pine Tree, Decatur, Charleston), and bifurcate-base (e.g., MacCorkle, St. Albans, LeCroy, and Kanawha) hafted bifaces. We note that detailed examination of blade and bipolar technologies reported for Dalton sites would augment this study, as in some sense Dalton represents a temporal-cultural transition from Paleoindian to Early Archaic. Such an examination is beyond the scope of this study.

A number of Paleoindian assemblages from the Southeast have well-accepted blade technologies, such as Big Pine Tree and Topper in South Carolina (Sain and Goodyear this volume); the Carson-Conn-Short and Nuckolls sites, Tennessee (Broster and Norton 1996:292; Ellerbusch 2004); and the Adams site, Kentucky (Sanders 1990). Identification of *pièces esquillées* in Dalton assemblages from the region is a common occurrence (e.g., Brookes 1979; Goodyear 1974; Michie 1996; Morse 1973). *Pièces esquillées* were also noted at several of the Tellico Early Archaic sites (e.g., Chapman 1973, 1975). Interestingly, we could not locate discussion of *pièces esquillées* from "early" Paleoindian sites in the Southeast; however, MacDonald (1968) describes the use of *pièces esquillées* at the Debert site in Nova Scotia.

In one of the more ambitious summaries of Southeast prehistory published over the past 20 years, Bense (1994:65) indicates continuity with the Paleoindian in her description of Early Archaic tool forms "made from blades and flakes struck from prepared cores." Others make general statements concerning continuity between Paleoindian and Early Archaic assemblages with regard to blade use. For example, Freeman et al. (1996:389), discussing "Aurignacian-like blades from prepared cores" at Paleoindian sites in Kentucky, make the point that "large prismatic blades also occur in some later Paleoindian and Early Archaic assemblages."

The major difference Bense notes between the lithic assemblages of these time periods is the addition of bipolar knapping during the Early Archaic. Somewhat confusingly, Bense (1994:66) states, "Flakes produced by the bipolar method, called *pièces esquillées*, are distinctively small, square in outline, and wedge-shaped in cross section." She previously discussed the use of *pièces esquillées* by Paleoindians as "small wedge-shaped stone flakes" for splitting bones (Bense 1994:45, 55–56). The only conclusion we can draw is that the production of Paleoindian *pièces esquillées* was by a method other than one employing bipolar forces, which only further clouds the relationship. Adding to the overall confusion, she uses the terms *bladelike flake* (Bense 1994:fig. 4.4) and *true blades* (Bense 1994:56). This is not a criticism specific to Bense, who did an admirable job summarizing a vast amount of information, but rather we are pointing to a symptom of the larger definitional issues in lithic analysis, which are particularly evident in the Southeast with blade and bipolar technologies. There are too many terms and too few definitions to make for reliable identifications and valid comparisons.

The role of blade and bipolar technologies is emphasized in the work of Kimball (1996) with the Early Archaic Tellico assemblages of east Tennessee. Like Bense, he points to similarity between "flaked stone tool portions of the Early Archaic technologies" and "preceding Dalton and Paleoindian" (Kimball 1996: 159). He concludes that Early Archaic people employed different technologies (blade, bipolar, bifacial) for the production of tools and the reasons for doing so were more complex than simple environmental factors such as raw material distributions and quality or type of procurement (Kimball 1996:167). Changes in the relative proportions in the use of blade versus bipolar technologies are attributed to settlement pattern changes during the Early Archaic (Kimball 1996:174).

Others have identified sites with Early Archaic blade and/or bipolar technologies such as the Taylor site in South Carolina "with a few blades and *pièces esquillées*" (Michie 1996:269). The Standing Boy flint industry in Georgia is described as an Early Archaic horizon that includes blades (Ledbetter et al. 1996:273). Futato's (1996:310) overview of Paleoindian and Early Archaic in Alabama indicates the Stanfield-Worley rockshelter Dalton and Big Sandy components include unifaces reportedly made on flakes and blades. Also in north Alabama, evidence of a blade technology was recovered from the Early Archaic occupation of Dust Cave (Driskell 1996:328; Sherwood et al. 2004). Moving farther south, the Beaumont Gravel Pit site of Mississippi has reported blades and *pièces esquillées* from a "late Paleoindian" San Patrice occupation thought "culturally" related to Dalton in part due to the presence of *pièces esquillées* (Giliberti 1995:146–147). Also associated with San Patrice are retouched blades at the John Pearce site, Louisiana (Webb et al. 1971). San Patrice includes a notched variant (Jennings 2008) and demonstrates that continued work is necessary to further define the cultural historical framework for the Southeast and the fuzziness of boundaries between time periods.

It is critical to recognize that blade and bipolar technologies are not ubiquitous during the Early Archaic. For example, a detailed analysis of flake debris from the Haw River site in North Carolina resulted in the identification of no blade or bipolar technologies, but rather demonstrated the variation in flake morphology produced by bifacial reduction, including "bladelike" flakes (Cable 1996:123). Additional Early Archaic sites with no reported blade or bipolar artifacts include the G.W.O. site, Mississippi (Jackson and Scott 1992); Tensaw Creek site, Alabama (Chase 1966); Hart site, Kentucky (Bradbury 2006); and 15CU31 and 15LO207, Kentucky (Bradbury 1998, 2007). Additionally, Carr et al. (2010:113) note that "blades and the waste products resulting from blade production are relatively uncommon on Clovis sites when compared to Upper Paleolithic and Epipaleolithic contexts. . . . While it is true to say that blades form a component of some Clovis assemblages, we believe they do not routinely approach the numbers reported for many Old World Upper Paleolithic and Epipaleolithic sites." Thus, while blades are known for Paleoindian sites, they are not found at all Paleoindian sites.

Interestingly, an examination of blade technologies and their distribution across space and through time in the Old World led to conclusions that went against well-accepted truisms (Bar-Yosef and Kuhn 1999); namely, that blade technology is strictly associated with anatomically modern humans. Bar-Yosef and Kuhn (1999:330) also make the point that it is not only the presence of blades that is significant but also the ubiquity. One goal of the current chapter is to lay the groundwork for a study that would include identifying the presence and ubiquity of blade and bipolar technologies in the Southeast during the Early Archaic.

Blades

The traditional, morphological definition of a blade is a flake that has twice the length of its width. Blade technology is considered a specialized method for producing elongated, parallel-sided flakes. A strict, technical definition focused on production would include a flake possessing one or more ridges running parallel to the long axis, such that it exhibits a triangular or trapezoidal cross section. Blades and blade-like flakes can be manufactured using several different methods (e.g., percussion, indirect percussion, pressure) (Crabtree 1972:42–47; Inizian et al. 1992:58–66).

Bar-Yosef and Kuhn (1999) point out that blades provide certain advantages such as an economy of raw material (once the core is prepared), standard product in terms of size and shape, and resharpening advantages when the working edge of the tool is the distal end of a blade. Parry (1994:94) discusses the reliability of a blade technology and its relationship to risk minimization. However, there are costs and difficulties in using a blade technology: blade production is risky with catastrophic errors causing a blade core to be discarded; it is best accomplished on high-quality material; there is preparation time for setting up platforms; and it is not a portable technology because sporadic use of a blade technology would be difficult (Bar-Yosef and Kuhn 1999:324). Whether blades are reliable or risky will require further study, but the manufacture of blades clearly indicates something of significance regarding prehistoric behavior.

Prior to attaining such behavioral insights, available data must be shown to be comparable and unbiased. What confidence can we place in the identification of Early Archaic blades if these artifacts are variously labeled and defined in the literature? Additionally, if Early Archaic people employed a blade technology, what is its relationship with Paleoindian blade manufacture? To answer these questions, a more in-depth understanding of blade manufacture in both time periods is needed.

Paleoindian Blades

Paleoindian assemblages in the Southeast are divided somewhat arbitrarily into three temporal periods that range from 12,500 to 10,000 B.P. with corresponding hafted biface types including fluted and unfluted forms. It is a rare discussion of Clovis material culture, the earliest of these, that does not include blades. However, the strict association of Paleoindian and blades is unwarranted. Just as the overly dramatic artist's reconstructions of mammoth hunting have skewed our picture of Paleoindian lifeways, the prominence of blades and blade cores in photos of Paleoindian assemblages has biased our perception, such that these items are considered a basic component of the Paleoindian toolkit.

One of the key conclusions one can draw from the *From Kostenki to Clovis* volume (Soffer and Praslov 1993) is variability in Paleoindian lifeways. This includes variation in subsistence as well as material culture, which has caused Haynes (2002:110) to state: "A typical Clovis 'toolkit' may exist only in the minds of archaeologists." Collins (1999) recently suggested that as more assemblages are deemed to be "Clovis," it becomes more apparent that there is not a single constellation of traits that defines Clovis. With specific regard to lithic technology, he points out that blades are common in some regions and absent in others (Collins 1999:5). This is not the first recognition of variation in the presence of blades in Paleoindian assemblages. For example, Bradley (1993) suggests that the presence of blades in the southern High Plains is the exception, not the rule. He further suggests that the flakes identified as blades are actually the result of biface reduction. As Parry (1994:91) comments, "It is important to note that blades and blade cores are extremely rare in Clovis sites. Most sites lack any evidence of true blades, although elongated thinning flakes and bipolar cores are plentiful and are sometimes misidentified as blades and blade cores." Blades and blade cores seem to be more common on sites in the Southeast as compared to the Southwest and Great Plains. Additionally, few Clovis sites in the Northeast, Great Lakes, and far western states have indications of a blade technology. Whether the distribution of Clovis blade industries indicates some regional specialization is unknown.

Early Archaic Blades

In contrast to Clovis and Paleoindian, the general picture presented of the Southeast Early Archaic is that of groups of hunter-gatherers who are adapting to a new, diverse, local environment and were using a variety of stone tools. Whether a blade technology was employed is debatable and specific analysts have differing opinions concerning the same assemblages. For example, Kimball (1996) notes blades and blade cores in all Early Archaic assemblages from Tellico. However, Chapman (1975:41) suggested that "the small sample of blade-like flakes relative to the total cryptocrystalline flake sample suggests that this artifact class, as far as the LeCroy and St. Albans phases are concerned, was merely an accidental byproduct of the flaking activities" in the Rose Island assemblage. A reanalysis of the Tellico assemblages by Carr (1995) indicated no or very few blades from these sites (between 0 and .3 percent of the assemblages examined). Of note, Carr employed a stricter definition for "blade" than that used by previous researchers.

At most Early Archaic sites with identified blades, other diagnostics of a blade industry are absent. For example, blade cores are rare or absent in most Early Archaic assemblages. This calls into question whether Early Archaic peoples used a blade industry or whether analysts are simply mistaking elongated flakes for blades. The reexamination of every Early Archaic assemblage controlling for interobserver and intraobserver error (sensu Beck and Jones 1989) would be a huge undertaking. Here, we employ a proxy method using published data that provides some insight into Early Archaic blade production in the Southeast.

Bipolar Technology

Bipolar reduction is defined by Crabtree (1972:42) as "a technique of resting a core, or lithic implement, on an anvil and striking the core with a percussor." Cotterell and Kamminga (1987:700) provide information concerning the fracture mechanics involved in bipolar flaking, which is characterized by wedging initiation, compression-controlled propagation, and a variety of terminations. Tsirk (cited in Flenniken 1981:31) notes the collinear nature of the forces emanating from percussor and anvil that often produces flakes almost the entire length of the core and can split the nodule into a set of equally long flakes.

Characteristics of bipolar flakes include the following: "shattered or pointed platforms with little or no surface area; evidence of force having been applied at opposite ends of the flake, and angular, polyhedral transverse cross section with steep lateral edge angles; the lack of a definite positive bulb of force; very pronounced ripple marks; and the lack of distinction between dorsal and ventral faces" (Ahler and Christensen 1983:187).

Bipolar technology has been the subject of debate (e.g., Bradbury 2010; Hayden 1980; LeBlanc 1992; Shott 1989, 1999; Solberger and Patterson 1976) and there appears to be little consensus regarding why bipolar technologies were employed. Shott (1999) refers to bipolar cores and debris as "splintered pieces" representing cores and flakes rather than tools. Conversely, LeBlanc (1992) argues that such items are wedges, and he agrees with Shott (1989) that bipolar reduction can be useful when raw material nodules are small. Goodyear (1993) suggests that bipolar reduction is employed to produce flakes when tool stone is in short supply. However, as Amick (2007:244–245) notes, "bipolar technology is frequently associated with the reduction of small pebbles and cores and may not necessarily reflect the lithic recycling of discarded waste." Clearly, raw material constraints (e.g., Andrefsky 1994a) and tool needs of prehistoric peoples have to be considered to fully understand the context of bipolar technology use at a site.

Interestingly, the reason for both bipolar knapping and production of *pièces esquillées* may be a lack of raw material or having only small-sized or low-quality stone available. If sufficient tool stone was lacking, people likely had to turn to other materials (e.g., wood, bone, antler) to produce needed tools. Wedges may have been useful in manufacturing these items. If sufficient tool stone was in short supply, then there would have been the need to conserve the stone that was available. Bipolar reduction to open small nodules or extend the use life of the available materials would be a likely consequence. Both of these situations would result in splintered (bipolar) pieces. In addition, if stone was in short supply, larger items that have been exhausted (e.g., hafted bifaces, bifaces, cores) may have been used as bipolar cores to obtain flakes for expedient tools.

A major problem is different conceptions of "bipolar pieces." In one case bipolar pieces are flakes and cores (e.g., Shott 1989, 1999), while in another bipolar pieces are tools, typically wedges (e.g., LeBlanc 1992). The latter are often referred to as *pièces esquillées*. There is certainly some overlap in the morphology of these items. In short, wedges and wedge-shaped bipolar cores may look similar because of similar production and damage patterns (Shott 1999).

Hayden (1980:2–3) distinguishes *pièces esquillées* from bipolar cores. The former are tools that may be mistaken for bipolar cores. Generally, *pièces esquillées* are made on flakes or tool fragments, crushing is exhibited at the ends (though the removals are small), flakes removed from either end only extend part of the way across the piece, the original ventral face of the flake is often discernable, and they are generally thin. Hayden (1980:3) suggests that the most likely use for such tools was the splitting of green bone. Bipolar cores, in contrast, are used for the production of flakes. These cores are often thick with flat bases, were typically not made on a flake, have flake scars extending the full length of the core, and often have cortex remaining on several faces. Hayden (1980:4) also notes that if bipolar cores were used on site, then bipolar flakes and shatter should also be present. Pitted anvil stones would also be common. *Pièces esquillées* do not require the use of an anvil stone and flakes removed from such tools would likely be small. This contrasts with a common idea in the Southeast literature that bipolar technology is used exclusively to create *pièces esquillées* (i.e., Bense 1994).

Several flintknapping experiments have been conducted with the goal of identifying debris produced from bipolar reduction. These experiments (e.g., Bradbury 2010; Jeske and Lurie 1993; Kuijt et al. 1995) have all noted problems in identifying individual flakes as bipolar. For example, in recent experiments with Burlington chert conducted by Bradbury (2010), only 13.7 percent of the flakes produced from bipolar reduction exhibited classic characteristics that would identify them as bipolar flakes. Several researchers have concluded that use of bipolar technology is best viewed at the assemblage level (e.g., Bradbury 2010; Jeske and Lurie 1993; Kuijt et al. 1995). For example, Bradbury (2010:98, 105) successfully used multiple regression analysis of the percents of blocky debris and broken platforms to estimate the percentage of an assemblage resulting from bipolar reduction. Additionally, Barham (1987:46) determined rounded nodules smaller than 50 mm could not be easily flaked using a direct percussion method. This size cutoff for a given shape can be used to suggest when the use of bipolar technologies would be expected given a particular raw material environment.

Given the above, it should be possible to discern *pièces esquillées* from bipolar cores. In addition, we might suggest that bipolar cores and flakes would be more common on residential sites. We also note that bipolar flakes were likely used for a variety of tasks and these may include wedging, which further confounds identification. Obviously, interpretation of splintered pieces as either *pièces esquillées* or bipolar cores has significant implications for inferences of social and economic strategies.

Problems and Solutions

Terminology and identification are both issues with regard to blade and bipolar industries. It is difficult to identify bipolar items, particularly flakes, at the individual artifact level. Liberal definitions of blades have resulted in long, thin flakes not produced using a blade technology being classified as blades. In both cases, other evidence of the technology should be present. If a blade industry was in place at a site, then we should identify both blades and blade cores in the assemblage. The same is true for bipolar industries: bipolar flakes, bipolar cores, and anvil stones should be present if a bipolar industry was in use at a site.

There is also a problem with analyst bias and classification. Identification of blade or bipolar industries may fit preconceived notions of what should be found in an assemblage or simply be a means of demonstrating something of interest about an assemblage. This is particularly true if the analysis is conducted by someone inexperienced (Carr and Bradbury 2000).

The crucial problem in any discussion of blades and blade technology is the differences in terminology used by various researchers and the manner each is conceived. As evidence, Kimball (1996:166) states: "The use of such terms as bladelike flake and true blade reflects a general disagreement over the defining attributes as well as the nature of blades in early lithic industries. In my opinion, it does not seem so important to agree upon a single definition of blade or 'blade-ness,' but that we recognize a blade as an intentionally removed, formalized flake, rather than the debitage of some other reduction sequence for the specific technologies one is studying." While we certainly agree that a blade is an intentionally removed, formalized flake, we would argue that there *does* need to be a single definition. Part of the problem, as we see it, is that there is a lack of standardization in the classification of these technologies. If there is no consensus in the definition of a blade, how are comparisons between various assemblages to be made? Issues of terminology such as the use of *blade, bladelike flake, prismatic flake, lamellar flake,* and so on extend back over 50 years (Solecki 1955; see discussion in Collins 1999:7–9).

With respect to blades, we suggest the definition of a blade should follow that of Johnson (1983:50) as a long, thin flake with a "prepared broad angle platform, parallel lateral edges, and dorsal flake scars that parallel the longitudinal axis of the blade and originate from the same platform." Sain and Goodyear (this volume) operationalize this definition through calculation of a "blade score," which we endorse. As an additional check of the data, at the assemblage level, at least half of the specimens produced from a blade technology will have two dorsal ridges and a trapezoidal cross section (e.g., Parry 1994). Further, distinctive blade cores, crested flakes, and platform rejuvenation flakes should be present in the assemblage, providing additional evidence of a blade technology. Finally, experimental reproduction of blade industries to produce blades, blade cores, and platform rejuvenation flakes would provide a comparative collection for use in identifying these artifact types in an assemblage. In addition, such experiments could produce baseline data for determining the relationship between the number of blades expected per core, amount of cutting edge expected, and similar technological aspects of blade production and use.

With regard to bipolar technology, terminology is likewise a problem. Various terms including *bipolar, pièces esquillées, splintered pieces,* and *strike-a-lights,* among others, are used to describe bipolar materials. In technical terms, *pièces esquillées* represent specific, manufactured tools, not the product of bipolar technology. There is some overlap between characteristics of *pièces esquillées* and bipolar cores, thus some confusion. At the assemblage level, bipolar technology should be associated with bipolar cores, bipolar flakes, anvil stones, and hammerstones. *Pièces esquillées* should not be associated with these artifacts. Complicating matters is the fact that both bipolar flakes/cores and *pièces esquillées* could be present in the same assemblage, as the consequences of similar conditions.

Examining the Evidence: The Organization of Early Archaic Lithic Technology

Blades

For this study, we compiled summary data from 47 Paleoindian and Early Archaic components concerning the number of blades and blade cores. Our sample is limited to those sites with specific counts in published reports.

A plot of the number of blades versus cores (Figure 6.1) for all of the assemblages in our data set indicates a very limited number of blade cores for Early Archaic assemblages. In contrast, there does appear to be a relationship for the Paleoindian data. The Sims and Big Pine Tree sites are possible outliers (many blades, few blade cores). Regression analysis using all of the data indicates a linear relationship between the numbers of blades and blade cores ($r^2 = .381$; $F = 7.4$; $df = 1, 12$; $p = .019$). This relationship is much stronger when Sims and Big Pine Tree are excluded from the analysis ($r^2 = .706$; $F = 24.057$; $df = 1, 10$; $p = .0006$).

The analysis of the Early Archaic data is somewhat more complex. Of the 18 assemblages in the analysis, six had no blades or blade cores identified. If all

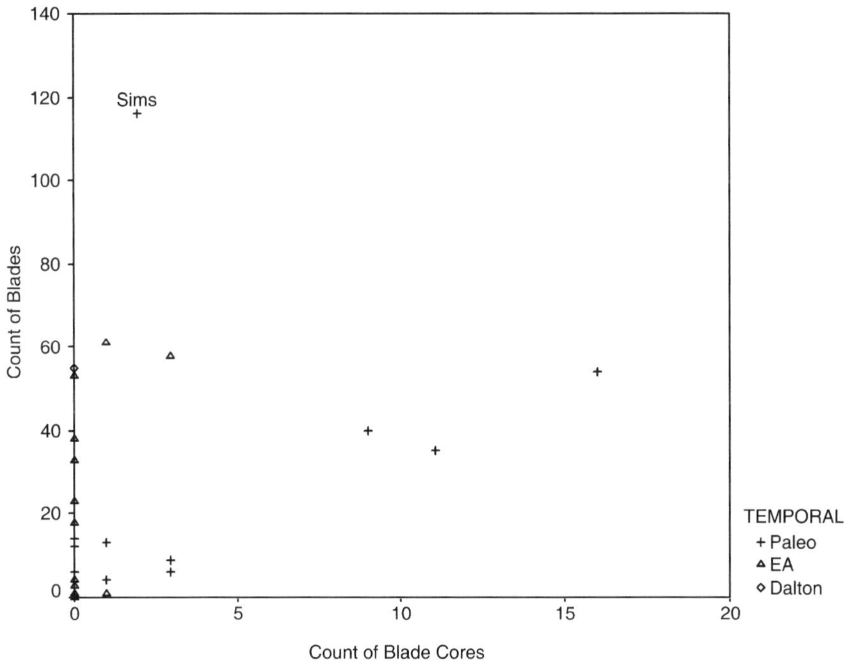

Figure 6.1. Plot of blades versus blade cores for all sites included in analysis.

of the Early Archaic assemblages are included in the analysis, then a weak, but significant, relationship is seen ($r^2 = .276$; $F = 6.09$; $df = 1, 16$; $p = .025$). If only those assemblages that include blades are considered, no relationship is indicated ($r^2 = .221$; $F = 2.84$; $df = 1, 11$; $p = .123$), meaning that the inclusion of assemblages with no evidence for blade industries is influencing the analysis. Overall, the data suggest that there is no relationship between the numbers of blades and blade cores in Early Archaic assemblages. Additionally, a one-way analysis of variance shows significant differences in the ratio of blade cores to blades between Early Archaic and Paleoindian assemblages ($F = 9.83$; $df = 1, 22$; $p = .0048$). Both blades and cores are present in most Paleoindian assemblages with blades, but blade cores are very limited or absent from Early Archaic assemblages. In our sample, 316 blades were associated with Early Archaic assemblages, yet only five blade cores were identified from these same assemblages (ratio of 63.2 blades per core). Only the Main site (n = 1 blade and 1 core), Calloway Island (n = 58 blades, 3 blade cores), and Bacon Farm (Kirk Corner Notched component, n = 61 blades, 1 blade core) had evidence of blade cores in addition to blades. In contrast, 1,040 blades and 81 blade cores (12.8 blades per core) were present in our Paleoindian data set.

Blade cores, like many tools, represent a time investiture and likely were curated. Therefore, one would not expect common recovery of these items unless they were exhausted. Additionally, if raw materials are scarce, blade cores may be recycled by some other means. Such is the case for a number of the Clovis sites (Collins 1999). However, some of the Early Archaic sites examined are large base camps with 50 or more blades reported. These numbers of blades are greater than for most of the Paleoindian assemblages in our study sample. In contrast, blade cores are scarce at the Early Archaic sites as compared to Paleoindian sites. In addition, many Paleoindian tools, such as unifaces, are manufactured on blades, but this is not seen in Early Archaic assemblages.

While there is certainly a relationship between blades and cores in the Paleoindian data, it is not a perfect relationship. Factors such as variation in manufacture, use, and curation of blades and cores, specialization, and gifting/exchange, as well as recovery methods, definitional issues, and analyst bias, will result in a less-than-perfect relationship. Our thinking is that if there was an Early Archaic blade technology in use, there should be a comparable relationship between blades and blade cores. Conversely, the lack of such a relationship in the Early Archaic data, in conjunction with the large numbers of "blades" reported for some Early Archaic sites, suggests that these items may have been misclassified in many cases.

While preliminary, several hypotheses can be suggested concerning the use of blades during the Early Archaic in the Southeast: (1) a true blade technology was not used; (2) blade manufacture played a minor role in the economy; (3) blade technology was organized differently than during Paleoindian times; or (4) a combination of the above. Our current assessment is that Early Archaic people did not use a blade technology.

Finally, in order to demonstrate this, lithic analysts who have an understanding not only of blade technologies but also of stone tool production in general must reanalyze existing assemblages. Our experience with going back to old collections is that even if the description of tools is thorough, much less care was taken with flake analysis. It is common to go through a bag labeled "flakes" and identify small biface fragments, unifacial tools, and cores. Our reanalysis of Early Archaic lithic assemblages has not produced an unrecognized blade industry, but quite the opposite. The fact remains that approaching an assemblage with an open mind concerning the methods of stone tool production will allow a better understanding of that assemblage.

Bipolar

While certainly not exhaustive, the bipolar data we collected provide a cross section of Early Archaic sites (Table 6.1; Hardaway site only screened through 12.7 mm). Several aspects of these data are noteworthy. First, with the excep-

Table 6.1. Summary of bipolar data for Early Archaic sites

Site	Distance to Material Source	Size of Material	Quality of Material	Component	Bipolar Cores	Bipolar Flakes
15LO207	100 m	Medium	High	Kirk	0	0
15CU31	100 m	Medium	High	Kirk	0	0
Hart site (15LA183)	7 km	Medium	Moderate	Bifurcate	0	0
Main site	6 km	Small	High	Bifurcate	15	37
12HR520	<3 km	Large	Moderate–high	Upper Kirk	0	0
12HR521	<3 km	Large	Moderate–high	Middle Kirk	0	0
12HR522	<3 km	Large	Moderate–high	Lower Kirk	0	0
12HR523	<3 km	Large	Moderate–high	St. Charles	0	0
12HR524	<3 km	Large	Moderate–high	Thebes	0	0
12HR525	<3 km	Large	Moderate–high	Early Side Notched	0	0
Icehouse Bottom	<1 km	Small	High	Lower Kirk	9	4
Icehouse Bottom	<1 km	Small	High	Upper Kirk	388	43
Icehouse Bottom	<1 km	Small	High	St. Albans	186	13
Icehouse Bottom	<1 km	Small	High	LeCroy	370	62
Rose Island	<1 km	Small	High	Upper Kirk	25	4
Rose Island	<1 km	Small	High	St. Albans	711	78
Rose Island	<1 km	Small	High	LeCroy	757	96
Rose Island	<1 km	Small	High	Kanawha	17	2
St. Albans	24 km	Large	Low–moderate	Charleston	0	0
St. Albans	24 km	Large	Low–moderate	Kirk	0	0
St. Albans	24 km	Large	Low–moderate	Bifurcate	0	0
Hardaway	8 km	Large	High	Kirk-Hardaway	33	0
G. S. Lewis	15 km			Kirk-Palmer	1	Present

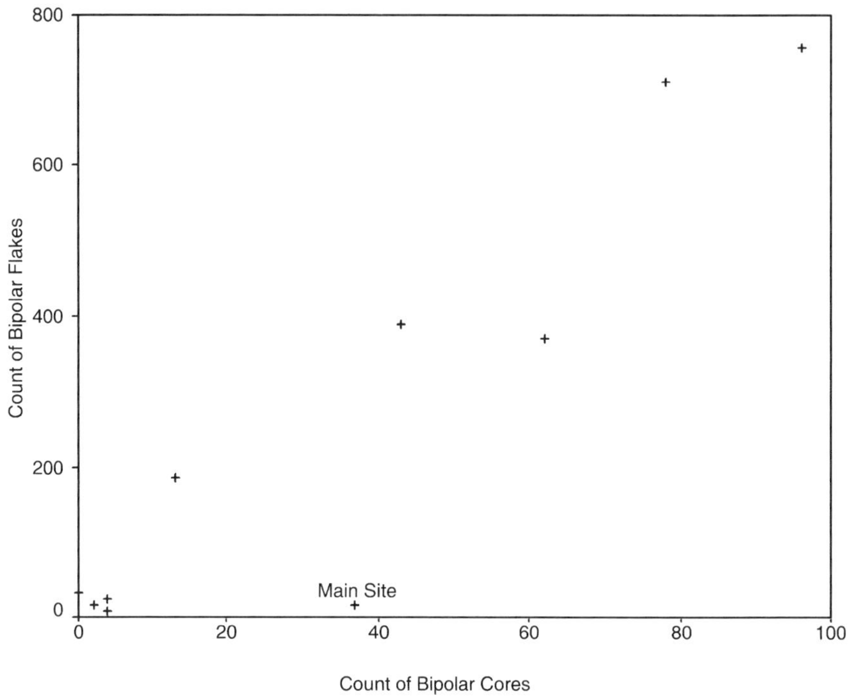

Figure 6.2. Number of bipolar flakes by bipolar cores for Early Archaic sites.

tion of the Main site, bipolar cores outnumber bipolar flakes. A linear relationship is indicated (Figure 6.2: $r^2 = .97$; $F = 606.8$; $df = 1, 19$; $p < .0001$ with Main removed; $r^2 = .9$; $F = 185.68$; $df = 1, 20$; $p < .0001$ with Main included). Second, bipolar materials predominantly are represented on sites with either limited access to raw materials or access to only raw materials of a small size. This suggests that the use of bipolar technology is related to the local raw material environment. For example, the Tellico Early Archaic sites inferred as residential camps have significant amounts of bipolar materials present. Local Knox chert, found in close proximity to these sites, is of high quality but available as small, rounded nodules. In contrast, the St. Albans site does not have bipolar materials. The local Kanawha chert, though of lesser quality, is of large size and abundant in the area. Also, Kimball (1996) and Carr (1995) both note a general increase in bipolar use from Kirk through the various bifurcate horizons at the Tellico sites. There is also a corresponding increase in the use of quartz and other non-chert materials during this time. This is a possible indication of suitable raw materials becoming scarcer over time, thus creating the need to conserve raw materials.

Economic/social strategies and environmental conditions are the impetus for the use of bipolar technology. For example, both the Main and Hart sites represent short-term residential sites dating to Early Archaic "bifurcate" times and both were located in areas with limited chert availability. Bipolar materials, both cores and flakes, were identified in the Main site assemblage, as well as anvil stones. Newman chert can be procured approximately 6 km from the site (Pecora 1995). In contrast, no bipolar materials were identified at the Hart site. There is, however, ample evidence for the recycling of materials at Hart. Bifaces were used until they were exhausted and small biface fragments show indications of use (Bradbury 2006). Brush Creek chert represents the closest material source and can be found some 7 km from the Hart site. Also of note are the high percentages of nonlocal materials (43 percent of flakes, 67 percent of tools) at Hart and the vast majority (99 percent) of local materials at Main. Looking at the geologic maps, the area surrounding Main would have had stone present, though these materials are generally of small size. Larger chert nodules are found around the Hart site, though they are not as abundant.

Overall, the data for the Early Archaic in the Southeast are suggestive of bipolar methods used when local materials are of small size. Bipolar technology allows a knapper to obtain the largest possible flake from a small nodule. In addition, bipolar methods may represent the best methods for producing flakes from small, rounded nodules.

Discussion

Blades represent patterned, highly controlled removals from a core of a standardized size/shape. If you are very mobile and keying on a specific resource, then your toolkit is likely to be highly specialized. In such cases, a standardized size/shape for blanks would be of use. For example, blades can be used as part of composite tools such that the stone component is easily replaced. The manufacture of blades does waste some material as the core must be prepared for blade removal. For this reason, we would not expect to see a blade industry in areas of limited raw materials unless the requirement for standardized blanks was considered crucial by prehistoric knappers. The potential for specialization (sensu Bar-Yosef and Kuhn 1999) as represented by blade manufacture is intriguing.

Bipolar reduction represents something of the opposite end of the continuum with regard to standardized products. This method of manufacturing flakes often is referred to as random and uncontrolled. It is useful in obtaining the last little bit out of a limited amount of material or opening small, rounded nodules (e.g., split cobble technique) that would be difficult to knap otherwise. While the goal of bipolar methods is to produce flakes, the cores, in rare cases, may also have been used as tools. With microwear analysis, it should be possible to separate bipolar cores from wedges used in the production of organic tools. Even without the aid of a microscope, morphological differences exist between wedges (or *pièces esquillées*) and bipolar cores and other bipolar pieces. Bipolar cores are thick with flat bases, not made on flakes, have flake scars extending the full length of the core, and often have cortex remaining on several faces. In contrast, *pièces esquillées* are thinner, are manufactured, and flakes removed from such tools during use are small.

Several patterns are evident in regard to the presence of bipolar technologies represented at Early Archaic sites in the Southeast. Sites with extensive evidence for bipolar technologies are located in areas with small raw materials. These materials can be located in close proximity to the site. Sites exhibiting extensive use of bipolar technology appear to represent larger residential camps. However, there are exceptions to these patterns. For example, at the Hardaway site, only quartz crystal (small pebbles) was used for bipolar reduction. The majority of the materials at the site were manufactured from Uwharrie rhyolite, a material source with larger pieces.

Summary

A problem of identification exists for both blade and bipolar products and byproducts. In the case of blades, a strict definition, the application of a blade score method, or both are needed to ensure that long, thin flakes produced by other means are not mistaken for true blades. With respect to bipolar materials, the problem is with identifying individual bipolar flakes. Our current methods allow bipolar debris to be identified at the assemblage level. In both cases, other indicators of the specific technology (e.g., blade cores, crested flakes, bipolar cores, anvil stones) should be identified to ensure that such industries are recognized. With the current data, we are unconvinced that a true blade industry was part of the organization of Early Archaic lithic technology. Bipolar materials are common on Early Archaic sites with raw material constraints. It is unclear whether *pièces esquillées* or wedges were used by Early Archaic inhabitants of the Southeast.

This work suggests that there is no continuity from Paleoindian to Early Archaic as evidenced by the use of a blade industry. Recent study of the Paleoindian blade industry suggests it was used only in certain areas and is not a hallmark of Paleoindian lithic technology. However, prehistoric knappers across space and through time appear to have relied on bipolar methods when they worked with small nodules. In general, there is great difficulty in using available Early Archaic site data due to the potential misidentification of blades and bipolar materials, inadequate reporting of metric and morphological data, and minimal drawings or photographs. Reexamination of existing collections by trained lithic analysts armed with comparative collections could establish the validity of these hypotheses. Microwear analysis would aid in identifying *pièces esquillées*. There is much lithic analysis yet to be accomplished in the Southeast.

Acknowledgments

We would like to thank Sarah Price for her thoughtful comments on various drafts of this chapter as well as acknowledge those of Jay Johnson and an anonymous reviewer. Any errors or omissions are the sole fault of the authors.

7

Provisioning Middle Archaic Places

Changing Technological Organization and Raw Material Economy in the Uwharrie Mountains

Paul T. Thacker, Joël Hardison, and Carolyn Conklin

Constructing hypotheses about past cultures based on flaked stone assemblages is a complex undertaking, requiring the collection of large data sets of observations and appropriate middle range theory linking organized patterns of attributes to human behaviors. Often the sample sizes are small, the assemblage or site representativeness open to question, and/or the linking arguments are weak. Nevertheless, the interpretation and integration of lines of evidence from lithic assemblages is an essential source of anthropological knowledge, especially in earlier periods of prehistory with poor preservation of organic artifacts and ecofacts.

This chapter is a response to Carr, Bradbury, and Price's challenge to generate new and broadly relevant interpretations of the archaeology of the southeastern United States using data primarily from lithic assemblages. Our work investigates changing technological organization and raw material economy at an important, stratified, prehistoric site (31MG328) in the Uwharrie Mountains of central North Carolina. Flaked stone artifacts typify the Archaic record of the Piedmont and also dominate the region's influence on archaeological space-time systematics in the eastern United States. The geographical area contains major geological formations of knappable rhyolite and dacite, including the famous Morrow Mountain rhyolite (Daniel and Butler 1996). The prehistoric exploitation of these raw material sources and the resulting distribution of artifacts at the end of their use lives have played major roles in formulating anthropological models of mobility of Late Paleoindian and Early Archaic hunter-gatherers on the Middle Atlantic Slope (Anderson 1996; Daniel 1998; Moore et al. 2004).

Given the important contributions of stone tool analysis to regional culture history in the Piedmont, surprisingly few sustained archaeological projects have proposed and evaluated anthropological hypotheses of Archaic and

Woodland period culture change in North Carolina using lithic artifact assemblages. Some of this hesitation is attributable to the Piedmont's poor preservation conditions for other types of corroborating archaeological remains such as organic artifacts and ecofacts or well-preserved features and site activity areas. However, it is our position that lithic analysts should not wait for a Middle Atlantic Koster to be found and excavated before building hypotheses of prehistoric culture change in the Piedmont after Early Archaic times. Rich assemblages from currently known stratified sites such as 31MG328 are appropriate data that, in combination with suitable middle range theory, facilitate an understanding of prehistoric Native American settlement and subsistence systems during the Mid-Holocene.

A Stratified Site in the Uwharries: Lithic Assemblages from 31MG328

Site 31MG328 is located in the Uwharrie National Forest, approximately 19 km from Troy, North Carolina, on a long, narrow ridge at the base of a large hill. The construction of roads and trails, as well as logging activities and tree fall, have all contributed to surface disturbance of the site. The location is not a quarry but is within a few hundred meters of both sizeable rhyolite outcrops and regionally ubiquitous quartz veins. Since the discovery of the site in 1978, several archaeological investigations have defined the boundaries through limited shovel testing and unit excavations (Abbott 1996; Cooper and Norville 1979; Cooper and Smith 1981; Harmon and Snedeker 1993). The most recent excavation at 31MG328 was conducted in 2006–2007 as part of the National Forest Service's Passport in Time public volunteer field training program. Led by Joël Hardison, the field program excavated more than 30 units, including a 20-m-long trench, and recovered a very large assemblage of over 35,000 stone artifacts. Projectile points and other diagnostic artifacts from the 2006–2007 excavations indicate a very long chronological sequence at 31MG328, spanning the entire Holocene and each subperiod from the Early Archaic to the Middle Woodland (Hardison 2007).

The stratigraphic integrity of the trench and units was assessed using vertical and horizontal patterning in diagnostic projectile points, ground stone tools, and ceramic artifacts (Conklin 2008). Tree throw and road construction contributed to the reverse stratigraphy present in the disturbed top levels along most of the trench. Cultural stratigraphy is intact along sections of the trench and in most of the 2-×-2-m units, a determination reinforced by the recovery of intact archaeological features.

Artifacts from each major chronological subperiod from the Early Archaic through the Middle Woodland have been found at 31MG328. The uppermost intact archaeological level is a palimpsest of artifacts mostly from the Middle Woodland subperiod. Yadkin points are common in this level, co-occurring with some Yadkin ceramics tempered with crushed quartz. The artifact assemblage, however, is certainly a chronological mixture resulting from long-term artifact accumulation, as Badin and a few Savannah River points (late Middle Archaic; LMA) are present. The middle cultural levels at 31MG328 contain numerous Morrow Mountain I and Morrow Mountain II points, along with less-frequent Guilford types. These middle levels are unambiguously Middle Archaic in date (Oliver 1999; Ward and Davis 1999). Site 31MG328 was a campsite of significant occupation duration at this time as several intact Middle Archaic features, including a hearth, were excavated in 2007. The lowest archaeological levels at the site contain Kirk (both corner-notched and stemmed variants) and Stanly points. These lowest levels appear to span the transition from the late Early Archaic to the Middle Archaic. Further chronological subdivision of the stratigraphy of some units is possible, but probably inappropriate given the relatively shallow overall deposit depth and the relative inexperience of some volunteer fieldworkers.

Lithic Assemblage Analysis and Individual Flake Attribute Results

A total of 9,552 flaked stone artifacts were analyzed from levels with stratigraphic integrity. Retouched tools, cores, and debris (including incomplete flakes and shatter) were analyzed separately from the more than 4,300 debitage pieces (complete flakes). Seventeen attributes reflecting reduction technology and lithic economy were recorded for each piece of debitage and retouched tool. Individual flake analysis included recording the following attributes: raw material type, percent dorsal cortex, cortex location, maximum length, maximum width, width at midpoint, maximum thickness, thickness at midpoint, platform type, platform length, platform thickness, presence of abrasion, cross-section morphology, termination type, flake profile type, weight in grams, and evidence of burning.

Metric flake dimensions are measured relative to the flaking axis, with a piece's midpoint defined as the location halfway between the striking platform and the most distal point along the direction of flaking. More than 99 percent of pieces have platform types considered cortical, simple (lacking cortex), crushed, dihedral, or faceted. Presence of platform abrasion is recorded if abrasion occurs along 25 percent or more of the dorsal platform edge. The categorical variable of cross-section morphology is assessed at the flake midpoint, with the cross section described perpendicular to the flaking axis. Flakes from

31MG328 (99 percent) have amorphous, triangular, and trapezoidal cross sections, with the trapezoidal forms often present on mid- and final-stage biface finishing flakes. Flake profile categories define the degree and direction of flake curvature along the ventral surface from platform to termination. Flakes from 31MG328 have profiles classified as irregular, straight, slightly curved, curved, very curved, or torqued. Burning is recorded as absent, partial (<35 percent of one surface), or extensive (>35 percent of one surface).

The thick weathered rinds that define cortical flakes in this analysis are distinguishable from surface patinations that sometimes formed on the rhyolite artifacts after flaking. Patination after manufacture is recognized by heavy weathering on multiple flaked surfaces and/or both dorsal and ventral sides of the piece.

This individual flake analysis supported the identification of different types of debitage produced during different reduction activities while also maintaining critical examination of the validity of these type distinctions (Andrefsky 2001). For example, the significance of an association between faceted or abraded platforms and flakes from later-stage biface reduction can be contextualized within overall trends of platform types across the entire assemblage.

Initial attribute analysis of debitage from 31MG328 was designed to explore changes in technological organization across the Archaic/Woodland boundary since this prehistoric transition supposedly marks major changes ranging from projectile propulsion and design to group subsistence economies, settlement strategies, and prehistoric social organization in the eastern United States. Categorical attributes such as platform type and several dimensional ratios were expected to reflect differences in reduction techniques related to functional constraints such as final projectile point form and hafting techniques (Shott 1997). As usual, the archaeological record did not cooperate with our preconceived notions. The overall diversity and prevalence of different knapping techniques, insofar as we can discriminate them, vary little through time at 31MG328 (Table 7.1). The relative frequencies of platform preparation types, platform dimensions, flake cross sections, profiles, and terminations are very similar or nearly identical between each archaeological unit. After much data exploration comparing tools, debitage, raw material use, and other characteristics between level assemblages, we conclude that the most significant lithic assemblage variability at 31MG328 stems from broad organizational differences between subperiods rather than from idiosyncrasies in knapping technique related to individual skill or site function. Put another way, prehistoric knappers at 31MG328 throughout the Archaic and Woodland periods were reducing bifaces or retouching unifacial tools using similar ranges of techniques, although final tool form and possibly even site function varied significantly.

Table 7.1. Site 31MG328 lithic assemblage characteristics

	Attribute	LEA/EMA (n = 1,942)	MA (n = 3,717)	LMA/Woodland (n = 3,893)
Raw material	% Rhyolite	95.4	94.1	91.8
	% Cortical rhyolite	13.4	9.9	8.5
	% Quartz	4.4	5.7	7.9
	% Other	.2	.2	.3
Platform type	% Cortical	3.1	2.7	2.4
	% Simple	34.6	35.1	33.2
	% Crushed	7.4	9.5	11.1
	% Dihedral	18.8	20.2	20.1
	% Faceted	36.1	32.5	33.1
Rhyolite flake cross section	% Amorphous	85.1	80.1	82.0
	% Triangular and trapezoidal	14.9	19.9	18.0
Quartz flake cross section	% Amorphous	88.9	78.5	75.7
	% Triangular and trapezoidal	11.1	21.5	24.3

When analyzed within a reduction sequence and lithic economy framework, however, 31MG328 reveals an abrupt and significant change in the flaked stone assemblages during the Early to Middle Archaic transition. Different activities were taking place on the site during the late Early Archaic/early Middle Archaic (LEA/EMA) and the Morrow Mountain Middle Archaic (MA) subperiods, and different choices were being made by knappers engaged in these activities.

The debris and debitage from shaping bifacial preforms and tools constitute most of the earliest assemblage (dating to the Early to Middle Archaic transition). Cortical flakes and debris are common, with few finished flake tools recovered. "Cortical flake" is technically a misnomer, since what we evaluated was the occurrence of a distinctive weathered rind that forms on exposed surfaces of rhyolite outcrops and cobbles. A decrease in "cortical flake" frequency during the Middle Archaic at 31MG328 cannot be attributed to changes in available initial cobble sizes given the geology of local rhyolite outcrops. This pattern stems from proportionally more initial shaping and early-stage lithic reduction in the Early/Middle Archaic assemblage.

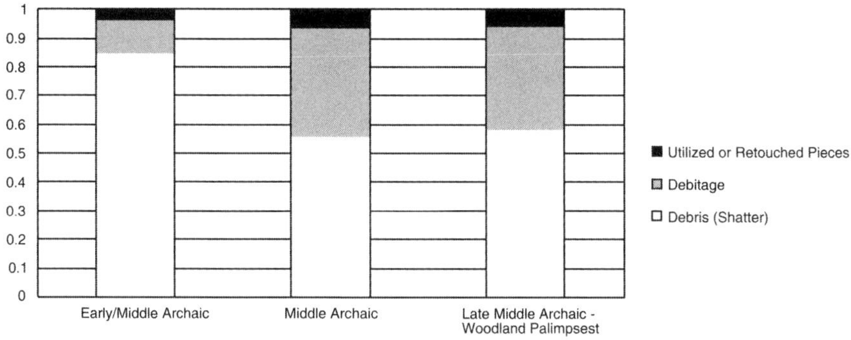

Figure 7.1. Proportions of lithic artifact classes by component.

All of the level assemblages contain large amounts of debris and shatter, an expected finding given the close proximity to rhyolite and quartz raw material sources (Brantingham 2003). The earliest assemblage, however, comprises a very large amount of debris compared to debitage or blanks (Figure 7.1). This high ratio also implies more early-stage reduction of rhyolite cobbles in the Early/Middle Archaic level.

Further along the reduction sequence, final-stage finishing activities and on-site tool use can be indicated by the relative frequency of utilized flakes and retouched tools. The Early/Middle Archaic level has the lowest percentage of these two artifact types, totaling only 3.8 percent of the assemblage (see Figure 7.1), implying less tool finishing/use on site and/or transport of finished tools away from the site. The lower density of artifacts and few finished tools (both bifacial and unifacial) from the earliest levels is consistent with an interpretation of the site as a special-purpose lithic procurement site.

Daniel and Davis (1996), Oliver (1999), Drye (1998), and other archaeologists investigating the Archaic period in North Carolina have established that the earlier Kirk and Stanly bifacial tools and finished projectile points on average are larger than (or more conservatively at least the same size as) Morrow Mountain I and II and other Middle Archaic bifacial tools. Our results confirmed this trend albeit with a small sample.

Logically, if 31MG328 is a gearing-up lithic procurement site for preparing larger finished tools during the earlier Kirk/Stanly occupation, and if reduction technique and raw material form do not vary between the chronological subperiods, then the Early/Middle Archaic assemblage should have larger debitage dimensions. There is the unexpected pattern of smaller flake sizes in the earliest assemblage (during the manufacturing of larger tools). The Early/Middle Archaic assemblage exhibits statistically significant lower mean flake lengths for all rhyolite flakes (12.7 mm, *s* = 5.9) and for those with "cortex" (13.7 mm, *s* = 6.3) as compared to the Middle Archaic assemblage (16.1 mm, *s* = 7.2; 19.2 mm, *s* = 9.3, respectively). A Welch's separate variance t-test results in t-values of −9.8534 for comparison of all rhyolite flakes and −4.7028 for rhyolite flakes with cortex. These t-values are considered extremely statistically significant, with p-values of less than 0.0001 and 0.001, respectively. Closer examination of debitage produced from the outer surface of the rhyolite cobbles (with weathered rinds) indicates that more than 40 percent of these flakes have about 10 percent dorsal cortex despite their smaller size as compared to fewer than 30 percent of the flakes from the Middle Archaic. As a set, these differences mean that in spite of the proximity to rhyolite sources, Early and early Middle Archaic reduction strategies were organized in ways that conserved raw material even during initial production.

In addition to the hearths and other features excavated in the Middle Archaic levels of 31MG328, the recovered lithic assemblage is dramatically different from that of the preceding levels, with much greater frequencies of utilized flakes, retouched tools, and bifacial implements. The complete Middle Archaic reduction sequence is present in both the rhyolite and quartz assemblages as confirmed by a more balanced ratio of debris to flakes. The Morrow Mountain debitage assemblages display greater proportions of triangular and trapezoidal cross sections (see Table 7.1), a characteristic found on flakes produced during middle- and late-stage reduction activities. The Middle Archaic assemblage also has a higher percentage of platform abrasion on flakes, at nearly 50 percent, as compared to the Early/Middle Archaic at just over 40 percent. Platform abrasion is a technique commonly associated with bifacial shaping and finishing although platforms were abraded during non-bifacial core reduction at 31MG328. More important, abrasion is not common in early-stage reduction. The higher ratio in Middle Archaic levels is consistent with other evidence of late-stage reduction in the later assemblage.

Stone Tool Manufacturing at 31MG328: Blank Selection Behaviors and Organizational Context

Retouched tool frequencies are relatively low in all levels at 31MG328, which makes statistical comparison of toolkit diversity difficult. The Early/Middle Archaic toolkit contains a large percentage (23 percent) of double tools (retouched pieces with two distinct edge preparations), but this is a small proportion of the total tool sample size. The Middle Archaic toolkit appears to contain larger proportions of informal tools, such as composite notches and exhausted final-stage cores on rhyolite, in addition to higher frequencies of retouched quartz. These toolkit configurations support our general interpretation of an Early/Middle Archaic emphasis on conserving raw material juxtaposed by a Middle Archaic organization structured by longer-duration occupation of a place well provisioned with local raw materials.

Beyond tool edge morphology, lithic economizing behavior is frequently evident in attributes connected to tool blank selection and use life (Odell 2003; Sellet 2004). At 31MG328, the overall dimensions of Early/Middle Archaic utilized flakes and flake tools were slightly smaller than their Middle Archaic counterparts (average lengths 33.9 mm and 37.3 mm, respectively), but these averages alone should not be interpreted as an indication of an organization of technology focused on conservation of raw material (Shott 2000). Demonstrating selection and reuse behaviors requires understanding the original form of the flake blanks selected for use and retouch. An important part of contextualizing blank choice is contrasting the dimensional variability of utilized pieces with available unretouched and unutilized blanks produced on site.

Ternary or triplot graphs are useful for examining the decision making of prehistoric tool users by exploring dimensional contrast between used flakes and unused debitage. Figure 7.2 plots the relative ratio of the three general dimensions of flake size (maximum length, width at midpoint, and maximum thickness). Contrasting plots of the utilized flakes/retouched tools with the overall assemblage reveals patterns in the morphological characteristics desirable for tool blanks. Debitage dimensional variability is plotted with small crosses and results in a background cloud of overlapping plots that represent all flakes produced at 31MG328 in each level.

In each period, the distribution of utilized flake plots overlaps with most of the debitage spread. If prehistoric people at 31MG328 systematically preferred certain types of flakes for tasks, for example, more elongated blanks for cutting, then the plots would not completely overlap. The plots in Figure 7.2 thus suggest that a wide range of flake proportions was considered suitable for use in basic expedient tasks.

Retouched tools present a clear contrast in selection between the two chronological periods. Early/Middle Archaic tool blank selection favored long and thick flakes, as the plots are skewed to the upper right side of the debitage spread. The brief occupation duration and special-purpose nature of the site during this period accounts for this configuration, consistent with the overall interpretation of the assemblage as exhibiting a truncated early-stage reduction sequence. In contrast, the full range of blanks available were used for expedient flake and unifacial flake tools during the Morrow Mountain (Middle Archaic) subperiod. This characteristic is expected at residential sites occupied for longer durations and/or at locations provisioned with plentiful raw mate-

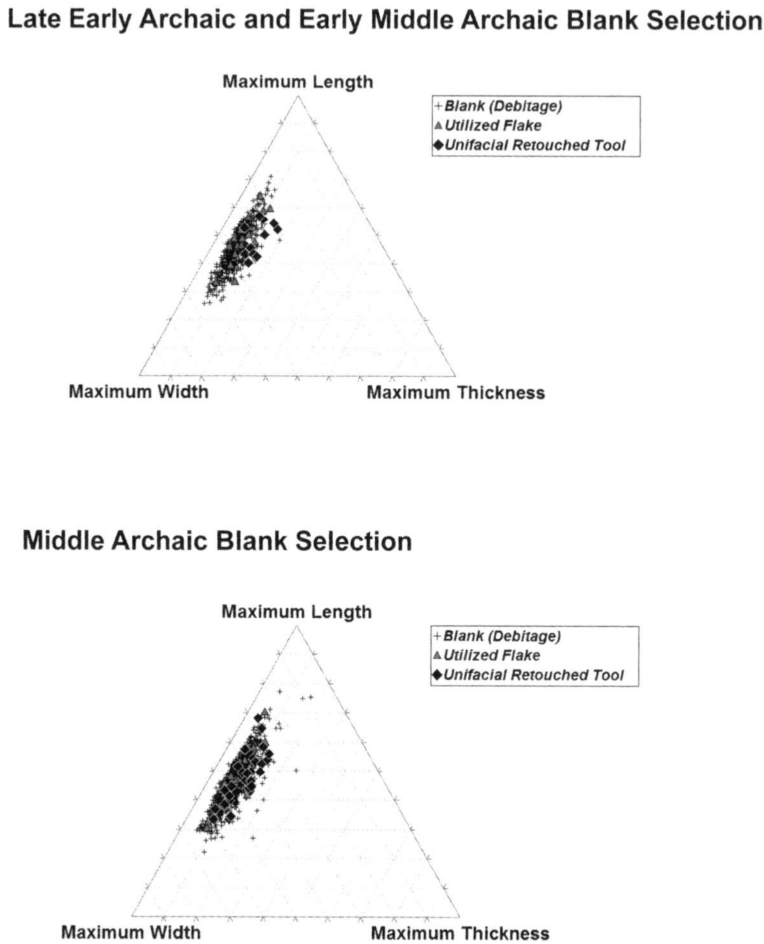

Figure 7.2. Retouched tool and utilized flake blank selection at 31MG328.

rials. A preliminary study of use and retouch intensity (Andrefsky 2009; Eren et al. 2005) found no statistically significant variability between the periods, with very few pieces exhibiting extensive, invasive retouch.

Archaic Raw Material Provisioning and Settlement System Organization: Bridging Arguments and Middle Range Theory

Anthropologically relevant lithic studies rely on robust and explicit middle range theory linking artifact or assemblage attributes to past human behavior. Interpreting past lithic reduction behavior, however, is not inherently anthropologically relevant, a point made by Binford (1981) three decades ago while debating the "Pompeii premise." Lithic assemblage patterns result from behavioral practices that are organized by cultural systems. Knowing how a single bifacial tool was knapped or the stage of manufacturing that took place at a specific location may interest or excite lithic analysts but too often these "just-so" behavioral interpretations are the end point of resultant archaeological studies. In the extreme cases, the substantial efforts of the lithic analyst are published as a stand-alone, descriptive chapter with little impact on the overall interpretation of the site. Ending interpretation at specific behavior rather than general organization greatly reduces the likelihood that archaeologists and prehistorians working to interpret other data sets will evaluate or integrate anthropological hypotheses generated from even the largest flaked stone assemblages. Beyond the lithic realm, the anthropological breadth of our interpretation of 31MG328 is determined by the potential of middle range frameworks to generate hypotheses of culture change rather than hypotheses explaining only lower-level behavioral change.

Steve Kuhn (1992, 1995, 2004) developed a specific interpretive heuristic for lithic raw material economies centered on the concept of technological provisioning behavior. Although Kuhn developed this provisioning-focused middle range theory while analyzing Paleolithic assemblages in Eurasia, the framework yields substantial insight into the broader anthropological significance of archaeological patterns at 31MG328.

Kuhn's middle range theoretical construct differentiates between provisioning people and provisioning places with stone raw material. The two lithic provisioning strategies represent the pathways from quarry to archaeological site, combining technological organization and reduction sequence with site location and function. Provisioning people "entails keeping individuals supplied with the artifacts and raw materials they are likely to use" (Kuhn 2004:432), whereas in a strategy of provisioning places, tools and raw materials are transported and stockpiled at activity areas for use at that location.

Transport cost of raw material packages and maximizing utility to mass is of primary importance in a provisioning strategy of supplying individuals with raw material. As a result, finished tools with long use lives are preferred technologies. Transport costs can be minimized by techniques such as reducing the carrying weight of cores or bifaces from quarries, embedded procurement, utilizing nearest or local raw material sources, and/or preforming to reduce waste generated during final reduction of stone cobbles, cores, or bifaces (see discussion and examples in Odell 1996b; Shott and Nelson 2008; Surovell 2009). In theory, conservation of raw material is a greater concern within strategies that provision the individual, resulting in more efficient reduction and longer tool use lives. A number of recent studies, however, illustrate the methodological difficulty in assessing technological efficiency of reduction (Eren et al. 2008; Jennings et al. 2010), and lithic analysts should not forget Torrence's (1994) reminder that energy conservation and risk management probably did not matter as much to prehistoric hunter-gatherers as having a stone tool that worked well when needed.

Because of conservation and economizing factors, site assemblages resulting from the strategy of supplying individuals with raw material have less unfinished raw material waste and more evidence of resharpening or reshaping of tools. Hunter-gatherers that provision individuals often expend more effort obtaining suitable raw materials and producing flexible tool forms for transport than groups that provision places.

Hunter-gatherers making stone tools at places that are deliberately provisioned do not need to economize raw material as extensively, and thus site assemblages display the entire range of production activities from barely worked cobbles to discarded finished tools. The availability of raw material on site reduces the amount of resharpening and reworking of pieces during use lives, and many tool forms are less formalized or have fewer design constraints. Because this strategy is associated with longer residential stays, large amounts of raw material are procured from the closest suitable stone source areas and stockpiled. The resulting debitage assemblage reflects this local raw material preference across a wide range of manufacturing stages.

A provisioning middle range framework has the potential to link patterns in technological organization with hunter-gatherer settlement system models. As the occupation duration of a campsite increases—usually for reasons unrelated to stone tool technology—it becomes increasingly more likely and cost effective to provision the place rather than the person with raw material. This systemic change occurs at an organizational level rather than an individual one. In other words, in both strategies hunter-gatherers leave campsites with the stone tools they need to perform necessary tasks. Provisioning strategies are more about how and where raw material is used than about how tools are fashioned.

In our interpretation, 31MG328 reveals a significant shift in lithic provisioning strategies between the Early Archaic and the Middle Archaic in the Uwharries. In the Early Archaic and the earliest Middle Archaic occupations, the short reduction sequence recovered is consistent with archaeological expectations for a strategy of provisioning people. The overall reduction strategy is efficient, producing less waste debitage and large bifacial preforms and projectile points that were transported from the site. In the few cases where flakes were utilized or retouched into tools, larger and thicker blanks were selected for use.

In comparison, the entire flaked stone reduction sequence is present in Morrow Mountain levels. Flake dimensions increase during the Middle Archaic and the full range of blank morphologies is selected for retouching into unifacial tools. These characteristics correlate with the technological strategy of provisioning places in the Middle Archaic. Hearths and other archaeological features substantiate the increased duration of site occupation at 31MG328.

The provisioning strategy concept focuses on the form of raw material transported to and from the campsite and on the activities performed on site using stone tools. It does not explain the reason for the different strategies. We hypothesize that the Middle Archaic change in technological organization at 31MG328 corresponds to a significant reorganization of regional settlement systems prior to the Morrow Mountain phase about 6,200 radiocarbon years ago (just before 5000 B.C.). If the 31MG328 assemblage sample is indeed representative of broader systemic organizational change, Middle Archaic hunter-gatherers in the Piedmont of the Mid-Atlantic increased occupation duration within favorable environmental locations or patches during the first part of the Middle Archaic.

Middle Archaic Organization at the Intersite Level: The Importance of Regional Analysis

Regional analysis provides an intersite comparative context for evaluating the systemic representativeness of site-based data (Johnson 1977; Kantner 2005). Models of changing settlement organization derived from a single stratified site such as 31MG328 can be susceptible to the fallacy of the "typical site." Archaeological patterns evident at one location may not be representative of the prehistoric system as a whole (Banning 2002; Binford 1982; Butzer 1982). It is thus important to consider how a changing technological strategy toward provisioning places would be archaeologically manifest at the regional level.

While Kuhn (2004) does not fully articulate his concept of provisioning behaviors with regional-scale assemblage patterning, some archaeological implications are clear. In strategies oriented by provisioning individual people with raw material, stone is more likely to be transported longer distances from each geological source in a hunter-gatherer range. Kuhn argues that when provisioning people, "distance to source may say much more about scales of individual mobility than about use of the site itself" (Kuhn 2004:434). In contrast, places occupied for longer durations and provisioned with raw materials should evidence an increased use of raw materials from the nearest suitable sources. As argued elsewhere (Thacker 2006), the organization of local raw material use rather than that of high-quality exotic stone may provide more insight for understanding the relationships between prehistoric technology, lithic economy, and settlement strategies.

Daniel (2001) demonstrated that Late Paleoindian and Early Archaic lithic economies on the South Atlantic Slope (including the Uwharries) exploited high-quality rhyolite to manufacture flexible and transportable toolkits within a settlement system with high residential mobility. He also examined the occurrence of raw material types within artifact assemblages at the regional level, resulting in his Uwharrie-Allendale settlement model. Daniel's Early Archaic "Uwharrie band" range covers most of central North Carolina with widespread availability of fine-grained rhyolite raw materials throughout the range, but he acknowledges that his archaeological "ranges" are probably not analogous to ethnographic hunter-gatherer settlement ranges. This Early Archaic pattern of transport and economizing of high-quality stone in the Uwharries is an organizational trait consistent with a strategy of provisioning people.

The archaeological record of raw material exploitation and use in the Uwharries becomes more complex in the Middle and Late Archaic. Two Middle Archaic archaeological patterns are recognized at the regional level: an increased use of lower-quality, but more widely occurring, porphyritic rhyolite (Daniel and Butler 1996) and higher numbers of recorded sites (McReynolds 2005), especially those containing Morrow Mountain types. The great number of, and geochemical variability within, rhyolite source areas has impeded the success of more detailed sourcing studies (Steponaitis et al. 2006). Yet, a cautious and parsimonious study of prehistoric rhyolite quarries at Three Hat Mountain and nearby archaeological sites by Abbott (2003) revealed diachronic change in Archaic lithic economies. His study demonstrated that, in marked contrast to Early Archaic patterns, Middle and Late Archaic sites contained very high proportions of rhyolite from nearby rather than distant quarries. At the regional level, Abbott verified a relatively rapid/short distance decay pattern of diagnostic Three Hat Mountain rhyolite use (which he interpreted as embedded procurement), a pattern that emerged in the Middle Archaic. This assemblage composition change is exactly what a shift to provisioning places rather than people would produce archaeologically at the regional scale.

These multiple lines of evidence are consistent with a reorganization of settlement systems and lithic economies prior to the Morrow Mountain phase of the Middle Archaic. Both Daniel's and Abbott's conclusions dovetail with our hypothesis of changing provisioning strategies during the Middle Archaic. As a set, these regional archaeological observations and studies corroborate that artifact assemblage patterns evident at 31MG328 are representative of broader changes in Middle Archaic technological organization and raw material use.

The Rising Importance of Place in the Middle Archaic: Environmental Context and Behavioral Shift at 31MG328

Identifying organizational differences in a lithic assemblage does not explain the underlying reasons for the change. Middle Archaic hunter-gatherers in the Uwharries increasingly employed a strategy of provisioning longer-duration campsites with local raw materials. But lithic provisioning does not determine broader subsistence and settlement behaviors; rather, provisioning strategies are integrated within these adaptations (Sellet 2006; Shott 1996b). Decreasing residential mobility in the Uwharries during the Middle Archaic may be related to regional Mid-Holocene environmental change and resulting impacts on the biotic habitats present in the Piedmont.

Many archaeologists have mentioned the possible correlation between the Mid-Holocene environmental change and the Middle Archaic (Anderson and Hanson 1988; Anderson et al. 1996; Anderson and Schuldenrein 1983; Claggett and Cable 1982; Sassaman and Anderson 1995; Seibel 2009). These hypotheses were mostly built using Coastal Plain data sets, are not specific to the Piedmont, and/or assume a marked Hypsithermal paleoclimatic event on the eastern side of the Appalachian Mountains. In these scenarios, the vegetational communities of the Piedmont are assumed to be geographically homogenous even at the height of Mid-Holocene warming and drying. New paleoenvironmental data are challenging these reconstructions.

Extensive paleoenvironmental research on the Atlantic Coastal Plain appears to indicate an Early Holocene (prior to 7,000 years ago) that was cooler, wetter, and stormier than present, with possible occasional short-lived periods of rapid aridity (Gorman and Leigh 2004; LaMoreaux et al. 2009; Liu and Fearn 2000). Throughout the first half of the Holocene, the Bermuda High was situated to the north and east of its current cycle location, a position that greatly magnified the movement of Atlantic moisture into the Southeast. The Coastal Plain was probably a closed mixed-oak forest. Unfortunately, no high-precision climatic and paleoenvironmental reconstructions based only on local proxies exist specifically for the Uwharries, largely because of geological preservation issues. The Piedmont as a whole experienced less, but perhaps more-seasonal, precipitation and cooler temperatures than the Coastal Plain, but this reconstruction is contentious (Otvos 2005). Early Holocene biotic communities in the Piedmont were probably more open than those of the Coastal Plain, but more closed and diverse than modern counterparts.

There is no clear Hypsithermal recognized for North Carolina comparable to that recorded in the midcontinent (Booth et al. 2005; Dean et al. 1996; Driese et al. 2008). However, circulation models, pollen records, and geomorphological data from river valleys concur that the gradual effects of warming and drying climate change peaked by at least 5,500 years ago (Leigh 2008), most significantly impacting forest communities between 7,000 and 4,000 years ago. Pine species become more prevalent than oak, and modern mixed southern pine/oak/hickory forest biomes were in place across the Coastal Plain by 5,000 years ago.

These recent paleoenvironmental reconstructions suggest that throughout the Uwharrie region, productive communities became more patchy (unevenly distributed across space) during the Mid-Holocene. We hypothesize that as this important climate change affected their subsistence base, Middle Archaic hunter-gatherers responded by establishing longer-duration residential camps in choice locations determined by water, biological communities, and raw material access. This settlement system change may explain the apparent explosion in the number of Middle Archaic sites recorded in the Uwharrie National Forest. If the hypothesis of Middle Archaic settlement system change is correct, this prominent archaeological visibility results not from a significant Mid-Holocene population increase (McReynolds 2005; Wholey 2009) but from a change in settlement system organization linked to environmental change.

If place was becoming an important feature of Middle Archaic environment and society in the Uwharries, 31MG328 may allude to a more dynamic influence of more sedentary, less egalitarian groups occupying other regions of the Mid-South on populations living in the North Carolina Piedmont (Sassaman 2001, 2005). Lithic assemblages from Middle Archaic occupation of 31MG328 document changes in technological organization inconsistent with prevalent descriptions of Morrow Mountain hunter-gatherer societies organized around generalized land use and frequent mobility except at the most general comparative level. Mid-Holocene cultural diversity subsumed under the Morrow Mountain phase may be more heterogeneous and complex than currently established.

Meeting the Challenge: Expanding the Anthropological Relevance of Southeast Lithic Assemblages

Carr, Bradbury, and Price began their symposium at the Mobile meeting of the Southeastern Archaeological Conference by decrying the separate publication of lithic studies as detached chapters or sections within archaeological reports. This poor structural integration of stone artifact interpretation with broader conclusions has the unintended consequence of marginalizing the anthropological significance of lithic results. Inadequate middle range theory further magnifies this problem of relevance (Carr and Bradbury 2000, 2001), yet stone artifact specialists often deliberately limit interpretation to lower-level lithic behavior for fear of overreaching their data. Middle range theory specific to flaked stone assemblages continues to expand through new experiments and analyses, a scientific process on display in many chapters of this volume (e.g., Pevny this volume; Potts this volume). As this study demonstrates, useful models or heuristics from other archaeological regions such as analytical techniques applied in Old World Paleolithic archaeology can be adapted for problems in southeastern prehistory. Hesitation to propose more integrated explanations based on stone artifact assemblages should be overcome since all anthropological interpretations of archaeological data take the form of abductive or inductive hypotheses and as such seek to generalize knowledge from specific data. Lithic artifacts matter because they "hold clues to these processes that can support other data sets and allow independent testing of behavioral models" (Odell 1998:568). Lithic analysts should be capable of proposing testable anthropological hypotheses about prehistory at the same rate as archaeologists who specialize in studying faunal/floral remains, intrasite organization, or settlement patterns.

Analysis of the large stone artifact assemblage recovered from the stratified site 31MG328 is the foundation for a hypothesis of significant Middle Archaic cultural change in the Uwharrie Mountains of North Carolina. Mobile hunter-gatherers of the Early Archaic employed a more curated lithic technology to provision people with flexible toolkits in a more homogenous, temperate environment. The Middle Archaic occupation at 31MG328 was for a much longer duration and has a stone artifact assemblage reflecting a strategy of provisioning the location. For subsistence and economic reasons, place became more important for Piedmont hunter-gatherers during the Middle Archaic. Both the changing lithic assemblage and varying site organization at 31MG328 are consistent with this hypothesis.

Increasingly, archaeologists recognize the significance of the Middle Archaic as a period of profound cultural evolution. Prehistoric Native Americans in other regions of the eastern United States were adapting in new ways to the changing social and environmental circumstances of the Middle Archaic (Emerson and McElrath 2009). From changing subsistence and increasing sedentism in the Midwest (Abrams and Nowacki 2008; Brown and Vierra 1983; Jefferies 1997; McElrath et al. 2009; Sheehan 2002; Stafford et al. 2000), to mound building and early domestication in the Lower Mississippi Valley (Gibson 2006; Kidder and Sassaman 2009; Saunders et al. 2005), and shell mounds and social status in Florida (Quinn, Tucker et al. 2008; Sassaman 2005), organizational change was altering and reshaping relationships between people and their social and natural environments. Flaked stone evidence from 31MG328 may point to important Mid-Holocene cultural changes in the Piedmont of North Carolina as well.

Acknowledgments

This research collaboration would not have been possible without the support of the USDA Forest Service—Uwharrie National Forest and the Archaeology Laboratories of Wake Forest University. We appreciate the enthusiastic fieldwork of numerous volunteers who participated in the Passport in Time excavations at 31MG328. Conklin's contribution to the assemblage analysis was facilitated by a Wake Forest University Summer Research Fellowship. We are grateful to Scott Ashcraft, Rodney Snedeker, Phil Carr, Andrew Bradbury, Sarah Price, Jay Johnson, and the anonymous reviewer for their valuable editorial comments.

8

Low-Quality Quartz and Implications for Technological Inferences

Tara L. Potts

Coarse-grained lithic raw materials are thought to present a myriad of problems for prehistoric knappers, and undoubtedly they present a different set of problems for lithic analysts. One such raw material, quartz, abundant throughout the Southeast and used for thousands of years, was the primary material for the manufacture of stone tools at some sites. Modern analysts faced with a lithic assemblage dominated by quartz must overcome multiple issues that range from discerning various flake attributes to making accurate type identifications of hafted bifaces and other tools. The coarse-grained nature of most quartz makes for a tricky technological analysis of tools and flakes because of the difficulty in identifying specific attribute states. This can result in some categories becoming catchalls and/or in a high level of interobserver and intraobserver error (e.g., Beck and Jones 1989). With regard to a technological analysis, there is a lack of comparative flintknapping experiments, especially using coarse-grained quartz, and this limits our ability to make well-supported inferences. For flake debris, multiple lines of evidence are preferred in technological analysis, yet due to the physical characteristics of quartz flakes it is difficult to make confident identifications. These issues have created a roadblock of sorts when dealing with sites on which quartz comprises the majority of an assemblage.

Here, I discuss the difficulties and potential of coarse-grained lithic assemblages with a focus on flake debris and coarse-grained quartz. Exploration of specific issues with Individual Flake Analysis (IFA) of coarse-grained materials aids in pinpointing appropriate methods for making valid interpretations. Preliminary results of a set of replication experiments using coarse-grained quartz are presented. Using aggregate analysis, these data are applied to two site assemblages from central Alabama. Quartz is locally available and the dominant raw material used by the prehistoric occupants at both of these sites.

Technological Organization and Quartz

Raw material availability and quality are basic considerations when employing an organization of technology approach (Amick and Mauldin 1997; Andrefsky 1994a, 1994b; Bradbury and Franklin 2000; Carr 1994a; Nelson 1991). A common supposition is that fine-grained (i.e., high-quality) raw materials were used preferentially for biface production (i.e., Hayden et al. 1996:24). Regarding tool design, the most desirable raw material for curated tools (portable and long use life) is one with high resharpening potential and durability (Bleed 1986; Carr 1994a; Hayden et al. 1996:28). Based on this thinking, low-quality quartz would not be used in the production of bifaces or curated tools. It is coarse grained and, while durable, does not have reliable fracture patterns to ensure multiple resharpenings. Data from some sites with locally available, coarse-grained material indicate that it is not used for formal tools, which are made from nonlocal, high-quality raw materials (Andrefsky 1994a:28, 1994b: 379). Further, Paleoindians as "high-technology foragers" focused on high-quality lithic materials (Kelly and Todd 1988). When coarse-grained materials are abundant, it is expected to be used primarily to make informal tools (Parry and Kelly 1987:299).

In general, locally available, coarse-grained raw materials are considered optimal for core and bipolar reduction (Hayden et al. 1996:30). Coarse-grained material is considered best suited for expedient tools. The argument is that raw material quality affects the technological strategy and design of tools. However, the exceptions to the rules are often the most informative. There are sites where locally available, low-quality quartz dominates the assemblage and was chosen for the manufacture of hafted bifaces, which are inferred to be curated tools. Further, in the two specific cases discussed here, a fine-grained chert, albeit available only in small pebbles, also was utilized for the manufacture of hafted bifaces, but not exclusively. The question becomes, what prehistoric decision making, in terms of implementing economic and social strategies, led to such a reliance on low-quality quartz?

As Odell (1996b) has argued, the relationship between raw material availability and curation is complex and must be taken on a case-by-case basis. I argue that this must be the same for reduction strategies and tool design. When dealing with a raw material that is abundant, yet coarse grained, some prehistoric peoples made the decision to use this raw material in the production of bifaces and curated tools. These people did not consistently seek a nonlocal, higher-quality raw material as an alternative, were prevented from doing so by other factors such as conflict with other groups, or their range was such that higher-quality materials were not encountered.

As diagramed by Nelson (1991:59) and discussed by Carr and colleagues (this volume), employing an organization of technology approach allows lithic analysts to consider raw material availability as one aspect of the environment. Additionally, artifact form and distribution provide insight into tool design and activities, thus leading to understanding of social and economic strategies. Therefore, if one studied a lithic assemblage laden with low-quality quartz with traditional assumptions regarding its usage, one would be biased toward identifying expedient tools and bipolar reduction strategies. Instead of using preconceived notions regarding technological strategies, tool design, and manufacture to drive our interpretations, we must work back and forth between the archaeological record and our theoretical approach to deal with assemblages containing a high frequency of coarse-grained material.

Low-Quality Quartz and Debitage Analysis

Accurate interpretations of coarse-grained lithic assemblages are not possible unless the data collected are reliable and replicable. The use of multiple lines of evidence is arguably the best means for the analysis of an assemblage of debitage (see Bradbury and Carr 1995, 1999, 2004b; Carr and Bradbury 2000; Franklin et al. this volume; Odell 2003). Quartz is especially problematic because of the difficulty in discerning specific attribute states. To examine the accuracy of IFA on quartz, three lithic specialists were asked to independently analyze a set of quartz flakes from a Late Woodland feature. The quartz flake sample (n = 30) was randomly chosen and included a range of sizes. All flakes were bagged separately and assigned an identification number. The analysts were asked to identify flake portion, platform configuration, facet count (if applicable), dorsal cortex, and dorsal scar count, as well as to rate their level of confidence in characterizing each flake (Carr and Potts 2008). Each specialist has studied lithics for no fewer than nine years, and together they have a combined 40 years of experience in conducting their own analyses. These three analysts also work together regularly coding lithic artifacts and have obtained at least a 95-percent agreement on attribute identification on prior assemblages (e.g., Odell 1989).

In this experiment, agreement among the analysts was not common in any attribute except cortex and no attribute was recorded with 95-percent agreement among all three (Table 8.1). Portion should normally be identified with ease by a lithic analyst (e.g., Sullivan and Rozen 1985), but complete agreement on quartz was achieved for only 12 flakes (40 percent). Concurrence is higher between pairs of analysts, but the level of interobserver error is unacceptable for the analysis of an archaeological assemblage. For pairs of analysts, platform characteristic agreement peaks at 67 percent. Analysts 1 and 3 have the highest concurrence on facet count at a mere 77 percent. Cortex is the only attribute

Table 8.1. Concurrence on attribute characteristics among three lithic analysts

	Attributes											
	Portion		Platform		Facet		Dorsal Cortex		Scar		Stage	
Analysts	n	%	n	%	n	%	n	%	n	%	n	%
1 & 2	23	76.6	17	56.6	16	53.3	27	80	19	63.3	1	3.3
2 & 3	14	46.6	17	56.6	19	63.3	26	86.6	15	50	15	50
1 & 3	16	53.3	20	66.6	23	76.6	29	96.6	21	70	8	26.6
1, 2, & 3	12	40	14	46.6	15	50	26	86.6	14	46.6	1	3.3
None	5	16.6	3	10	2	6.6	—	—	3	10	2	6.6

Table 8.2. Confidence level frequencies per analyst

	Analyst					
	1		2		3	
Confidence	n	%	n	%	n	%
Very	14	46.6	15	51.7	11	36.7
Somewhat	9	30	9	31	16	53.3
Not	7	23.3	5	17.3	3	10
Total	30	100	29	100	30	100

for which 95-percent agreement was met, but only between Analysts 1 and 3. In regard to stage determination following methods outlined by Magne (1985), all three agree only on one flake from this assemblage. For other raw materials, one would expect better results than random assignations of reduction stages (Bradbury and Carr 1995).

The analysts recorded their confidence level for their overall characterization of each flake as very confident, somewhat confident, or not confident (Table 8.2; the number of artifacts for Analyst 2 is 29 because the analyst did not agree one artifact was a flake). While overall the analysts felt confident doing the analysis, the results indicate otherwise as they rarely agreed on specific attribute states. The results of this test suggest that IFA is not a reliable and replicable method for low-quality quartz regardless of the analyst's experience level.

Some researchers (e.g., Jeske 1992; Kuijt et al. 1995; Magne 1985; White 1968) have argued that a high frequency of non-orientable flakes (ventral and dorsal faces are not distinguishable) is an indicator of bipolar reduction. While not tested in this experiment, this highlights further problems using IFA on assemblages dominated by coarse-grained materials. The assemblages may have a higher number of flakes in the non-orientable category because of material quality rather than reduction activities. Additional experiments are necessary to examine this issue.

Experimental Data: Not Just Bipolar

In light of the previous discussion, aggregate analysis appears better suited for making inferences regarding manufacture stages or reduction type when working with coarse-grained materials. Replication experiments are commonly used for interpretation of debitage assemblages (e.g., Ahler 1989a, 1989b; Amick et al. 1989; Andrefsky 1986, 2006; Bradbury and Carr 1995, 1999, 2004b; Dibble 1997; Maudlin and Amick 1989; Morrow 1997), but published quartz replication experiments generally focus on expedient flake production or bipolar reduction (e.g., Ahler 1989a). Bifacial tool replication experiments generally use higher-quality raw materials (e.g., Ahler 1989a, 1989b; Amick and Mauldin 1989; Amick et al. 1989; Andrefsky 1986, 2006; Bradbury and Carr 1995, 1999, 2004b; Dibble 1997; Morrow 1997). Without a broad range of experiments with a variety of raw materials, lithic analysts will perpetuate misconceptions rather than make accurate inferences of prehistoric technology.

With the help of Andrew Bradbury as the flintknapper, experiments using quartz were completed. I collected nodules in cobble beds along the Coosa River, Tallapoosa River, and a secondary creek of the Coosa in central Alabama. From the samples collected, raw material quality similar to that observed in the archaeological assemblages (1MT318 and 1EE639) was chosen for the experiments. Raw material from the assemblages ranged from high-quality quartz to low-quality quartz/quartzite but was predominately low quality.

Eight experiments were conducted using hard-hammer bipolar percussion (n = 2), hard-hammer freehand core reduction (n = 3), soft-hammer biface production (n = 2), and soft-hammer uniface production (n = 1). Hard-hammer percussion was conducted with a quartzite hammerstone. For the bipolar experiments, a flattened quartzite nodule was used as an anvil. Soft-hammer percussion was conducted with antler billets. Pressure flaking experiments were not conducted due to failure during soft-hammer percussion on the bifaces and uniface. From the eight replication experiments, a total of 6,159 flakes were collected. Size grade analysis was conducted for each experiment. Size grades were 25.4 mm (1 inch), 12.7 mm (.5 inch), 6.35 mm (.25 inch), and 3.17 mm (.125 inch), using standard geologic sieves. Flakes were hand manipulated through screens. Data from each type of reduction, bipolar, freehand core, uniface, and biface, were combined to create a suitable sample for comparison. The goal of these experiments was to create a data set of manufacturing debris specific to this raw material that can be used to interpret archaeological assemblages.

Flakes from every size grade were produced from the bipolar experiments (Table 8.3). A majority of the flakes were caught in the 3.17-mm screen (n = 153; 78.5 percent). Mean weights for all size grades are high, especially the 6.35-mm size grade (.98 g), indicative of early-stage reduction. Generally with aggregate analysis, a low average weight of 6.35-mm flakes is associated with tool production and a relatively high average weight is associated with core reduction (Bradbury and Carr 2004a; Carr and Koldehoff 1994:table 4). Percentage of cortical flakes in the 6.35-mm aggregate is high (60.6 percent) for the bipolar experiments. The 3.17-mm flakes make up a small percentage of overall weight of flakes, and the weight percentages are somewhat evenly distributed among the three largest size grades.

Flakes from the freehand core reduction experiments distribute across all size grades (Table 8.3). A majority of the flakes were caught in the 3.17-mm size grade (n = 457; 74.6 percent). Mean weights for all size grades are high, especially the 6.35-mm aggregate (.86 g), indicative of early-stage reduction (Baumler and Downum 1989:106), and lower than the bipolar data. Cortical flake percentage per size grade reduces as the flakes get smaller. Similar to the bipolar reduction data, flakes from the 3.17-mm aggregate make up less than 10 percent of the total weight, but almost 50 percent of the total weight is found in the 12.7-mm size grade.

Flakes from the soft-hammer uniface production experiments were present in the smallest three size grades (Table 8.3). A majority of the flakes were caught in the 3.17-mm screen (n = 17; 85 percent). Mean weights for all size grades

Table 8.3. Experimental data

Size Grade (mm)	n	Weight (g)	% Count	% Weight	% Cortical	Mean Weight (g)
			Bipolar			
3.17	153	12.7	78.5	9.6	29.4	.08
6.35	33	32.5	16.9	24.5	60.6	.98
12.7	7	38.6	3.6	29	57.1	5.51
25.4	2	49	1	36.9	100	24.5
			Freehand Core			
3.17	457	40.7	74.7	8	15	.08
6.35	116	100.2	18.9	19.6	42.2	.86
12.7	35	245	5.7	48	65.7	7
25.4	4	124.5	.7	24.4	75	31.12
			Soft-Hammer Uniface			
3.17	17	1.4	85	4.5	17.6	.08
6.35	1	.4	5	1.3	—	.4
12.7	2	29.4	10	94.2	50	14.7
25.4	—	—	—	—	—	—
			Soft-Hammer Biface			
3.17	81	6.3	81.8	37.5	6.1	.07
6.35	16	6.5	16.2	38.7	31.2	.4
12.7	2	4	2	23.8	100	2
25.4	—	—	—	—	—	—

are low, especially the 6.35-mm aggregate (.40 g), indicative of late-stage reduction. Very few flakes exhibit cortex in this assemblage. The weight percentage is very high in the 12.7-mm aggregate, almost 95 percent, while the smallest size grades make up little of the total weight for the sample. It should be noted that this sample is small, potentially skewing the data.

Flakes from the soft-hammer biface production experiments were present in the smallest three size grades (Table 8.3). A majority of the flakes were caught in the 3.17-mm screen (n = 81; 81.8 percent). Mean weights for all size grades are low, especially the 6.35-mm aggregate (.40 g), indicative of late-stage reduction. Interestingly, the 12.7-mm flakes exhibit cortex (albeit only two were recovered), and very few flakes in the remaining size grades exhibit cortex. The weight percentages are somewhat evenly distributed across the smallest three size grades, although flakes from the 12.7-mm size grade have the lowest total proportion of weight.

Experimental studies by Ahler (1989b) indicate that the ratio of 3.17-mm flakes to the sum of the larger flakes can indicate type of reduction. Low ratios (less than 2.8) suggest a focus on early stages of reduction (hard hammer) and high ratios (ranging from 2.87 to 83.0) indicate late stages (soft-hammer reduction and pressure flaking). Bipolar reduction ratios (3.93 and 4.00) tend to fall between late and early. It is noted that there is some overlap in the ratios provided by Ahler; therefore, these should be used in conjunction with other flake data to interpret an assemblage. This overlap also may be caused by raw material and/or the nature of the experiment. The quartz experimental data provided by Ahler is from Kalin (1981), in which quartz experiments include bipolar flake production (ratio 4.00) and stemmed point production from a flake blank (ratio 22.25).

In the quartz bipolar experiments presented here, the ratio (3.64) of 3.17-mm flakes to the combined totals of the larger size grades is lower than those for biface (4.5) and uniface (5.6) reduction but higher than that for core reduction (2.95). While the trends are similar to those in Ahler's experiments, the overall ratios for quartz tool production and core reduction (2.95) tend to be higher, suggesting that raw material and cobble size play a role when using these data to interpret archaeological assemblages.

In regard to mean flake weight from the 6.35-mm aggregate, an interesting pattern occurs. As demonstrated in other experiments, the mean flake weights for the biface and uniface experiments are relatively low (both .40 g) compared to the core reduction weight (.86 g). The bipolar mean flake weight (.98 g) is higher than that of soft-hammer reduction flakes and core reduction flakes. In another recent experiment, the core (.94 g) mean flake weight was considerably higher than that of bipolar (.76 g) (Bradbury and Carr 2009: table 1). The ambiguity and lack of distinct separation between bipolar and soft-hammer reduction could most definitely create problems when interpreting an assemblage.

Flake weight percentage within each size grade also exhibits an interesting pattern (Figure 8.1). The majority of flake weight from bipolar reduction is evenly distributed between the 12.7-mm and 6.35-mm flakes. The majority of the core flake weight is found in the 12.7-mm size grade. For soft-hammer biface production, the majority of the flake weight is somewhat evenly distributed between the 3.17-mm and 6.35-mm size grades. Almost all of the soft-hammer uniface weight was recovered from the 12.7-mm size grade.

As a preliminary step, the aggregate analysis data were used in a stepwise discriminant function analysis using Mahalanobis distance to determine the best variables for separating the reduction groups. Given the small data set, the reduction groups were collapsed into core reduction (bipolar and freehand)

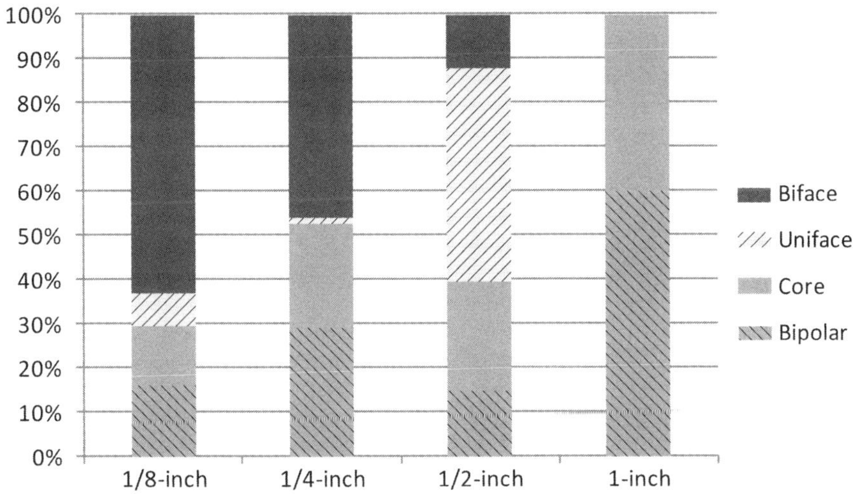

Figure 8.1. Weight percentage per size grade for replication experiments.

and tool production (uniface and biface). The cross-validation summary indicates 100-percent correct classification was achieved. A plot of Functions 1 and 2 (Figure 8.2) indicates excellent separation between core reduction and tool production experiments. However, a distinction between core and bipolar as well as uniface and biface reduction was not possible. While in this instance the data are limited, this result illustrates that these data combined with more quartz experimental data may lead to better insights into quartz reduction.

The Archaeological Assemblages

Two quartz-heavy lithic assemblages from central Alabama were used to test the applicability of the experimental data. Both sites are located near the Coosa River and they are approximately 10 km apart. The first site (1MT318) was a portion of a Late Woodland settlement extensively occupied from A.D. 978 to 1023 (Potts 2008). In addition to being somewhat earlier (A.D. 645–772), the Late Woodland occupation at the second site (1EE639) was ephemeral and no evidence of structures or any long-term occupation was documented (Potts 2010). While Late Woodland peoples used the sites for different purposes, stone tool reduction using coarse-grained raw material predominated in both assemblages.

Madison Park

The Madison Park site (1MT318) was excavated in 2002 by staff at the University of South Alabama's Center for Archaeological Studies. The chipped-stone

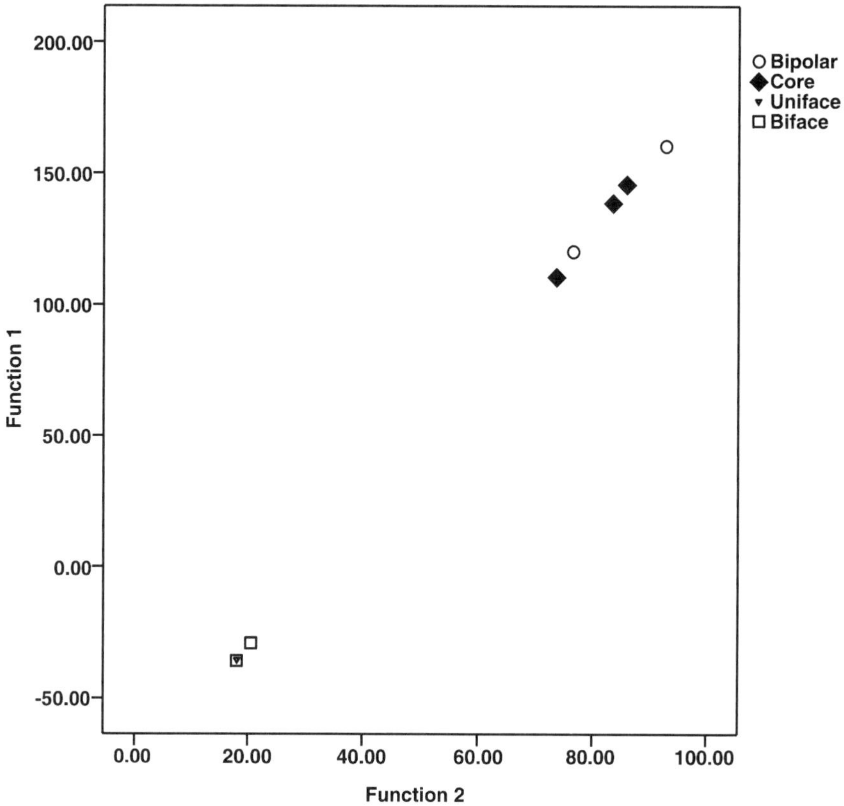

Figure 8.2. Discriminant analysis scatter plot of experimental data.

lithic assemblage of this Late Woodland site is primarily locally available quartz (n = 50,455; 85.1 percent). Only one other raw material in the lithic assemblage is locally available, Knox chert (n = 8,822; 14.9 percent). Quartz is available in the gravel bars of Sevenmile Creek adjacent to the Madison Park site. While the Knox chert formation is approximately 260 km north of the site, the Coosa River transports cobbles to the gravel bars near Madison Park approximately 10 km away.

The remaining raw materials (Tallahatta agate, Tallahatta sandstone, Hollis quartzite, Coastal Plain chert, and Fossiliferous Bangor) are considered nonlocal raw materials. The closest Tallahatta formation is approximately 80 km south of the Madison Park site. Tallahatta agate (n = 58; <.1 percent) and Tallahatta sandstone (n = 3; <.1 percent) can both be found in this formation. Coastal Plain chert (n = 241; .4 percent) is available in the most southeastern counties of Alabama. The Hollis quartzite formation (n = 70; .1 percent) is in

Table 8.4. Quartz flake size grade distribution at 1MT318

Size Grade (mm)	n	% Count	Weight (g)	% Weight	Mean Weight (g)
3.17	37,299	74.5	5,175.4	17.5	.1
6.35	11,419	22.8	7,930.0	26.9	.7
12.7	1,279	2.5	15,494.1	52.6	12.1
25.4	24	.05	855.9	2.9	35.7

east-central Alabama approximately 81 km from the site. However, this formation is located along the Tallapoosa River, suggesting that hydraulic transport of materials closer to the site is possible.

Importantly, none of the Hollis quartzite recovered from Madison Park exhibits weathering from transport. The Fossiliferous Bangor flake (n = 1; <.1 percent) recovered from Madison Park is high-quality, blue-gray chert with fossilized Bryozoa inclusions (Meeks 2000:157). The Fossiliferous Bangor formation is located in northeastern Alabama, in Colbert and Franklin counties (Meeks 2000:157). Interestingly, most of the nonlocal raw material (by count) comes from southern Alabama.

A majority of the recovered cores are quartz (n = 380; 84.6 percent) followed by Knox chert (n = 65; 14.4 percent), Coastal Plain chert (n = 2; .5 percent), and Hollis quartzite (n = 2; .5 percent). A total of 107 unhafted bifaces were recovered from 1MT318. The majority (n = 58; 54.2 percent) are Knox chert, while quartz is the second most abundant raw material (n = 32; 29.9 percent). The remaining unhafted bifaces are of Coastal Plain chert (n = 12; 11.2 percent), Tallahatta sandstone (n = 3; 2.8 percent), Hollis quartzite (n = 1; .9 percent), and an unidentified raw material (n = 1; .9 percent). For the 113 hafted bifaces, Knox chert is also the preferred raw material (n = 69; 61.0 percent) with quartz as the second most common (n = 22; 19.5 percent). Other hafted bifaces are made of Coastal Plain chert (n = 18; 16.0 percent), Tallahatta agate (n = 2; 1.7 percent), Hollis quartzite (n = 1; .9 percent), and an unidentified material (n = 1; .9 percent). The majority (n = 50,021; 84.5 percent) of the debitage is quartz (Table 8.4). Knox is the second most common, totaling 8,822 flakes (14.9 percent). The remaining debitage is composed of Coastal Plain chert (n = 209; <.1 percent), Hollis quartzite (n = 66; <.1 percent), Tallahatta agate (n = 56; <.1 percent), Fossiliferous Bangor (n = 1; <.1 percent), and unidentified material (n = 12; <.1 percent).

For quartz, the average weight in the 6.35-mm aggregate is high and supports a focus on core reduction (.69 g; Table 8.4). The flake weight, percentage by count per size grade, and size grade ratio (2.93) suggest core reduction. A similar distribution to that of the core experimental data presented above was also seen. These data, combined with the number of quartz cores recovered, indicate quartz core reduction as a primary activity at Madison Park (Carr and Potts 2008). The abundance of quartz cores is probably due to easy access to this raw material from Madison Park. Most quartz cores are bipolar (n = 127; 33.4 percent) or tested cobbles (n = 121; 31.8 percent). The remaining quartz cores are bidirectional (n = 32; 8.4 percent), bifacial (n = 30; 7.9 percent), tested bipolar (n = 27; 7.1 percent), amorphous (n = 21; 5.5 percent), and indeterminate (n = 22; 5.8 percent).

In sum, the quartz flakes and cores from Madison Park suggest a focus on early-stage or core reduction (see Table 8.4). The more formal the tool the less likely it would be made of quartz at this site. The abundance of bipolar cores, the biface data, and the size grade data do suggest that quartz was used primarily for expedient tools. However, it should be noted that quartz bifaces and hafted bifaces do appear in the assemblage. The higher-quality materials may have been preferred during this occupation; however, the low-quality quartz minimally was used for tool production. Recognizing tool production in the debitage assemblage using aggregate data appears impossible for this site. As exemplified in the work of Ahler (1989a, 1989b), size grade data may be best suited for identifying the reduction method for specific contexts. The "mixed assemblage problem" looms large in the case of Madison Park (see Andrefsky 2007). Recent experiments illustrate that the mixing of flakes from different reduction activities masks the presence of different reduction activities to such an extent that proper interpretation beyond "mixing" is impossible (Bradbury and Carr 2009).

Site 1EE639

In 2008, site 1EE639 was investigated by staff at the University of South Alabama's Center for Archaeological Studies. Site 1EE639 was a multicomponent site with occupations dating from the Late Archaic to the early twentieth century. The site was extensively plowed, resulting in the mixing of the prehistoric and historic assemblages. For this reason, deciphering episodes of occupation was dependent on feature excavation and analysis. The Late Woodland occupation was represented by a single feature, Feature 44.

Although cores could not be separated by occupation, the overall trends in the quartz assemblage can be useful, if considered cautiously. A majority of the cores (n = 252; 95 percent) are quartz. Similar to 1MT318, the abundance of quartz cores can be attributed to the close proximity of the raw material in creek beds adjacent to the site. The majority of the quartz cores are amorphous (n = 74; 29.4 percent) or bipolar (n = 72; 28.6 percent). The remaining quartz

Table 8.5. Quartz flake size grade data for Feature 44, 1EE639

Size Grade (mm)	n	% Count	Weight (g)	% Weight	% Cortical	Mean Weight (g)
3.17	867	76.3	74.7	17.5	—	.86
6.35	226	20	179.5	42.1	—	.79
12.7	43	3.7	172.1	40.4	4.6	4
25.4	—	—	—	—	—	—

cores are bidirectional (n = 40; 15.9 percent), tested cobbles (n = 37; 14.7 percent), bifacial (n = 23; 9.1 percent), and indeterminate (n = 6; 2.3 percent). The bipolar core count is high, indicative of expedient tools, although the number of amorphous cores suggests that flake production for the manufacture of formal tools was also a focus with this raw material. Since there is a mixture of Archaic and Late Woodland cores in the assemblage, it is difficult to differentiate which cores correspond to which occupation.

Considering the hafted bifaces, which can be separated by occupation, a total of 13 Late Woodland projectile points were recovered. Of these, 10 (76.9 percent) are quartz. Therefore, locally available quartz clearly was used by Late Woodland populations for tool production and arguably for expedient flake tools.

Due to component mixing, the discussion of quartz debitage from 1EE639 is confined to Feature 44, a quartz flake and tool concentration. A radiocarbon date places this feature in the Late Woodland. Overall, the size grade distribution of flakes from this feature suggests bipolar reduction (Table 8.5), but no bipolar cores or distinctive bipolar flakes were identified. The high mean flake weight in the 6.35-mm aggregate does support the bipolar interpretation. The ratio of 3.17-mm flakes to the sum of the larger flakes is relatively high (3.22), which suggests bipolar percussion. Additionally, the majority of the flake weight is evenly distributed between the 6.35-mm and 12.7-mm size grades, as seen in the bipolar experiments presented earlier in this chapter.

Additionally, two quartz bifaces were recovered from Feature 44. One biface exhibited hard-hammer percussion with a longitudinal reverse failure. The other quartz biface exhibited soft-hammer reduction and retouch with an incipient failure and a lateral snap. Interestingly, when all debitage and biface data from Feature 44 are considered, something more complex is evident. In comparing the debitage from Feature 44 to the experimental data set, Feature 44 is consistent with bipolar reduction, but it also matches a mixture of biface and core reduction. How do the two discarded failed bifaces mesh with a strict interpretation of bipolar reduction? With this consideration in mind, multiple types of reduction (core and biface) likely created the debitage assemblage recovered from Feature 44.

Conclusions

Current assumptions of raw material quality preference may apply to many archaeological assemblages, but they do not apply to all, as seen at 1EE639 and 1MT318. Preconceived notions of coarse-grained material usage, particularly in bipolar reduction, should be recognized as biased assumptions. Bipolar reduction must be demonstrated, but this is not always a simple task.

Bipolar experimental data derived from aggregate analysis tend to fall between early- and late-stage reduction in regard to size grade ratio. Mean weight of bipolar flakes is higher than for soft-hammer percussion. Bipolar reduction creates an assemblage that cannot always be clearly differentiated from early-stage (core) and late-stage (biface) reduction. Conversely, a mixed assemblage (biface and core) might also appear as bipolar reduction using aggregate analysis. Accompanying bipolar cores, hammerstones, and anvils provide additional evidence of a flake assemblage that resulted from bipolar reduction (Bradbury and Carr this volume).

Recent experiments examining "mixed assemblages" (Bradbury and Carr 2009:table 4) indicate that aggregate proportions vary depending on what is in the mix and the average weight of flakes in a specific size grade can add diagnostic power. For example, if core reduction flakes are added to biface edging flakes, the mean flake weight increases. Although bipolar reduction was not one of these investigators' experiments (Bradbury and Carr 2009), the message is clear: mixing of flakes from different reduction types blurs the divisions using these size grade data.

The work presented here is preliminary and I note that there are a few issues that should be addressed. First, no pressure flaking of quartz was reported from the experiments and such data would certainly help in interpreting the archaeological assemblages. Due to the low quality of the material, it was difficult to reduce the material without manufacturing failures. Therefore, the experiments were halted prematurely. Based on the assemblages from 1EE639 and 1MT318, failure at this stage was common with this material in prehistory. Second, the experimental data set is small and further experimentation with more knappers and with a greater variety of low-quality materials is necessary. Given the small size and preliminary nature of this experimental data set, further statistical testing could not provide reliable results.

As discussed here, low-quality material is used for multiple reduction techniques in the Late Woodland of central Alabama. At 1MT318, stone tool manufacture appears to depend on core and bipolar reduction, although some bifaces are produced using the low-quality quartz. With similar raw material availability, quartz was used for biface and core reduction at 1EE639. Reliance on this low-quality material for tool production is apparent despite the availability of high-quality material suitable for tool production in the area.

This situation begs the question, how do these bifaces fit into the toolkit of Late Woodland people? The material quality hinders resharpening, therefore prohibiting long-term curation of these artifacts. When the entire Late Woodland lithic assemblage from 1MT318 is taken into account, the quartz bifaces may fall somewhere between expedient tools (bipolar and flake tools) and curated tools (hafted bifaces with the potential for multiple resharpening episodes). While time is spent manufacturing low-quality bifaces, they may not have been made with the intention of long-term curation and multiple resharpening episodes. Rather, these tools were intended for use away from the place of manufacture (not expedient) but were disposed of when broken or dulled. Such bifaces can be made in quantity because of the abundance of material. These curated yet disposable tools demonstrate that our current dichotomy between expedient and curated tools may be oversimplified and may deserve further consideration (see Nash 1996; Odell 1996b).

This study does not answer all questions regarding interpreting assemblages with low-quality raw material, and it may actually increase uncertainty in interpretation of these assemblages. Without taking all quartz artifacts into account for both of these assemblages, the interpretations would never approach the actual events that created the record. Fully understanding these lithic assemblages of low-quality material, while tedious at times, is critical if we are to move toward a better understanding of the specific complex behaviors that created them and of prehistoric lifeways more generally.

Acknowledgments

I would like to thank Andrew Bradbury, Philip Carr, and Sarah Price for requesting my participation in this volume. Andrew Bradbury knapped the experimental assemblage and assisted with statistical analysis. Thank you to George Odell, William Andrefsky, Jay Johnson, and one anonymous reviewer. Any errors are my sole responsibility.

9

An Integrated Approach

Lithic Analyses and Site Function, Eagle Drink Bluff Shelter, Upper Cumberland Plateau, Tennessee

Jay D. Franklin, Maureen A. Hays, Sarah C. Sherwood, and Lucinda M. Langston

After four excavation seasons at Eagle Drink Bluff Shelter, a small sandstone rockshelter in the highlands of the Upper Cumberland Plateau (UCP) of Tennessee, components ranging from the Middle Archaic through the Late Woodland have been identified. Here we present the results of technological and use-wear analyses of the Late Archaic lithic assemblage, which contained more than 180 finished and reworked stone tools. In general, rockshelters have been viewed as special-purpose sites, though this interpretation has largely been applied to rockshelters in lowland regions where they are comparatively rare (e.g., Hall and Klippel 1988). The technological and functional analyses of the flaking debris and tools at Eagle Drink support the interpretation of a base camp or residential location. While each of the methods employed in this study alone contributes to the site interpretation, confidence in the interpretation lies in their integration. We further believe that if lithic analysts working in the Southeast wish to fully address site function and identify specific activities in the archaeological record, then they should routinely employ use-wear studies.

Approach—*Chaîne Opératoire*

The framework we employ in our investigations is in various contexts simultaneously referred to as the *chaîne opératoire* approach and the organization of technology approach, while in others significant distinctions are strongly debated (Andrefsky 2009; Bleed 2001; Shott 2003; Simek 1994; Tostevin 2006). It is not our intent to try to resolve this debate here. We believe the *chaîne opératoire* concept provides a slightly broader perspective from which to address the system within which stone implements are a part. Therefore, we briefly outline our perception of *chaîne opératoire* as applied in our research at Eagle Drink.

Yogi Berra once said, "In theory, there's no difference between theory and practice. In practice, there is." Often when a debate is polarized, the theoretical realm and the practical application are two different things. When it comes to the application of the concepts to lithic analysis, organization of technology and *chaîne opératoire* in many cases are very similar. They both, for the most part, purport to investigate the relationship between raw material procurement, the technology of production, use, recycling, and discard/loss and incorporation into the archaeological record (e.g., Kelly 1988; Sellet 1993). Odell (2001:81) contends that "the *chaîne opératoire* comes closest to Schiffer's behavioral archaeology, which considers objects within their systemic contexts from procurement to discard (and beyond)." We believe this statement brings us closer to the concept of *chaîne opératoire* as it was originally conceived of by André Leroi-Gourhan (1993[1964]) before it was adopted by lithic analysts (Boëda 1995; Geneste 1985, 1991; Inizian et al. 1992). *Chaîne opératoire* is just one aspect of a much broader holistic approach to understanding humans past and present (Audouze 2002).

Though Leroi-Gourhan was concerned with individual gestures, he argued that the level of analysis was not that of the individual but rather the group (Audouze 2002): "Everything humans make—tools, gestures, and products alike—is impregnated with group aesthetics. . . . Individuals introduce their personal variations into the traditional framework and, safe in the knowledge of belonging to the group, draw some of their sense of existing as individuals from the margin of freedom allowed them" (Leroi-Gourhan 1993[1964]:253). This is important given the nature of archaeological assemblages and our analyses of technological traditions. When we analyze an assemblage technologically or typologically we are looking at a palimpsest of the actions of multiple individuals over an undefined period of time (Leroi-Gourhan's "group aesthetics"). Refitting analysis can bring us closer to understanding the individual technological gestures (Leroi-Gourhan's "personal variation" or "gestures"). When we examine use, we are actually looking at the action or gesture, if you would like, of a single individual at a specific time. However, when we look at the assemblage function as a whole, we return full circle to that group collective.

Using the *chaîne opératoire* approach, we work to consider the entire life history of the assemblage. In so doing, we also try to keep in mind that this is part of a much broader system that includes the acquisition of other resources, other technologies, and movement on the landscape. Because our work at Eagle Drink represents the first long-term systematic archaeological excavation on the UCP of Tennessee (Franklin 2008), comparative data are rather limited. We can now begin to address the hypotheses relevant to Eagle Drink. First, cultural historical models developed in lowland regions are not appropriate models when applied to the UCP (e.g., Des Jean and Benthall 1994). Second, rockshelters in highland regions (e.g., the UCP) were not simply special-purpose sites (e.g., Hall and Klippel 1988).

Table 9.1. Archaic AMS radiocarbon determinations from Eagle Drink Bluff Shelter

Sample #	Material	Provenience	14C Age (B.P.)	2σ Ranges (B.P.)	1σ Ranges (B.P.)
AA77117	Wood charcoal	Fea. 1, XU6, L7	3066 ± 40	3164–3186 (.032); 3205–3377 (.968)	3248–3349
AA80690	Wood charcoal	Fea. 4, XU4, L8	2886 ± 55	2868–3168 (.962); 3179–3208 (.038)	2929–2939 (.038); 2941–3080 (.847); 3093–3108 (.062); 3127–3139 (.053)
Beta-265068	Wood charcoal	Fea. 6, XU10, L21	4790 ± 40	5333–5348 (.024); 5353–5362 (.010); 5366–5371 (.005); 5464–5601 (.961)	5476–5540 (.836); 5576–5588 (.164)
Beta-250290	Wood charcoal	TU2, 45 cm bs	2880 ± 40	2879–2912 (.060); 2917–3084 (.822); 3088–3157 (.117)	2951–3074
Beta-250292	Wood charcoal	TU2, 80 cm bs	5240 ± 40	5917–6031 (.676); 6039–6073 (.070); 6075–6120 (.157); 6148–6177 (.906)	5927–6005 (.807); 6083–6101 (.125); 6159–6170 (.068)

Site Background

Eagle Drink is a small, self-contained place on the landscape. Located within the Sewanee Conglomerate, the shelter is a small bluff overhang situated just below an upland gap at the head of a steep gorge. The shelter faces southeast and measures approximately 12–14 m wide by no more than 3 m deep from the back wall to the drip line.

The excavation consisted of 28 1-×-1-m units with all sediments screened through 6.35-mm (.25-inch) mesh. Numerous diagnostic artifacts and 10 chronometric age measures indicate intermittent occupation of the site from the late Middle Archaic through the Late Woodland. The Late Archaic radiocarbon dates (Table 9.1) are consistent with the diagnostic bifaces in these deposits.

The majority of the excavation took place in the northeast portion of the shelter. In general, the southwest side of the shelter is higher, sloping down slightly to the northeast side. The dripline marks a diagenetic shift in the deposits, with organic material only present within the shelter. We collected intact block samples for micromorphology to study the sediments in thin section (standard descriptive terminology used from Bullock et al. 1985; Courty et al. 1989). The results relevant to the Archaic at Eagle Drink are summarized here and reported in detail elsewhere (Sherwood 2010).

Beginning at the base of the profile, Layer 1 consists of yellow sand with silt aggregate clasts (most likely highly weathered shale) and common secondary clay both as coatings and hypo-coatings along vertical and horizontal cracks and channels. This layer is of interest up and down the plateau as it is the typical sterile yellow sand that marks the base of most excavations in these sandstone shelters. We expect that this is a highly weathered saprolite, in situ sandstone where the cement has been removed and just the sand grains and gravel inclusions remain. In thin section, the upper 10 to 20 cm of Layer 1 appears to be mixed, probably due to trampling and bioturbation. The clay coatings suggest that seepage from slope wash and lateral groundwater flow periodically move through this layer. There are no organics save a few charcoal fragments, likely introduced through bioturbation.

Layer 2, a variable layer of brown sand, contained Middle Archaic artifacts at the base and Terminal Archaic artifacts toward the top. This deposit is composed of sand from bedrock attrition, anthropogenic sediments in the form of burned soil aggregates, occasional microdebitage, and nut and wood charcoal fragments, some incorporated into aggregates of organics-rich sediments. Layer 2 has been bioturbated based on the microstructure. In profile there are large clasts of the matrix that appear to have been dislodged and broken, most likely due to burrowing activity.

The microstratigraphy revealed in the Eagle Drink thin sections is surprisingly homogenous. Typically, in a rockshelter environment the microscale will reveal concentrations of anthropogenic materials or lenses that show localized human activities (Goldberg and Sherwood 2006). This homogeneity in sediment source suggests to us that the function of the shelter changed very little over time. Localized bioturbation is evident throughout the shelter but otherwise the sediments above the yellow sand of Layer 1 changed very little. Bedrock attrition from the shelter roof appears to be relatively consistent. Slope wash would have contributed to the deposits, but most of the original microstructures related to these processes have been reworked by localized bioturbation.

Methods

Because we identified no specialized activity areas within this already very small bluff overhang, we selected certain excavation units and levels for lithic flake debris analyses. Specifically, we targeted units and levels where we recovered diagnostic Late Archaic artifacts and associated radiometric determinations to provide a representative sample of the Late Archaic lithic assemblage.

The lithic flaking debris analyses were conducted by Franklin and Langston (who learned from Franklin). A mass analysis of the lithic assemblage following Ahler (1989b) was completed (Franklin et al. 2008). An experimentally generated lithic assemblage is optimal for mass analysis (Ahler 1989b:98, 112). For our analysis, we used an experimental assemblage made of Monteagle chert nodules from nearby 3rd Unnamed Cave. This raw material was used because the vast majority of lithic artifacts recovered from Eagle Drink are made from Monteagle chert and the chert quarry in 3rd Unnamed Cave was contemporaneous with the occupation of Eagle Drink (Franklin 1999, 2001; Franklin and Simek 2008; Simek et al. 1998). An assemblage comprising materials from 53 experiments was generated. The lithic reduction experiments were conducted by Andrew Bradbury, a highly skilled flintknapper, and Jay Franklin, an adequate knapper. Efforts were taken to replicate the range of reduction possibilities noted in the archaeological record of the region. In other words, following Amick et al. (1989), we tried to move back and forth between the experiments and the archaeological assemblage in an effort to more fully understand each. Thus, the experimental reduction groups were as follows: Group 1—hard-hammer freehand cobble testing (n = 13); Group 2—hard-hammer freehand core reduction (n = 15); Group 3—hard-hammer bipolar core reduction (n = 18); and Group 4—soft-hammer tool production (n = 7). For Group 1, experiments were terminated when the quality (or lack thereof) could adequately be judged. If the cobble testing experiment revealed high-quality or suitable-quality chert relatively free of internal fracture planes, the cobble or nodule was retained and used in either the hard-hammer freehand or bipolar core reduction experiments. For experimental Groups 1–3, comparatively large uniform flakes were subjectively removed from further analysis and used for the soft-hammer experiments. The soft-hammer experiments replicated both projectile points/knives (hafted bifaces) and unifacial scrapers (see Bradbury and Franklin 2000; Franklin 1999; Franklin and Simek 2008 for specifics on the experimental assemblage).

We also analyzed the Eagle Drink lithics using an individual flake attribute analysis. Our approach is modeled after Magne's (1985, 1989) debitage stage approach. Magne (1985:120) initially found that the number of platform facet scars on individual flakes with complete platforms is the most robust indicator of reduction stage. Subsequent experimental work by Bradbury and Carr (1995:108) also has shown this to be the case, but largely for early-stage reduction (e.g., core reduction). However, their experimental results also suggest that the number of dorsal scars may be the better indicator of late-stage reduction (e.g., tool production), particularly for flakes with no platforms. Both lines were employed in our study (our method of analysis for lithic flaking debris allows for recording 13 different dimensions, or attributes, on each individual piece).

Within the *chaîne opératoire,* tool use and reuse are often bypassed due to the technical skills of the analyst and/or time constraints. However, we believe a critical element of addressing tool function, and more broadly site function, should be accomplished through the methods developed for use-wear analysis. The methods used in this study are predominantly those developed by Keeley (1980) for assessing polishes, though attributes such as scarring, edge rounding, and striations as identified to be significant indicators of use by Odell (1977) were also recorded. An Olympus BH-2 metallurgical microscope with an incident-light attachment and magnification capabilities from 50× to 500× was used. Interpretations were made with reference to an experimental collection believed to be representative of the archaeological record (Hays 1998; Hays and Lucas 2001). Types of use wear, to name a few, include projectile damage, butchering or meat processing, hide processing (fresh and dry), bone and antler working (dry and soaked), and woodworking.

Results and Interpretations

Typology and Chronology

Most of the diagnostic bifaces from the site are typical for the Middle and East Tennessee regions. These include Ledbetter, Cotaco Creek, Iddins, and Wade. There are also a number of bifaces that we simply refer to as Late Archaic asymmetrical stemmed. Many of these have been reworked to varying degrees. In short, the stone tool assemblage is consistent with Late Archaic to Terminal Archaic typologies. Some diagnostic bifaces, while indicative of the Late Archaic, are more typically described as midwestern types such as Matanzas and Merom (Justice 1987:120, 132). In the Midwest, Matanzas dates from 4,000–5,700 years ago (Justice 1987:119–120). These bifaces have been recovered from many sites on the UCP, including 3rd Unnamed, and those at Eagle Drink date to around 5,000 years ago. We also have recovered Merom bifaces from other shelters in the area, further supporting Franklin's (2002) and others' (Watson 2001) contentions of north–south relationships along the Cumberland and Allegheny plateaus in prehistory. Finally, Adena bifaces were recovered at Eagle Drink. While the Adena culture area is located in the central Ohio Valley, it is common to find Adena in Middle Tennessee. Interestingly, on the UCP, the raw materials used in their manufacture, far more often than not, are local Monteagle and other Mississippian aged cherts. It may be better to view Matanzas, Merom, and Adena as "Eastern Woodland" types rather than midwestern types. This is but one example of why we believe that cultural historical models developed in other (mostly lowland) regions do not fit the UCP or at the very least need to be tested here.

Raw Material Procurement

In general, the rockshelters of the UCP are located in high-elevation sandstone formations. Because these formations do not contain outcrops of siliceous stones, it might be assumed that suitable lithic raw materials would not be readily available to the prehistoric inhabitants of these shelters. Results from Eagle Drink and regional surveys on the western escarpment of the plateau indicate that lithic raw materials were plentiful in the area. Most of these sources are Monteagle chert outcrops, which occur primarily in the East Fork Obey River gorge at an approximate elevation of 890 feet. Third Unnamed Cave is the largest outcrop and source location we have identified to date (Franklin 1999, 2001; Simek et al. 1998). Interestingly, 15 radiocarbon dates from a mining chamber more than 1 km underground in 3rd Unnamed Cave are contemporaneous with three AMS dates from Eagle Drink at about 3,000 years ago. The cave is less than 7 km from Eagle Drink shelter (Figure 9.1). While this also involves a 300-m change in elevation across rugged terrain and a 1-km trip into the dark-zone mining chamber, the prehistoric hunter-gatherers who inhabited this region were likely well aware of the raw material distribution.

We have identified at least seven more source locations in the vicinity of Eagle Drink: five of these are Monteagle outcrops. Further, in our surveys of the Obey bottom, we have collected Monteagle, Fort Payne, and St. Louis cherts as well as chalcedony in the Obey riverbed and from gravel bars of its attendant streams (see Figure 9.1). Finally, given the proximity to the Eastern Highland Rim, it is reasonable to assume that the vast majority of lithic raw material came from within a 30-km radius of the rockshelter.

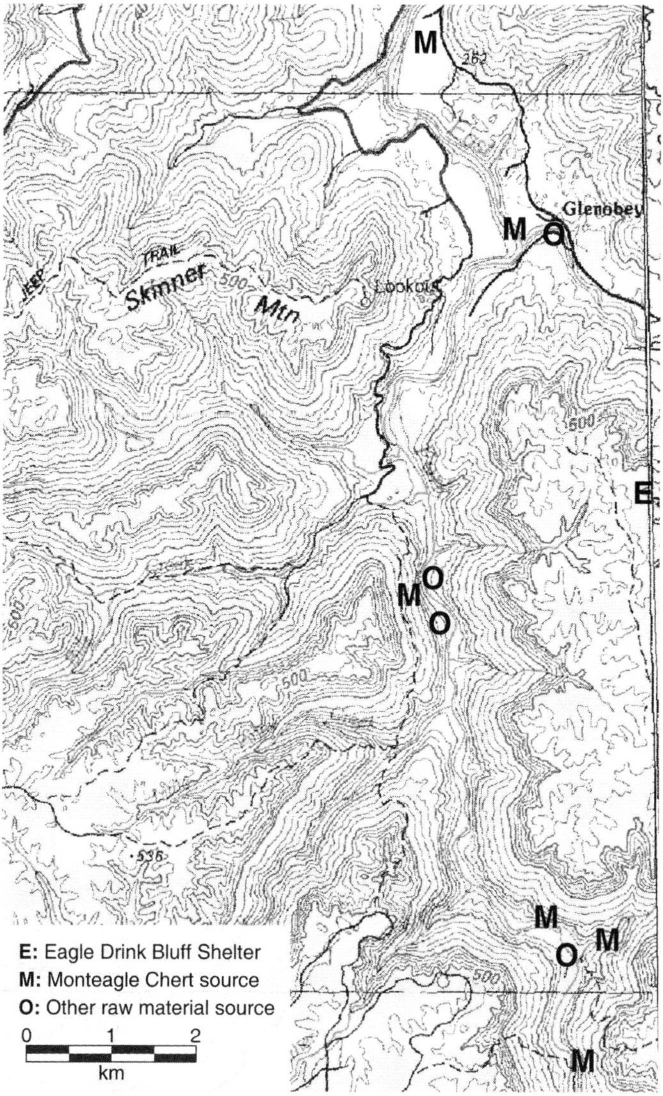

Figure 9.1. USGS 7.5' Wilder, TN, topographic quadrangle showing location of Eagle Drink and other chert locations.

Highland regions such as the UCP have been labeled as marginal zones, occupied more out of necessity than preference (e.g., Swanton 1946). It is clear, however, that Late Archaic hunter-gatherers successfully and routinely navigated these rugged upland environments. As Walsh (2005:299) argues, "notions of marginality are contingent on place and time." As these prehistoric peoples were successfully adapted and familiar with this environment, this fact then renders these regions not marginal at all, and suitable lithic raw materials are ubiquitous.

We have also recovered numerous steatite vessel sherds from myriad shelters in the area, including several from Eagle Drink. While this material was widely traded in the Eastern Woodlands during this time, it is clear that the UCP was involved in this regional exchange.

The Technology of Production

All stages of lithic reduction are present at Eagle Drink. We have already noted the large numbers of finished, broken, and reworked bifaces recovered from the site. We also recovered at least seven large bifaces/bifacial core fragments in the Late Archaic deposits. Several chert core fragments (more than 10) were recovered, as were at least six chalcedony core fragments (it is possible that the chalcedony nodules were also/alternatively used as hammerstones). Finally, many large fragments of tabular chert were recovered in the Late Archaic deposits. Some bear flake scars; some do not. It is clear that they were brought to the site because the shelter is in sandstone hundreds of meters above chert-bearing limestones. For two reasons it is also possible that raw materials entered the site as large flakes: (1) we recovered many and (2) based on the refitting analysis at the contemporary 3rd Unnamed Cave, products of export from the cave were mostly large flakes.

Mass Analysis

In terms of mass analysis, there is little to no variation in the Eagle Drink flaking debris. All assemblages from Late Archaic levels were classified as the result of bipolar reduction. This is not surprising. Monteagle chert nodules at identified source locations, including 3rd Unnamed Cave, occur in small rounded and amorphous shapes. Franklin's (1999, 2001; Franklin and Simek 2008) refitting analysis of the 3rd Unnamed Cave quarry assemblage indicated an invariable bipolar technology. For mass analysis discriminant functions, the overall correct classification rate is 66 percent. While this is far better than correct classification by chance alone (25 percent), it is not robust. Franklin's (1999, 2001) previous work in the analysis of 3rd Unnamed Cave materials demonstrated that when the experimental assemblage is simply separated into two groups, core reduction and tool production, the correct classification rate improves to 98 percent. Therefore, several discriminant function analyses were conducted in this manner. The Eagle Drink Late Archaic lithic assemblage is now classified simply as the result of core reduction, again not surprising given that core fragments were common at the site. The results are not displayed graphically because only one function was generated. The mass analysis is informative and identified core reduction as a major activity on the site. However, given the high number of tools, particularly bifaces, we believe the mass analysis did not capture all of the variation in the lithic assemblage, and mixed technologies can be problematic for mass analysis, particularly with regard to tool production (Ahler 1989b; Andrefsky 2004:204). The discriminant function analyses were conducted on the combined raw materials because sample sizes of other raw materials (e.g., Fort Payne) are inadequate to do the analyses separately. Clearly, this factor also is responsible for masking variation in the mass analysis. Given our concerns, we also conducted another line of analysis to augment the mass analysis.

Individual Flake Analysis

We conducted attribute analysis on 574 pieces of flake debris from several levels of four excavation units. Monteagle chert dominates the assemblage, making up nearly 70 percent. Unidentified local chert makes up 15 percent. The unidentified category was largely employed for very small nondescript gray pieces of chert and/or pieces exhibiting significant thermal damage. The remainder of the assemblage consists of chalcedony (11 percent), Fort Payne (3 percent), and St. Louis and Knox Black together (<2 percent).

Following Magne (1985), we first used platform facet counts (PFCs) on complete and platform remnant bearing (PRB) flakes with complete platforms as an indicator of reduction stage. In this line of analysis, the assemblage appears to be skewed toward early-stage reduction (Table 9.2). This is not surprising given that experiments by Bradbury and Carr (1995, 1999) show that platform facet counts are a conservative measure such that misclassifications are more likely to overrepresent core reduction. Further, this line of analysis is consistent with the results of our mass analysis, which determined the assemblage to largely be the result of bipolar (core) reduction. This interpretation holds for all raw material types.

Using dorsal scar count (DSC) on flakes without complete platforms as the primary indicator of reduction stage, the Eagle Drink materials are heavily skewed toward late-stage reduction for all raw material types (see Table 9.2). However, using Magne's (1985) method of examining platform facet counts, 65 percent of the assemblage could not be assigned a stage for several reasons including lack of a platform, a broken platform, or the piece was either blocky or thermal shatter. Further, using dorsal scar counts, 28 percent could still not be classified because it was either blocky or thermal shatter. Carr and Bradbury (2001:129) maintain through experimentation that higher percentages of blocky shatter are produced in all types of core reduction. Further, their experiments indicate 10–20 percent blocky shatter results from core and bipolar reduction (Bradbury and Carr 2004a). Some researchers have argued that very high percentages of blocky shatter distinguish bipolar reduction (e.g., Kuijt et

Table 9.2. Summary information per raw material for the individual flake attribute analysis

Monteagle

	n	Size	Count	Weight				n	
Complete	76	1″	2	26.7	Heat damage			84	
PRB	90	3/4″	9	80.5	Lipped platform			19	
Broken	145	1/2″	101	297.1	Pressure flake			3	
Blocky shatter	43	1/4″	283	174.3	Biface thinning flake			9	
PFCs	1/4″	1/2″	3/4″	1″	DSCs	1/4″	1/2″	3/4″	1″
0	66	25	2	1	0	2	3	0	0
1	23	7	1	0	1	12	1	0	0
2	16	8	1	0	2	20	5	0	0
3 or more	3	0	0	0	3 or more	82	27	2	0

Chalcedony

	n	Size	Count	Weight				n	
Complete	6	1″	2	43.1	Heat damage			4	
PRB	9	3/4″	9	101.7	Lipped platform			2	
Broken	21	1/2″	15	49.62	Pressure flake			2	
Blocky shatter	23	1/4″	35	23	Biface thinning flake			0	
PFCs	1/4″	1/2″	3/4″	1″	DSCs	1/4″	1/2″	3/4″	1″
0	9	2	0	0	0	0	0	0	0
1	0	1	0	0	1	0	0	0	0
2	0	2	1	0	2	8	1	4	0
3 or more	0	0	0	0	3 or more	2	4	1	0

Fort Payne

	n	Size	Count	Weight		n			
Complete	5	1″	0	0	Heat damage	1			
PRB	4	3/4″	0	0	Lipped platform	1			
Broken	7	1/2″	3	6	Pressure flake	1			
Blocky shatter	1	1/4″	15	7.4	Biface thinning flake	1			
PFCs	1/4″	1/2″	3/4″	1″	DSCs	1/4″	1/2″	3/4″	1″
0	3	2	0	0	0	0	0	0	0
1	2	0	0	0	1	1	0	0	0
2	1	0	0	0	2	0	0	0	0
3 or more	0	0	0	0	3 or more	5	1	0	0

Local

	n	Size	Count	Weight		n			
Complete	5	1″	1	14.4	Heat damage	27			
PRB	13	3/4″	2	11.8	Lipped platform	1			
Broken	18	1/2″	14	42.39	Pressure flake	0			
Blocky shatter	28	1/4″	72	66.01	Biface thinning flake	0			
PFCs	1/4″	1/2″	3/4″	1″	DSCs	1/4″	1/2″	3/4″	1″
0	10	3	0	0	0	1	0	0	1
1	1	0	0	0	1	2	0	0	0
2	1	0	1	0	2	4	0	0	0
3 or more	0	0	0	0	3 or more	8	2	0	0

al. 1995). However, our experiments with Monteagle chert demonstrated that blocky shatter was the least useful variable in determining the *type* of core reduction (Franklin and Simek 2008:116). In any case, blocky shatter accounts for more than 12 percent of the Eagle Drink Monteagle chert assemblage and for approximately one-third of the chalcedony and unidentified local chert assemblages (see Table 9.2). Given that the mass analysis and platform facet counts both indicate core reduction, it is reasonable to believe that core reduction was a common activity at Eagle Drink during the Late Archaic. Late-stage reductions (e.g., tool production and maintenance) also appear to have been common. These results are consistent across all excavation units and levels. Based on both lines of lithic analyses conducted, it appears that Eagle Drink during the Late Archaic was a location where all stages along the continuum of lithic reduction were practiced.

Function

Initially all (n = 179) retouched pieces were to be analyzed for microtraces due to use. While the materials from Eagle Drink were in good condition for analysis, upon closer investigation 8 percent of the pieces were removed from analysis for one or more reasons (e.g., significant postdepositional alterations such as heat damage—common on both tools and flaking debris at Eagle Drink). The final assemblage analyzed microscopically consisted of 164 pieces. The activities represented at the site range from butchering/processing meat, to early-stage hide processing, to woodworking. The overall functional composition of the assemblage indicates that 40 percent of the pieces had some evidence of use (10 percent butchering/processing meat, 21 percent early-stage hide working, and 9 percent woodworking) while for 60 percent of the pieces no wear could be detected. It cannot be said conclusively that these tools were not used; rather, there is no macroscopic or microscopic evidence.

This is not a surprisingly high percentage for "unused pieces," because most of the tools in the assemblage were stemmed bifaces (61 percent). When considering site function, stemmed bifaces pose some interesting problems. The site of discard is often the site of secondary use or the location of multiple uses (Ahler 1971; Greiser 1977; Kimball 1994) and/or the site of retooling in the case of armatures. If stemmed bifaces were used as knives, damage from cutting soft substances such as meat is often ephemeral. If the stemmed bifaces were used as armatures, damage from projection is rarely represented by polishes given there is little repetitive motion. While various fractures are indicative of impact, fractures due to impact in hunting activities are difficult to distinguish from fractures caused by other means (Dockall 1997; Fisher et al. 1984; Odell and Cowan 1986). This study focused on the final use of the tool prior to discard.

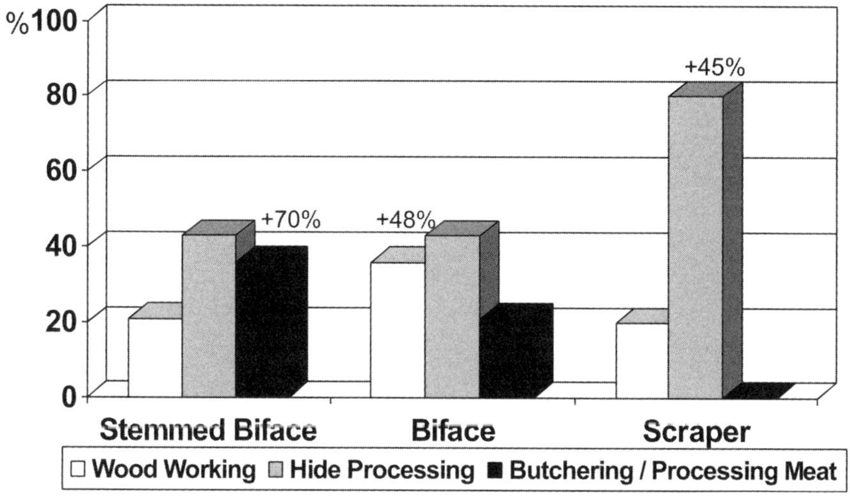

Figure 9.2. Activity by tool type.

Use

For analytical purposes three basic tool types were defined: stemmed bifaces, bifaces, and scrapers. When a chi-square test of independence is used to investigate the variables use and type, the null hypotheses of mutual independence can be rejected in favor of the alternative hypothesis that these variables are dependent with a p-value of <.0001. This probably can be accounted for by a very high discrepancy between the observed and the expected values in the scraper category. Scrapers were used 122 percent more often than would be expected by chance alone.

When we investigate the relationship between specific activities and type given the low counts in several cells, Fisher's exact probability test is more appropriate. The exact probability of an association between activity and type is $p = .012$, rejecting the null hypothesis. A bit more information can be teased out by looking at specific activities. It appears that scrapers were used 45 percent more often for early-stage hide processing, bifaces 48 percent more often for woodworking, and stemmed bifaces 70 percent more often for butchering/meat processing than we would expect due to chance (Figure 9.2). However, the overall pattern is that stemmed bifaces and bifaces were used for multiple purposes while scrapers were used in early-stage hide processing.

Recycling

Given the assemblage is dominated by pieces that can be classified as stemmed bifaces (61 percent), this category was further investigated to look for possible indications of recycling prior to discard. Assuming the original intent for some of the stemmed bifaces was to be projected (a big assumption) then breakage and usage might be dependent variables. For 10 pieces recycling was clearly evident due to a distinctive hafting element, presumably from previous use as an armature, and the end subsequently having been retouched into a piece that would be typologically classified as a scraper. Ninety percent of these were used (eight in hide working and one for woodworking).

If broken stemmed bifaces were being recycled after breakage as other analysts have observed (Kimball 1994), then breakage and use should not be independent. Broken pieces should be used more often than whole unbroken pieces. Here pieces were simply classified as broken or unbroken and a chi-square test of independence was run to test the null hypothesis that tool usage and breakage are independent. With a p-value of .590, the null hypothesis of mutual independence cannot be rejected.

When the relationship between breakage and activity category is investigated, the activity patterns for broken and unbroken stemmed bifaces are very similar with the exception of butchering/meat processing, for which a higher percentage of unbroken pieces (40 percent) are used relative to only 18 percent of the broken pieces. However, when the chi-square test was run, the null hypothesis of mutual independence was not rejected ($p = .435$). This is important because it demonstrates that if we are going to discuss recycling in the *chaîne opératoire,* then we should not rely upon typology alone. We need to understand use and its relation to technology (Soressi and Hays 2003). As has been observed at other sites (Ahler 1971; Greiser 1977), the stemmed bifaces at Eagle Drink, broken or not, were recycled and/or used for multiple purposes.

Assemblage Formation

Magne (1989) expanded his debitage stage approach to develop a model of assemblage formation processes. This model is predicated on assemblage diversity (variety in tool types) and frequencies of tools and tool fragments vis-à-vis the percentage of late-stage debitage recovered. In short, archaeological sites with high numbers of tools and a greater diversity of tools, but low percentages of late-stage debitage, were residential locations. Sites with few tools, low diversity, and low late-stage flaking debris were manufacturing sites. Locations with low diversity, few tools, but higher late-stage debitage are interpreted as situational "emergency" camps. Finally, sites with large numbers of tools, relatively high diversity, and higher percentages of late-stage flaking debris were repeated logistical camps.

For the Late Archaic at Eagle Drink, we recovered more than 180 tools and tool fragments. The percentage of late-stage flaking debris for the Late Archaic is 29.3 percent. When these are plotted against each other, it is clear that Eagle Drink Bluff Shelter served as a repeated residential camp (Figure 9.3).

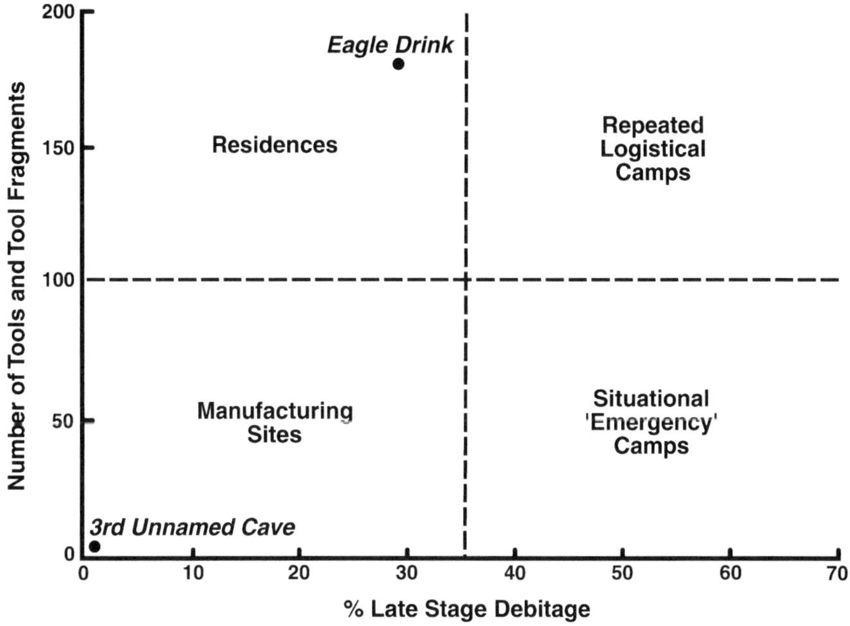

Figure 9.3. Site function diagram for Eagle Drink Bluff Shelter and 3rd Unnamed Cave (diagram adapted from Magne 1989:figs. 3 and 7).

For comparative purposes, we have included in the illustration 3rd Unnamed Cave, from which we recovered only two stone tools and where late-stage debitage made up less than 2 percent of the lithic assemblage. Without question, 3rd Unnamed Cave was a quarry and workshop (i.e., manufacturing) location (Franklin 1999, 2001; Franklin and Simek 2008; Simek et al. 1998). The results of the technological and functional analyses presented herein are consistent with the interpretation of Eagle Drink as a repeatedly used residential (base) camp based on the frequency of tools and late-stage flaking debris.

Discussion and Conclusion

Many archaeologists (e.g., Binford 1962; Flannery 1968; Leroi-Gourhan 1993 [1964]) consider culture as a system and worked to conceive an integrated multidisciplinary approach to the study of humanity. Lithics are simply a single part of that much broader system. Here we only have focused on this single aspect and thus fall short of fully implementing the concept of *chaîne opératoire* as Leroi-Gourhan proposed it. However, we hope that by integrating several different methods we gain a broader and more accurate perspective on the site.

The UCP region is dominated by rockshelters. While models have been proposed for the lowland regions that view rockshelters as special-purpose sites, we caution against this wholesale view for all rockshelters, especially in upland regions. The results from Eagle Drink support our contention. For several thousand years, hunter-gatherers used a small bluff overhang as a residential base camp. Activities represented include the entire range of lithic reduction, early-stage hide processing, woodworking, and butchering/meat processing. Sherds from several steatite vessels, perhaps for cooking and/or storage, were also recovered. In short, a wide range of activities are represented—exactly what we would expect at a residential location (albeit one used perhaps by small family groups). We recovered very small quantities of charred hickory, walnut, and acorn nutshells from the Late Archaic features; curiously, however, we did not recover any obvious nutting stones (a majority of shelter sites on the Cumberland Plateau contain nutting stones). Further, we have no faunal remains from the site due to poor preservation conditions. Though we cannot address seasonality, we believe that Eagle Drink was part of a larger system of rockshelter exploitation on the plateau, which involved differential and varied use of shelters for both special-purpose activities such as hunting and butchering as well as longer-term residential sites with no need to seasonally "retreat" to the low-elevation sites away from the plateau. This is a hypothesis we will test as we proceed with our work: that by the Late Archaic, prehistoric hunter-gatherers were living year-round on the UCP.

By further considering a survey of raw material source locations, we understand that not only was raw material locally abundant but also it outcropped in rugged, sometimes underground, locations. Therefore, little lithic reduction was accomplished at the source, rather the material was carried away to more favorable locations, such as Eagle Drink, where ambient conditions were more suitable. Some of the open-air outcrops in the gorge are located on slopes so precipitous that one can hardly stand upright. However, it is clear that the outcrops were used based on evidence including localized bashing and negative flake removals, bulbs of percussion, and so on. The dark-zone quarry in 3rd Unnamed Cave presented its own problems. However, Walsh (2005:299) reminds us that prehistoric hunter-gatherers in rugged highland landscapes, whether hunting or procuring raw materials, were not necessarily constrained or influenced by relief. Their notions of risk and marginality are virtually beyond our comprehension.

Refitting analysis of the 3rd Unnamed Cave assemblage indicated that items of removal were relatively large cortical flakes and split cobbles—early-stage removals, in effect. If such items were taken to shelter locations to fashion into stone tools, then we would expect an assemblage such as that from Eagle Drink: early-, middle-, and late-stage reduction debris with the emphasis on early stage. We recovered only a few middle-stage bifaces. However, the large number of formal bifaces were clearly used for a variety of purposes on site based on our use-wear analyses. Thus, it seems likely that the bifaces recovered from the site were coming in as more or less finished products.

It is clear that the Southeast has a rich and varied lithic environment. However, be it a lack of comparative data, inattention to analytical biases, the lack of integrated use-wear analyses, or a myriad of other obstacles, the potential of lithic studies to contribute to our understanding of prehistory is not being fully realized. It is our hope that this work demonstrates how an integrated *chaîne opératoire* approach can provide a robust interpretation of a small assemblage from this rather unassuming site on the UCP of Tennessee.

Acknowledgments

We wish to extend our sincere thanks to the Estate of Bruno Gernt, Inc., in particular Jerry Gernt, for allowing us to conduct the excavations and subsequent research at Eagle Drink and 3rd Unnamed Cave. Jay Franklin wishes to thank the Research Development Committee, Office of the Vice Provost for Research and Sponsored Programs, the College of Arts and Sciences, and the Department of Sociology and Anthropology, East Tennessee State University. The AMS determinations were done by the NSF-Arizona AMS Facility and Beta Analytic, Inc. (all radiocarbon measures were calibrated using Calib 6.0 with Intcal 09 atmospheric data). We would like to thank the folks at the Hangin' Hog BBQ for providing food for our crews while in the field. We appreciate the suggestions and cogent comments provided by Bill Andrefsky, George Odell, Phil Carr, Andrew Bradbury, Sarah Price, Jay Johnson, and an anonymous reviewer.

10

Shifting Strategies in Chert Use from the Late Archaic to the Early Fort Ancient at Elk Fork in Eastern Kentucky

D. Randall Cooper

Raw material studies have been a key component of lithic analysis in the Southeast for decades, mainly because of the mosaic of geologic formations with recognizable varieties of useable stone and the fact that broad gaps between these resources required logistical planning by prehistoric groups. While lithic analysts have long recognized the potential of these signature lithic types for interpreting the movement or interaction of people over the landscape, they have struggled to accurately identify these materials and to determine specific sources for materials found in archaeological contexts. Analysts also have struggled at times to assign meaning to raw material data from a particular site or study area. The complex interplay of geology, biota, and culture does not lend itself to a static mathematical model, and consequently there is no single formula for divining past behavior from ratios of local and nonlocal chert, or early- versus late-stage flakes. In the sort of exploratory archaeology that occurs so often in cultural resource management, interpretation of lithic artifacts demands a broad view of multiple data sets, any one of which could be crucial, or virtually useless, in a particular case study.

For most samples of lithic artifacts from intact contexts, the analytical value can be increased exponentially by an understanding of the natural lithic sources within the reach of those who left the artifacts. Lithic resource distribution is one of the few areas in which an absolute baseline can be established; thus lithic resource distribution can provide a much-needed independent variable in the science of prehistoric archaeology. Establishing this baseline presents two fundamental problems: finding out where useable raw material occurs naturally and learning to recognize it when it is found elsewhere. As simple and obvious as these problems may appear, resolutions are usually beyond the scope of any single project, and few lithic studies adequately account for these important

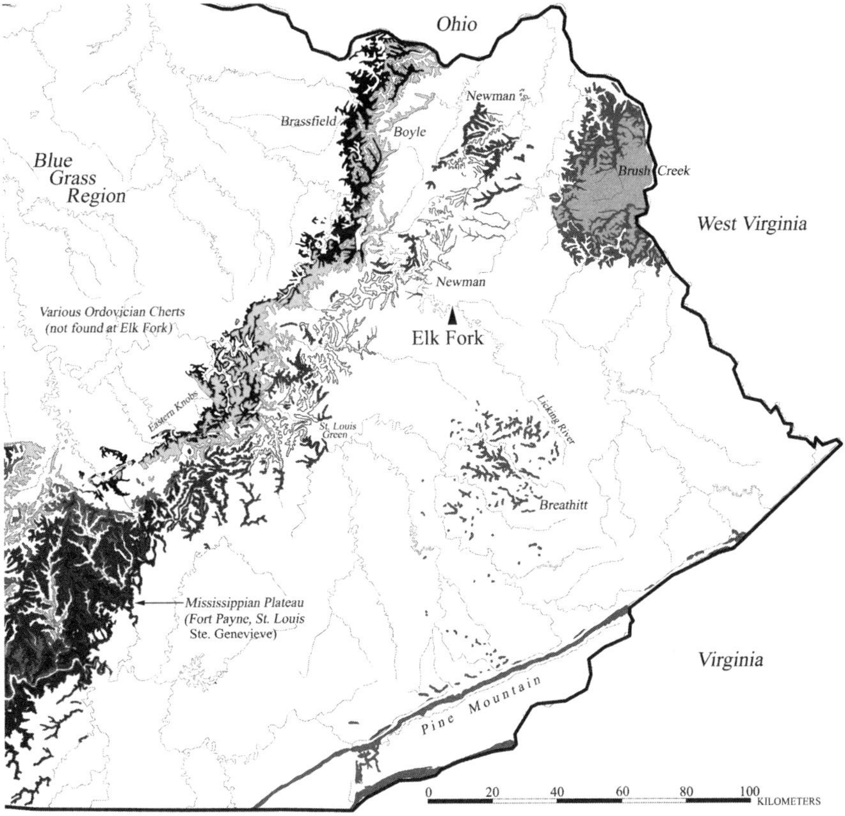

Figure 10.1. Chert-bearing formations in eastern Kentucky.

variables. The analysis of lithics from the Elk Fork site (15MO140) is presented here as one example of how these problems can be addressed and how the resulting data contribute to interpretations of behavior during the different occupations of the site, as well as provide implications for broader patterns of behavior in the region. Though we have not yet achieved an absolute baseline for lithic resources in the region, we have sufficient data to refine our understanding of the different strategies used to exploit lithic resources by two distinctly different groups occupying the same terrace along Elk Fork.

The Elk Fork site is a multicomponent prehistoric site in the upper Licking River drainage of eastern Kentucky (Figure 10.1). The data recovery project at Elk Fork (Herndon 2005) yielded more than 15,000 lithic artifacts. Most of this was flake debris, and 389 stone tools and 41 cores were included (Table 10.1). The bulk of the material was recovered from unit excavation using 6.35 mm

Table 10.1. Elk Fork lithic artifacts by component

Component	Bifaces	Cores	Cobble Tools	Ground Stone	Flake Tools	Manuports	Debitage
Early Archaic	7			3			121
Late Archaic	32	2	11	1	1		1,977
Early Woodland	1						15
Early Fort Ancient	292	36	15	4	5	5	12,442
Indeterminate	7	3	4			1	75
Total	339	41	30	8	6	6	14,630

(.25-inch) screens, but nearly half of the flakes were recovered from flotation samples. Ninety-eight percent of the lithic items recovered from Elk Fork came from Late Archaic and Early Fort Ancient components.

The two major occupations at Elk Fork were separated in time by at least 2,000 years, over which major culture changes occurred. Much of what we know about the Late Archaic in eastern Kentucky is based on inferences from work in adjacent regions, especially southern Ohio (Vickery 1976, 1980) and the Green River area of western Kentucky (Jefferies 1996, 2008a, 2009). Late Archaic sites in the Ohio Valley generally show a continuation of the regional specialization that characterized earlier subperiods of the Archaic, but there are signs of increasing use of cultigens and evidence for increasing sedentism, population size, and social complexity at several sites. Copper and marine shells at sites in western Kentucky demonstrate some level of interregional trade. Various models have been proposed for Late Archaic settlement systems (Boisvert 1986; Granger et al. 1992; Janzen 1977; Jefferies 1996; Vickery 1980; Winters 1969), but most suggest a high degree of residential mobility, with some kind of sustained occupation for part of the year.

At least 76 Late Archaic sites have been documented in the upper Kentucky and Licking river drainages of eastern Kentucky (Jefferies 2008b). Research has focused on a few of the more intensively occupied sites, especially in rockshelters where organics are well preserved. Sites such as Cloudsplitter Rockshelter (Cowan et al. 1981) and Cold Oak Shelter (Gremillion 1998; Ison 1988), approximately 30 to 50 km southwest of Elk Fork, have evidence of sustained occupation, but probably by small groups. The Bluestone and Skidmore sites (Brooks et al. 1979; Cowan 1985) are open habitations with middens and other evidence of sustained occupation, but similar sites are rare in the east (Jefferies

2008b). Late Archaic sites in this mountainous region generally lack the dense midden deposits, exotic trade items, and status burials of some contemporaneous western Kentucky sites.

The second major component at Elk Fork dates to the transition from Late Woodland to Fort Ancient. Radiocarbon dates place this later material within the time frame of Fort Ancient (A.D. 1000–1200), but elements of the Late Woodland are still present in the material culture, especially in the ceramics. The question of whether the site was used by Woodland or Fort Ancient people is discussed by Herndon (2005). Here it is considered Early Fort Ancient, with the radiocarbon dates serving as the primary guide.

Fort Ancient people were "sedentary village farming peoples" of the middle Ohio River valley (Henderson 2008:739). Fort Ancient is contemporaneous with Mississippian cultures to the south and west but lacks the ranked society and settlement hierarchy (Pollack 2008:7). Henderson (2008) suggests Early Fort Ancient society was egalitarian and villages were probably small (40–50 people). In contrast to the Late Archaic, the Early Fort Ancient period is one of the best studied in the eastern half of Kentucky. Several sites from this narrow time range have been excavated, mainly in the Bluegrass region to the west of Elk Fork and in the Big Sandy drainage to the northeast, in addition to a few in the upper Kentucky and Licking river drainages. These sites show a high degree of regional variation, relative to later Fort Ancient manifestations (Henderson 2008). Most of the sites were open habitations, but rockshelters were still being used in eastern Kentucky as hunting camps and probably base camps in some cases. Early Fort Ancient people in this region continued to rely on wild foods and native cultigens as well as maize and squash.

Geology

Both the Late Archaic and Early Fort Ancient occupants of Elk Fork faced a lithic raw material shortage in the immediate vicinity of the site. Flaked stone artifacts in Kentucky are made almost exclusively of chert, but the site lies within a mostly chert-free corridor that runs between Pine Mountain to the southeast and the western escarpment of the Cumberland Plateau to the northwest (see Figure 10.1). Bedrock on the plateau is predominantly Pennsylvanian aged sandstone. The nearest possible chert source is 21 km downstream from Elk Fork, or 8 km over mountainous terrain, where chert-bearing Newman limestone is exposed in bluffs along the Licking River. Geologic maps show no chert-bearing formations upstream from Elk Fork in either the Elk Fork drainage or the Licking River drainage, except for a small area where the upper reaches of some tributaries of the Licking River overlap with the reported distribution of Breathitt chert in southern Magoffin County. It is unlikely, however, that this chert would have been transported closer to the site in any significant quantity by stream action. Chert resources are rich to the west, as streams flow off the Cumberland Plateau and cut into a variety of older chert-bearing formations of Silurian, Devonian, and Mississippian age. More cherts are available on the Mississippian Plateau in south-central Kentucky and in the Pennsylvanian Conemaugh formation of extreme northeastern Kentucky. Cherts from all of these areas made their way into the Elk Fork lithic assemblage.

Chert-bearing formations are well documented in central and eastern Kentucky, thanks in large part to the work of Thomas Gatus, who collected and described chert samples during several projects in the 1980s (e.g., Gatus 1980, 1981, 1985, 1987). These are now curated at the University of Kentucky's (UK) William S. Webb Museum. Cultural Resource Analysts, Inc. (CRA) has also amassed a large collection of regional cherts in the course of archaeological surveys throughout the state. Kentucky cherts have a wide range of variation, even within the same geologic formation. The samples demonstrate the range of variation and in some cases allow analysts to associate varieties of chert with a more specific geographical area than geologic maps alone.

Analysis

Chert types for Elk Fork artifacts were determined primarily by macroscopic comparisons with the CRA geologic samples. Types were identified by color, color patterns, translucency, luster, texture, inclusions or structures, and sometimes type of cortex (Cooper 2005; see also Gatus 1980; Graham 1990). Identification was not attempted for flakes smaller than 6.35 mm because of the amount of time involved and the questionable reliability of identifications for such small pieces (especially considering the similarity of some cherts used at Elk Fork), but small flakes of rare or seemingly exotic chert were described in comments. As both Price (this volume) and Edmonds (this volume) point out, small debitage carries important information about raw material use and site formation, and their research will provide justification to funding agencies for expanding the scope of analysis on future projects.

The effects of wide variation within types and overlapping characteristics between types, as seen in geological samples, were mitigated somewhat by liberal use of "indeterminate" categories and consultation with a regional expert (see Carr and Stewart 2004). Admittedly, some materials from outside of Kentucky were unidentified (including two flakes of suspected Ohio Flint Ridge flint). Also, recent samples of Breathitt chert acquired from the primary source area demonstrate a wider range of variation than was known at the time of the analysis. However, most "indeterminate" cherts from Elk Fork are well within the range of variation of known Kentucky cherts.

Using the CRA collection, along with published descriptions, we were able to confidently identify several cherts in the Elk Fork sample. These were Pennsylvanian aged Breathitt and Brush Creek cherts; Mississippian aged Newman, St. Louis, Ste. Genevieve, and Fort Payne cherts; and Devonian Boyle chert and/or Silurian Brassfield chert. Boyle and Brassfield are both fossiliferous cherts, and one is hard to distinguish from the other, but their geological distributions are very similar, and for the sake of this analysis they were considered a single type. However, St. Louis Green chert was separated from all other varieties of St. Louis chert. This distinctive material is believed to outcrop only in the Eastern Knobs area of east-central Kentucky (Gatus 1980).

The most important chert, in both of the major components at Elk Fork, was Newman. Newman is a highly variable chert, and exposures of Newman limestone are scattered over a wide area of eastern Kentucky. Two varieties of Newman that have been described as different chert types are Paoli and Haney. These two varieties overlap, both in geographic distribution and in visual characteristics. We did not try to differentiate between Paoli and Haney per se. However, we did separate oolitic Newman chert from all other forms of Newman. Oolitic Newman varies widely in color and translucency, but it consistently contains oolitic fossils. It also tends to have a brown, leathery cortex, while other Newman chert generally has a thin, white cortex. Based on written descriptions and material samples at UK and CRA, it seems that all oolitic Newman chert has been traditionally classified as Haney, but not all Haney is oolitic. The only oolitic Newman chert in the CRA type collection is from Menifee County to the west of Elk Fork. All non-oolitic varieties of Newman were classified simply as "Newman."

To determine the general lithic reduction activities represented by the flake debris from Elk Fork, all flakes from each provenience unit were sorted by raw material type, and mass analysis variables were recorded as described by Ahler (1989b:102). Discriminant function equations were then used to classify flake debris aggregates as the result of either core reduction or tool production. These discriminant functions were developed by Bradbury and Franklin (2000) using data from experimental reduction of several Ohio Valley and Mid-South cherts, including some of the cherts used at Elk Fork. The cherts used in experimental reductions were generally similar to the Elk Fork cherts in their range of quality and nodule size (Bradbury, personal communication 2009). In the Bradbury and Franklin study, the discriminant functions yielded a 92-percent correct classification rate when tested on a second experimental data set, which was generated using the same Ohio Valley and Mid-South cherts.

In addition to mass analysis, certain technologically diagnostic flakes (e.g., biface thinning flakes, alternate flakes, notching flakes, bipolar flakes) were noted in comments, but only when they were obvious examples. Wherever possible, ratios of flakes from different size grades were used to help distinguish between primary and secondary deposition (Behm 1983; Wandsnider 1996: 348). Finally, the type of cortex, if any, was recorded (primary geologic cortex, waterworn/alluvial cortex, or patination/indeterminate cortex).

Late Archaic Component

Within the Late Archaic component, lithic material was recovered from three different concentrations (Figure 10.2; map arrows indicate magnetic north; text discussion refers to grid north). The first was associated with a cluster of features in the southwest corner of the site, the second was in Block 4, and the third was in adjacent Blocks 5–9. Radiocarbon dates from the three areas suggest the concentrations were the result of separate occupations, all during the Maple Creek phase of the Late Archaic (Table 10.2; table source, Herndon 2005). The earliest occupation (Maple Creek 1) was centered on Feature 30 (a pit hearth). A carbon sample from this feature yielded a calibrated date of 1950 to 1750 B.C. at the 2-sigma range (3530 ± 40 B.P.). The Maple Creek 2 occupation occurred in the area of Block 4 and dated from 1200 to 940 B.C. at the 2-sigma range (2890 ± 40 B.P.). The Maple Creek 3 concentration, which was actually second oldest, yielded a 2-sigma calibrated range of 1740 to 1400 B.C. (3280 ± 80 B.P.). Other occupations, possibly related, are indicated by post mold alignments to the north of these concentrations, but unfortunately no concentrations were identified in exploratory tests in this area and the post molds were not discovered until the area was mechanically stripped. Their stratigraphic position suggests they also date to the Late Archaic.

Maple Creek 1

The concentration of material at Feature 30 (Maple Creek 1) included three bifaces, one cobble tool, and 26 pieces of flake debris. A Merom cluster hafted biface from Feature 30 is consistent with the radiocarbon date and supports an early Maple Creek phase occupation. Interpretation of this concentration is limited by the small sample, which did not include material from outside of the features. Without material from the old surface surrounding these pits (probably lost during backhoe stripping), the specific lithic reduction activities that took place remain unknown.

Maple Creek 2

In the Maple Creek 2 horizon, identified in Block 4, the lithic assemblage consists of three hafted bifaces, five cobble tools, one flake tool, one ground stone tool, and 504 pieces of flake debris. These were recovered from 36 1-×-1-m units. These artifacts were associated with two pit features near the center of

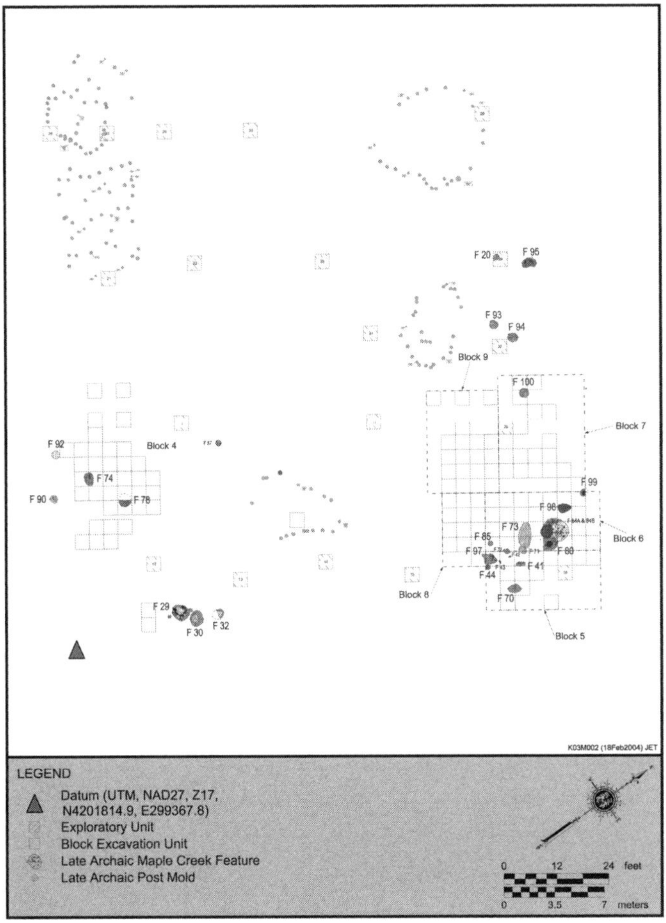

Figure 10.2. Distribution of Late Archaic features (Elk Fork site).

the block (Features 74 and 78). Two of the hafted bifaces match descriptions of the Iddins tradition cluster, which dates from about 2200 to 900 B.C. (Chapman 1981). A concentration of flake debris, made up entirely of Newman chert, was identified near the middle of Block 4. Although Newman chert is highly variable, the concentration shows a narrow range of Newman, mostly fine gray chert with some faint banding and very little color. This debris includes a notching flake, indicating a hafted biface was finished here.

The few flakes of other cherts were recovered from the outer units of Block 4. These were Ste. Genevieve, oolitic Newman, Breathitt, Boyle, Brush Creek, and indeterminate chert (some burned and some unburned). Mass analysis of Newman and Ste. Genevieve cherts suggests the flake debris was mainly from

Table 10.2. Summary of Elk Fork radiocarbon dates

Lab No.	Provenience	Measured Radiocarbon Age	$^{13}C/^{12}C$ Ratio	Conventional Radiocarbon Age	Cal. 2σ	Cal. 1σ
Beta-192112	Feature 30	3550 ± 40 B.P.	−26.5	3530 ± 40 B.P.	1950–1750 B.C.	1910–1770 B.C.
Beta-192114	Feature 74	2890 ± 40 B.P.	−25	2890 ± 40 B.P.	1200–940 B.C.	1120–1000 B.C.
Beta-192115	Feature 84A	3280 ± 80 B.P.	−25	3280 ± 80 B.P.	1740–1400 B.C.	1650–1450 B.C.
Beta-192110	Feature 12	930 ± 50 B.P.	−25	930 ± 50 B.P.	A.D. 1010–1220	A.D. 1030–1180
Beta-192111	Feature 18	880 ± 60 B.P.	−25	880 ± 60 B.P.	A.D. 1020–1270	A.D. 1040–1230
Beta-192113	Feature 60A	930 ± 50 B.P.	−25	930 ± 50 B.P.	A.D. 1010–1220	A.D. 1030–1180

late-stage reduction (i.e., tool production). However, in one of the two adjacent units where the concentration of Newman was found, mass analysis indicates early-stage debris (core reduction).

The lithic remains from Maple Creek 2 reflect a variety of domestic activities focused around the features in the south half of Block 4. The bulk of the lithic material is from a concentration of flakes related to an episode of tool production on the north side of Feature 78 (a shallow basin with sparse wood charcoal). With this concentration and the feature as the nucleus of the Maple Creek 2 horizon, various activities are present around the perimeter. Three large sandstone blocks were found on three different sides of and roughly equidistant from this nucleus (2–3 m away). Two of these are nutting stones and one is an anvil stone. A fragment of ground sandstone on the north side appears to be from a carved vessel. Three hafted bifaces were also collected from this northern perimeter, including two Iddins cluster bifaces. This perimeter is further defined by flakes of nonlocal cherts, with Boyle chert to the west and Ste. Genevieve and Breathitt cherts to the south. It is not clear whether material along this perimeter represents peripheral activities, a discard zone, or a combination of the two. It might be a "displacement zone" as discussed by Stevenson (1985:75, 1991). This is a zone where larger items, after being dropped near use areas, are inadvertently (and incrementally) pushed toward the perimeter of the occupation area by foot traffic (or "scuffage") and possibly by children playing with objects left by adults.

The Maple Creek 2 lithic remains are from a discrete concentration of material with evidence for task organization within the concentration. This concentration probably relates to a single occupation, or a series of short occupations by a single group. Hafted biface forms are consistent with the radiocarbon date that places this in the middle of the Maple Creek phase.

Maple Creek 3

In the Maple Creek 3 horizon, encompassed by contiguous Blocks 5–9, lithic material was most concentrated near a cluster of features in Block 6 in the southeast part of the group. The features were mostly pit hearths (at least five within Block 6), but there was also one post mold and a fire-cracked rock concentration that apparently resulted from cleaning a pit hearth. The lithic material from this cluster consists of 22 bifaces, four cobble tools, one core, and more than 1,300 pieces of flake debris. Three of the bifaces match descriptions of the Merom cluster, one falls within the Late Archaic Stemmed cluster, and one falls within the Brewerton cluster. At least 11 of the remaining bifaces appear to have been hafted, but they are mostly small fragments and could not be assigned to a cluster. Some of the other bifaces appear to be production failures, but they were all in the later stages of manufacture. At least six of the 14 hafted bifaces were made from nonlocal cherts. The four cobble tools are all sandstone fragments, including a nutting stone, an anvil stone, a whetstone, and a small grooved abrader. All of these were found to the north of the main concentration of features and lithic debris. The core is one of only two cores associated with the entire Maple Creek assemblage. It was found on the eastern fringe of the main concentration in Block 6.

The raw material for most of the flakes (approximately 85 percent) is Newman chert. Other raw materials, in order of abundance, are Ste. Genevieve chert, Brush Creek chert, Breathitt chert, Boyle chert, Fort Payne chert, oolitic Newman chert, chalcedony, St. Louis chert, and indeterminate chert. For all material types, the highest concentrations of flakes were in Block 6, especially in and around Features 84A and 84B. Most of the flakes and bifaces were found within 3 m of these features. The cobble tools, however, were found to the north and northwest of the main concentration, 4 to 6 m away. Mass analysis of Blocks 5 and 6 suggests that flake debris from both blocks was produced mainly during tool production.

Lithic reduction in the Maple Creek 3 occupation occurred primarily near a cluster of features, and ground stone and cobble tools were left at the perimeter of the concentration. This suggests separate areas for lithic reduction and food processing, similar to the organization of the living space in the Maple Creek 2 component. Spatial patterning is not as clear, however, in Maple Creek 3. The central concentration is denser, and it includes a mix of artifact classes and raw material types. The greater volume of material and the multiple flaking episodes (indicated by the various chert types) suggest a longer occupation, or a longer series of occupations, in Maple Creek 3. Yet, the volume of material and variety of artifact types fall short of what would be expected from a long-term occupation.

Early Fort Ancient Component

The Fort Ancient assemblage was deposited on top of the Maple Creek remains with a nearly sterile stratum of about 30 to 40 cm between the two (Figure 10.3). Approximately 85 percent of the lithic artifacts from the site came from this upper component (see Table 10.1). Most of the material was associated with a cluster of post molds in the northern part of Block 2, which was designated Structure 1. A smaller concentration was identified to the south in Block 1.

Bifaces dominate the tool assemblage in the Fort Ancient component. Unlike findings in earlier components, early-stage bifaces are present, but later-stage bifaces remain more common. Most bifaces appear to be finished or nearly finished. Finished bifaces include 110 hafted bifaces and two drills. Ninety of

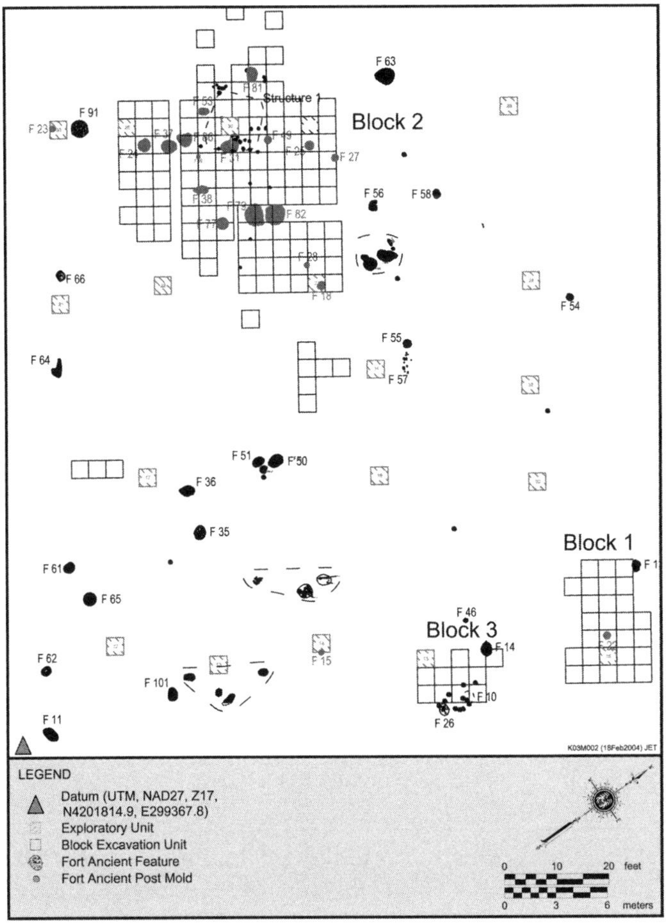

Figure 10.3. Distribution of Fort Ancient features (Elk Fork site).

the hafted bifaces are small triangular arrow points. These were found scattered across the site, but most were recovered from the general lithic concentration in Block 2. Other hafted bifaces from this horizon include a Jack's Reef corner notched and two Jack's Reef Pentagonal points. At least five hafted bifaces appear to be recycled older forms. These fall within four different clusters: two in the Copena cluster (a Middle Woodland form), one in the Early Woodland stemmed cluster, one in the Terminal Archaic barbed cluster, and one in the Motley cluster (also from the Terminal Archaic). Some of these show signs of having been burned since their initial manufacture then flaked again.

At least 12 different lithic raw materials were flaked during the Early Fort Ancient occupation at Elk Fork. The material used most often was Newman

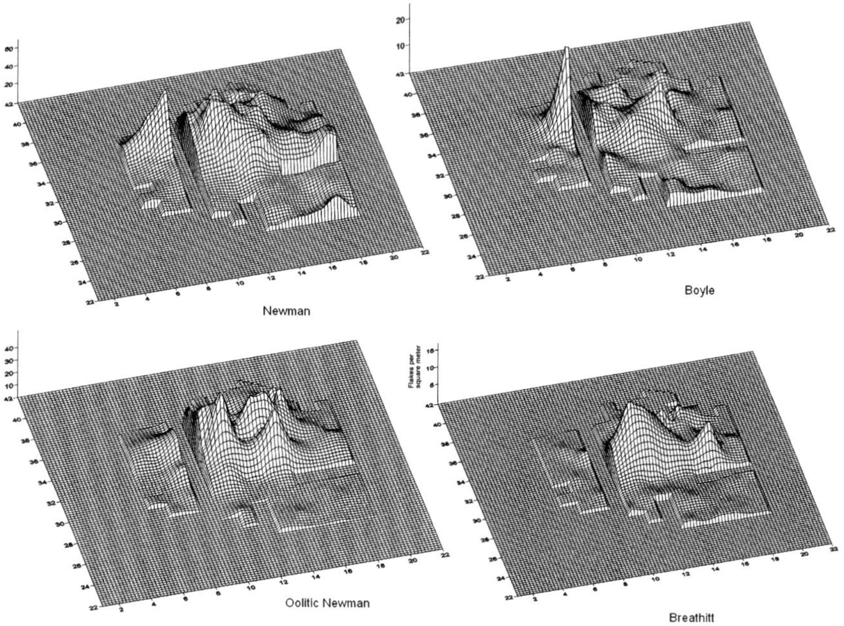

Figure 10.4. Flake debris distributions for the four most common materials in the Fort Ancient component.

chert, which makes up 57 percent of the flake debris in the analysis. For flakes of all materials, the densest concentrations correspond to the general lithic concentration in the northern part of Block 2. In Blocks 1 and 3, where densities are much lower, nearly all flakes identifiable to raw material are of Newman chert. In Block 2, the four most common cherts are concentrated in roughly the same area (Figure 10.4).

Because the scatter was thin over most of the site, mass analysis was employed for about half of the units. In most cases, mass analysis indicates tool production. This is consistent with the relatively small number of cores recovered. When units with small samples are combined for analysis, the results are the same, except for a small group of units at the north edge of the site, where mass analysis indicates core reduction.

Comparisons

The differences in lithic remains between the two main components at Elk Fork are consistent with the traditional view of Archaic peoples as more mobile and living in smaller groups than people at the start of the Fort Ancient period, who had become increasingly sedentary. A substantially higher artifact density in the Fort Ancient component indicates a more intensive occupation. The concentration of lithic artifacts in the area of Structure 1 shows sustained occupation of a confined area. Late Archaic remains, on the other hand, were found mainly in the form of small, discrete clusters with evidence for a variety of activities (pit features, fire-cracked rock, and stone tools of various classes), but without evidence for a long series of repeated activities in the same living space. The distribution of flakes of different material types helps highlight the organization of the living space in the Late Archaic, especially in the Maple Creek 2 concentration.

In addition to differences in site structure, the various raw materials show dissimilar geographic affinities between Late Archaic and Early Fort Ancient peoples at Elk Fork. While there is broad overlap in the materials used, as would be expected from prehistoric groups occupying the same site, Late Archaic occupants were bringing in more material from the Mississippian Plateau, such as Ste. Genevieve and Fort Payne cherts. This pattern persisted through at least the later two Maple Creek occupations. Early Fort Ancient people, on the other hand, show a much greater affinity with the Eastern Knobs and Outer Bluegrass, as seen in the greater abundance of Boyle and oolitic chert and also the presence of St. Louis Green chert, which is absent from the Maple Creek assemblage. They also show more connection with the Big Sandy/Ohio River area of northeastern Kentucky, as shown by the presence of Brush Creek chert.

Beyond the differences in frequencies of chert types, this analysis showed distinctions in the ways the various materials were used. The local Newman chert was the most common material in both components, but the percentage of non-Newman is much higher for debitage in the Fort Ancient component, while non-Newman accounts for a much higher percentage of the tools in the Late Archaic component (Figure 10.5). For Fort Ancient, chert type percentages are almost identical for flakes and bifaces. In this case, tools were made, maintained, and discarded at the same site. In the Late Archaic, the materials are strikingly different between bifaces and flake debris. Flakes indicate that most new tools were made of chert from the nearest source (Newman), while most of the discarded tools were made of chert from distant sources. This pattern suggests a subsistence range in which local chert sources along the way were exploited in a fashion similar to the local plant and animal communities. Tools made elsewhere in the seasonal round were replaced with new tools of local chert at Elk Fork. Small amounts of nonlocal flake debris also suggest some of these tools made elsewhere were being repaired, not replaced, at Elk Fork.

Raw material procurement during Fort Ancient is not as easy to interpret. Different materials were used in much the same way, regardless of distance from source. Chert was more of a commodity during Fort Ancient, imported from distant sources and stockpiled for later use. This suggests the possibility of indirect acquisition of chert from people in the surrounding areas where the different materials occur naturally. However, another line of reasoning suggests

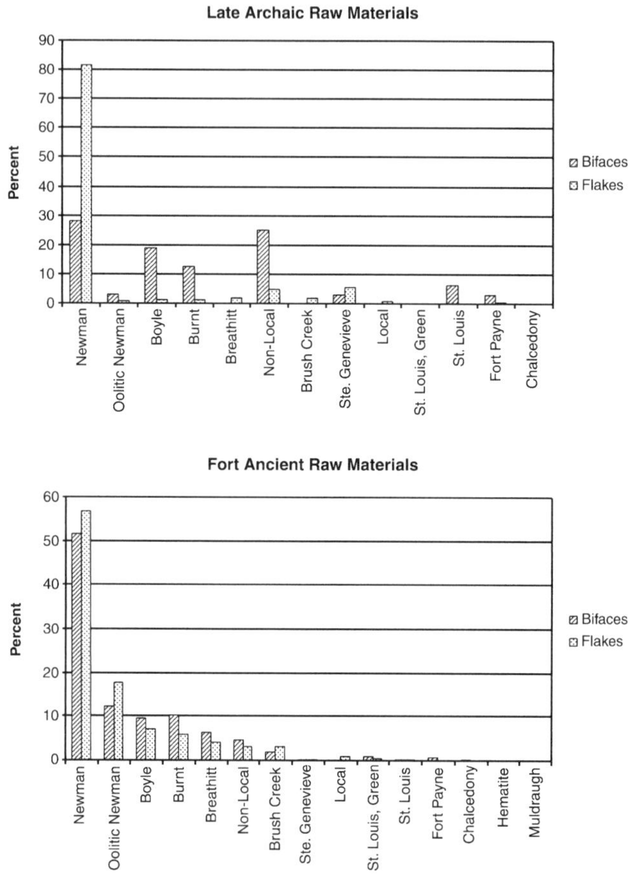

Figure 10.5. Proportions of debitage and bifaces by raw material types by component.

indirect acquisition was unlikely. Newman is a high-quality chert available at several sources within 20 km of the site and was probably acquired directly. If the other materials were obtained as gifts or trade items, there should be differences in manufacture and use-life profiles. Instead, the different cherts are remarkably similar in spatial distribution, frequencies across artifact classes, and predominance of tool manufacture debris (with minor amounts of core reduction debris).

Other than the greater quantity of Newman, this analysis showed few differences with other cherts. Newman is the material for a slightly higher proportion of Fort Ancient cores (67 percent, compared to roughly 55 percent of flakes and bifaces), but several other materials also were used for cores. At least five other cherts are represented by one to three cores each. Newman also has a higher percentage of primary cortex. Although the cortex type was indeterminate for most cortical flakes, Newman is the only chert in the Fort Ancient component with more primary cortex than waterworn cortex (at least 8:1 for those with identifiable cortex). Except for Ste. Genevieve, which has two of each, all non-Newman cherts have more alluvial cortex than primary cortex (Table 10.3). The reason for the difference is not clear, but Newman and Ste. Genevieve also have more primary cortex than other cherts in the Late Archaic assemblage.

The similarities in technology and spatial distribution between the different chert types in the Fort Ancient component suggest a uniform system of acquisition and use of materials from different sources. In other words, if some materials were acquired from neighbors and others directly from geologic sources, we could expect to see more substantial differences between chert types in frequencies across artifact classes, ratios of tools to flakes, reduction stages, and/or spatial distributions. Such spatial or technological differences would not argue specifically for trade, but the lack of them argues against some materials being acquired indirectly and some being acquired directly from geologic sources.

While chert might have been obtained by "direct acquisition," as described by Meltzer (1989), it almost certainly was not obtained through a "direct procurement" strategy as described by Binford (1979). That is, the Fort Ancient people at Elk Fork were not traveling away from the site specifically to collect chert. If this was their strategy they would have exploited the nearest source, and materials other than Newman chert would be rare. As in the Late Archaic, chert was obtained in the Fort Ancient period as part of an embedded procurement system. Unlike in the Late Archaic, most of the nonlocal material was transported to the site early in the production process. The evidence favors an interpretation of opportunistic procurement in the course of targeting other resources over a wide area. They were traveling to distant camps, too far away to return in a day, and collecting raw material along with other resources, but not staying long enough in those areas to "consume" the material.

At least some of the lithic material was brought back to Elk Fork in the form of nodules or cores, but the small number of cores compared to tools and the relatively small amount of core reduction debris suggest some arrived in the form of flake blanks or unfinished bifaces. Taken in isolation, the relatively small number of cores in the Fort Ancient material does not mesh well with the idea that use of expedient cores increased through time with sedentism, as suggested by Parry and Kelly (1987). Johnson (1989:132) also reported a higher ratio of amorphous cores to bifaces at Late Woodland sites in Mississippi, compared to earlier sites created by more mobile groups. Odell (1996a:207) has suggested that greater "technological entropy" results from a decreased need for more sedentary groups to use raw material efficiently, especially in chert-rich areas. If there was an increase in the importance of expedient raw material use at Elk Fork, it might manifest itself not in greater numbers of cores but in

Table 10.3. Cortex type by raw material

Component	Material	No Cortex	Primary Geologic	Alluvial	Patination/ Indeterminate	Total
Late Archaic	Boyle	8		3	3	14
	Breathitt	12		4	5	21
	Brush Creek	19	1	3	1	24
	Chalcedony	2				2
	Fort Payne	4				4
	Newman	633	47	55	233	968
	Oolitic Newman	6		1	2	9
	St. Louis			1	1	2
	Ste. Genevieve	46	4		17	67
Fort Ancient	Boyle	325	2	65	40	432
	Breathitt	204	2	16	29	251
	Brush Creek	135	3	44	9	191
	Chalcedony	2			1	3
	Fort Payne	4		1		5
	Muldraugh	2				2
	Newman	1,923	468	246	836	3,473
	Oolitic Newman	798	8	178	96	1,080
	St. Louis	16		4	1	21
	St. Louis, Green	11		14		25
	Ste. Genevieve	12	2	2	2	18
Total		4,162	537	637	1,276	6,612

more intensively used cores. Intensive use is suggested by the average weight of the Fort Ancient cores, which is just under 21 g. Only three weigh more than 40 g. By comparison, each of the two Late Archaic cores weighs approximately 40 g. Most of the Fort Ancient cores are multidirectional freehand cores or indeterminate fragments. Only two show signs of bipolar reduction.

More intensive use of cores actually lowers the count relative to flake debris, and possibly relative to bifaces in this case, since several small triangular points could be produced from a single core. The ratio of bifaces to cores in the Fort Ancient material is 8:1. The ratio of bifaces to cores in the Late Archaic material is 16:1. Thus, the seemingly small number of cores in the Fort Ancient component is still high compared to the remains left by a more mobile group (i.e., Late Archaic) operating under the same raw material constraints. This highlights the need to consider raw material availability when interpreting the lithic assemblage (e.g., Andrefsky 1994a; Bamforth 1986; Carr 1994b).

The lack of a chert source nearby also seems to have motivated Fort Ancient inhabitants to recycle older lithic artifacts at the site. This "secondary recycling" (Amick 2007) is indicated by the presence of at least five hafted bifaces from earlier periods among the Fort Ancient remains. Some of these show signs of having been burned since their initial manufacture then flaked again. This has obvious implications for investigations of other multicomponent sites in chert-poor areas.

Conclusion

As Andrefsky (2009) has noted, every site has a unique context and understanding that context is crucial to an accurate interpretation of the stone artifacts. In the case of Elk Fork, the regional geologic context is particularly important. The Elk Fork site has no immediate chert sources, but it lies within a region of many, and the chert types vary widely. The raw materials at Elk Fork can be seen as geologic residue, reflecting the geographic range exploited, directly or indirectly, by inhabitants of the site. The availability of a raw material comparative collection makes it possible to trace that residue back to its source. Using the baseline data provided by the geological samples, the Late Archaic and Early Fort Ancient lithic assemblages from Elk Fork provide an opportunity to isolate dependent and independent variables in a regional lithic study. Broad similarities in lithic procurement and technology through the various occupations (i.e., relatively small amounts of cores and core reduction debris, large amounts of local Newman chert) can be seen as a consequence of the lithic landscape shared by both groups, and variation ("consumption" of raw material in the course of seasonal movement versus stockpiling material at a long-term residence) highlights some of the different ways these groups operated in a similar environment.

Newman chert was the favored raw material for both groups as they lived along Elk Fork, but their use of outside sources is dissimilar, and they have distinct strategies to exploit those areas derived from differing settlement systems. A wider variety of materials was used in the Fort Ancient occupation than in the Late Archaic. These materials were brought to the site from different parts of the Cumberland Plateau, the Outer Bluegrass region, and the Eastern Knobs. Most would have been available within a 50-km radius, but in several different directions. These materials apparently arrived at the site in much the same form and all were used in the same way. While Late Archaic occupants used fewer cherts, some of the materials traveled a greater distance to reach the site. Several discarded tools were made of Mississippian cherts from at least 100 km away, but flake debris suggests they were replaced with new tools made of Newman. The Late Archaic material indicates a more linear pattern of seasonal movement. Site structure, defined in part by raw material distributions, supports the interpretation of shorter occupations, and hence greater residential mobility, by the earlier group.

Although the sample of lithic artifacts from Elk Fork is relatively small, it sheds light on regional patterns of lithic raw material acquisition and use, and it highlights the importance of understanding regional geologic context when interpreting lithic artifacts. Knowledge of regional cherts helps define analytical units, and it adds leverage to arguments about changing use of resources within a particular region. In an area with as much raw material diversity as Kentucky, and in the Southeast in general, further development of chert type collections and chert type definitions can add finer resolution to our view of settlement patterns, social networks, and migration patterns, as well as changes in these systems through time.

Acknowledgments

Special thanks are given to Rich Herndon, who directed the data-recovery project at Elk Fork and provided graphics and information and general support for this study. Thanks to George Crothers for making UK's geologic samples available for examination and photographs, and to Andrew Bradbury for help with chert identification and comments on the initial analysis, as well as drafts of this chapter. I would also like to thank Russell Quick, Jason Anderson, and Eric Thomason for help with graphics, and The Kentucky Transportation Cabinet for support of this project. Finally, this study would not have been possible without the databases and geologic maps made available on-line by the Kentucky Geological Survey.

11

Lithic Reduction at a Middle Woodland Site in Mississippi

Scale, Classification, and Explanation

Jason L. Edmonds

Woodland period research tends to focus on ceramic artifacts, likely due to their usefulness in chronology construction. While lithic tools, such as projectile points, have proven to be chronologically sensitive as well, within the Woodland period as well as in other periods in northeast Mississippi (Burris 2006; Edmonds 2009; Rafferty 1994), reliance only on artifacts useful for chronology construction masks the variability within the period in question. All classes of artifacts vary through time, either in form or proportional representation, and it is this variation that provides evidence of the cultural change that is the hallmark of the archaeological record. Simply because some classes of artifacts are difficult to place into a temporal framework because of a lack of stylistic traits (Dunnell 1978), this should not be taken to suggest that such artifacts do not vary through time as well. Close associations of temporally less-sensitive artifacts, such as lithic debris, with temporally sensitive artifacts can help highlight archaeologically useful patterns and changes within both classes of artifacts.

A study sample of lithic debitage was drawn from 18 randomly selected excavation levels from investigations at the Cork site (22OK746). The primary occupation of the Cork site was during the Middle Woodland, as determined largely from the presence of sand-tempered fabric- and cord-marked ceramics (Rafferty and Galaty 2002). This investigation involved a comparison of macrodebitage and microdebitage samples, based on a somewhat similar study by Eerkens et al. (2007), to determine whether raw material representation varied between the two size classes. The presence of nonlocal materials within the Cork site Middle Woodland assemblage suggested that a targeted investigation could yield more information on exotic raw materials. Further, differences in lithic raw material proportions between macrodebitage and microdebitage samples might provide information on the acquisition and use of those materials.

As Sherwood (2001) has noted, much disagreement exists within the literature on the definition of microartifacts, most notably concerning the issue of size (see Price this volume). Indeed, a brief overview of the microartifact literature (following Sherwood 2001) shows that there are almost as many size definitions as there are authors writing about the subject (Dunnell and Stein 1989; Fladmark 1982; Hassan 1978; Metcalfe and Heath 1990; Nicholson 1983; Peacock 2004; Rosen 1993; Sherwood et al. 1995). This study does not attempt to resolve this issue, nor does it address whether in fact this is an issue that requires resolution. Rather, this chapter will highlight the necessity of theoretical considerations such as scale, applied to the dimensions of time, space, and form, and classification in archaeological research questions as applied to the Cork site lithic sample. A brief discussion of these two considerations is presented below. This is followed by an overview of how choices within scale and classification affect our ability to explain archaeological phenomena.

The Cork Site, Oktibbeha County, Mississippi

The Cork site (22OK746) is situated in an area lacking knappable lithic materials (Figure 11.1). Sandstone and siltstone are likely the most immediately available materials, as they naturally occur within the uplands of the region. Due to their generally large grain sizes, however, these two materials are probably better suited for ground—rather than flaked—stone tools. The nearest source of knappable material is found in the Tuscaloosa formation along the Tombigbee River (Bruce 2001; Yedlowski and Vento 1992), located roughly 30 km to the east near Columbus, Mississippi.

Field recovery during excavation was primarily by the use of water screening with nested 6.35-mm (.25-inch) and 1.58-mm (.0625-inch) wire mesh screens, in order to recover small artifacts such as animal bone, charred plant remains, and small lithic debris. Due to the presence of small amounts of exotic materials such as copper, galena, and quartz crystal noted in some analyzed portions of the 6.35-mm sample, a limited investigation of the fine-mesh lithic sample was undertaken to determine whether more exotics were recovered at that scale. This study draws on lithic material from 18 randomly selected excavation levels, representing a 10-percent sample.

Scale

Scale specifications were given particular attention in this study. Whether scale is fully defined or explicitly dealt with or not, all archaeological investigations place arbitrary limits on the phenomenological world. Determinations of scale were made for each of the three dimensions of archaeology: through time, across space, and within form.

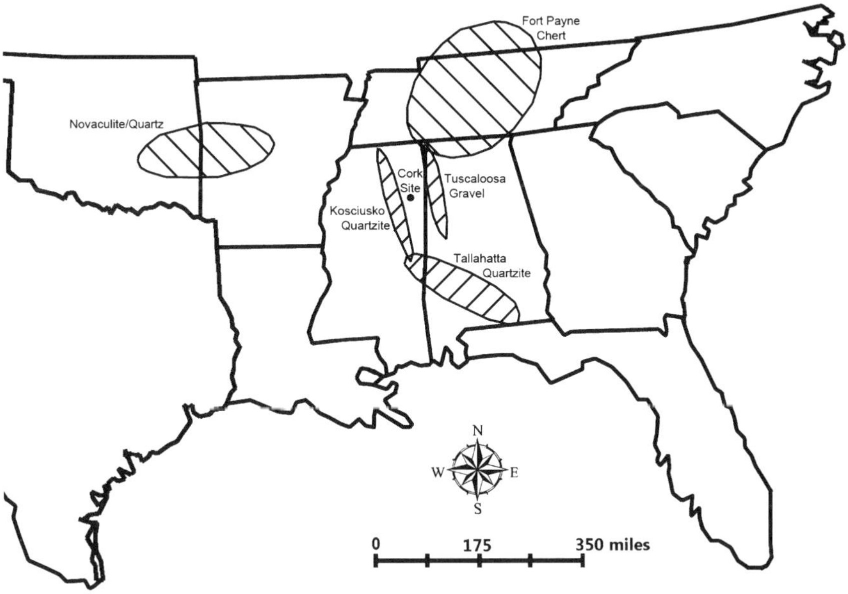

Figure 11.1. Cork site location and lithic raw material source areas.

Because archaeological observations are indirect observations of the past, the recognition of intentionally modified objects and patterns within and among groups of those objects requires a reliance on aggregate data. As such, it is essentially impossible for the resolution of such observations to become so fine grained as to reliably determine specific moments in time (Bailey 2007). Furthermore, behaviors in the past cannot be directly observed and are only "visible" using inferences drawn from aggregate patterning in artifacts. It is, therefore, the observer who decides how to order the data into aggregates, whether explicitly or implicitly. Scale is defined for the purposes of this discussion as the limitations imposed by the individual researcher upon the variability of the archaeological record. However, scale is often presented in nebulous terms, such as the "human scale" (Stein 1993:4–5), which is never fully operationalized and appears to place emphasis on deriving explanations from archaeological data in the framework of individualized perceptions of people in the past.

Different time scales can, as Bailey (2007) notes, provide the researcher with opportunities to observe a variety of phenomena that may be visible only at certain scales or that may operate only in the long or short term. While this study is limited in time to the duration of the Middle Woodland occupation, perhaps a few centuries, no single time scale will work in every instance. Microartifact studies have spanned the synchronic, including a study of a Mississippian period house floor in eastern Tennessee (Sherwood et al. 1995) and the investigation of site function and occupational intensity at two Woodland period sites in north Mississippi (Peacock 2004), and the diachronic, including the investigation of destruction and occupational episodes at a tell site in Israel (Rosen 1993).

Microartifact studies within smaller spatial scales may include those involved with understanding community or household organization (Metcalfe and Heath 1990; Sherwood et al. 1995) or site function (Peacock 2004) but are not necessarily confined similarly in time. Long-duration occupations may include many alterations to community structure, including those associated with changes in technology or other behaviors. Those encompassing larger portions of the landscape, such as patterns in settlement or resource exploitation, may require broader context among sites of varying sizes, durations, and occupational intensities. The latter example of resource exploitation is of key importance for studies addressing the use of nonlocal materials, as is the case with this study. Given these different scales, appreciation of context is necessary in defining the spatial scale for an investigation. Fine-grained provenience control is probably most important on the small-scale side of the coin, while a broader understanding of the distribution of archaeological materials over the landscape is integral to the larger scale. Because this study is at a fairly low spatial scale, relationships among artifacts are important at a similarly small scale; provenience here is based on 1-×-1-m excavation units. All samples were taken from the same zone and level across the excavation for purposes of comparability.

The pursuit of exotic materials, however, places this study in a conceptually broader spatial framework. Some studies (Eerkens et al. 2007; Johnson and Brookes 1988; Meltzer 1989) dealing with nonlocal or exotic raw materials have tended to perceive of such terms implicitly, without formal definitions, as more or less distant from the sites or areas in question. This question can be a very complex one, especially when dealing with the artifacts from populations that were mobile and may have directly acquired distant materials as a part of their settlement pattern. The designations of local versus nonlocal/exotic should not be rationalized by what researchers believe may accord with perceptions in the past, as there is no realistic way of determining such information. At a very basic level, designating local versus nonlocal is simply an act of classification, as the source location of any material is an attribute of that artifact. As an act of classification, this parsing of the spatial scale is simply a way of conceptually limiting the variability of distance, as anything above a certain threshold is considered nonlocal and anything below is considered local. While any number of classes can be derived from within that variability, this study will limit the discussion to the two basic classes. The current analysis follows the lead of Gibson (1994) in dealing with exotic materials at Poverty Point by defining local materials as those available within 100 km or less of the Cork site and nonlocal/exotic as those materials available at a distance greater than 100 km.

This distance was not chosen to draw direct corollaries between the Cork site and Poverty Point, although some similarities do exist. Both represent sedentary hunter-gatherers within the Southeast, and both contain raw materials from similar source areas (Carr and Stewart 2004); nonetheless, differences also exist. The distance of 100 km was chosen to limit the variability and provide a more concise discussion of the materials. Given these classes, the local materials consist of the following: sandstone and siltstone, both of which are immediately available in the vicinity of the Cork site; Tuscaloosa gravel, available approximately 30 km to the east; and Kosciusko quartzite (McGahey 1999), available some 60 km to the west. Nonlocal materials include Fort Payne chert, the nearest source of which lies in the extreme northeastern portion of Mississippi (Merrill et al. 1988), roughly 160 km distant from the Cork site; Tallahatta quartzite/sandstone and Coastal Plain/Tallahatta agate, both of which are available in the Tallahatta formation (Dunning 1964), the nearest portion of which is approximately 140 km to the southeast of the Cork site; and novaculite and quartz crystal, the nearest source of both lying in the Ouachita Mountains of Arkansas, about 360 km to the west (see Figure 11.1).

Because this study is placed at relatively low scales within the dimensions of space and time, direct conclusions must be limited in scope to phenomena at the occupation level and within a fairly narrowly focused period of time. Such low-level temporal and spatial scales, however, do not preclude useful comparisons over space and through time. Rafferty and Galaty (2002) have shown, via changes in frequencies of ceramic styles, that the focus of the Middle Woodland occupation shifted eastward across the landform over time. While this aspect of the occupation was not explored for this study, differences in exotic lithic presence in the study samples as compared to Rafferty and Galaty's (2002) data could potentially provide information on change in raw material use over time and within the spatial extent of this occupation.

Finally, the dimension of form relates most directly to the basic unit of archaeology, the artifact. Following Dunnell and Stein's (1989) discussion of microartifacts, artifacts at increasingly smaller scales are not just smaller versions of larger artifacts, but contain complementary information. As artifact scale is decreased, the information denoting an object's nature as an artifact becomes increasingly locational. Artifacts at very small scales may only be recognizable as concentrations, and, as such, recognition of very small artifacts becomes more probabilistic. Researchers working with small-scale artifacts should be keenly aware of the ways in which microartifacts should be conceptualized and of the information that such artifacts possibly contain.

With regard to the scale of artifacts, this study draws on comparisons between two scales, chosen for convenience and purposes of potential future comparisons with similar materials. The artifact scales were chosen essentially based upon common field recovery methods, as the wire mesh sizes are in common use. This should not be taken to suggest that other scales are inappropriate for other, or even for similar, research questions (see Price this volume). Nor are the previously noted (Sherwood 2001) differences among microartifact-based research projects approached as problems to be solved. Scale determinations should be conducted on a case-by-case basis, and the scales chosen by various researchers should only be called into question if they do not appear to be theoretically justified. Also, as stated previously, different scales allow for different kinds of questions to be addressed and different kinds of information to be studied (Dunnell and Stein 1989). Different studies could be conducted on the same basic data, particularly in the case of this analysis, as the scales were determined solely by recovery methods, and the artifacts at the two scales have the same provenience. Given this, the two could be collapsed or expanded into different scales as deemed appropriate.

Classification

Classification was a fairly simple process for this study as a specific question was being addressed: Are there differences in the representation of macrodebitage and microdebitage raw materials at the Cork site that can be used to inform us on how the stone was acquired? Following Dunnell (1971), classification, at its simplest, is a way of organizing artifacts into groups. This action is separate from that of determining the scale of the observation to be considered; however, scale determinations may place some constraints on classificatory schemes. A paradigmatic classification scheme was used whereby objects are ordered into groups by interception of attributes that have been determined to be appropriate at a certain level for the question at hand. Level, as used here, refers to the level at which certain artifacts are to be considered the same and, conversely, what attributes are dissimilar between or among groups. Artifact definitions should include attributes that are mutually exclusive and exhaustive, that is, paradigmatic. This prevents ambiguous, confusing, and potentially overlapping artifact classes that can obfuscate useful variability. Additionally, paradigmatic classes allow for the inclusion of all artifacts of a certain scale and level in the classification. Because the attributes used are mutually exclusive and exhaustive, unexpected types of artifacts or newly discovered types can be easily included within the classification without a complete reevaluation of definitions being necessary. Specifics of the classification used in the Cork site analysis are outlined below.

In an effort to prevent inclusion of portions of larger flakes that were broken during the production and life history of tools, postdepositionally, or during recovery, only pieces of debitage having recognizable flake characteristics of either a striking platform or a bulb of percussion (Cotterell and Kamminga 1987) were chosen for analysis. While this might exclude flakes produced through other reduction strategies such as bipolar reduction (Cotterell and Kamminga 1987; Peacock 1989), these attributes were chosen to maintain comparability between the two artifact scales, as any broken portions of larger flakes could bias patterns in the microdebitage sample. Also included in the classification was the raw material of the flake and, by extension, the designation of local or nonlocal, inasmuch as this applied directly to the research question at hand.

Size grades were determined by mesh sizes (6.35 mm or .25 inch and 1.58 mm or .0625 inch) used in the field and subsequent washing of artifacts. Screens were constructed of wire mesh, and material was processed through the screens by hand manipulation. No further processing of the materials was undertaken at this stage, given the generalized nature and purpose of this study. All flakes were analyzed using a 10× hand lens, and raw material types were determined by texture, opacity, grain size, inclusions, and color. As Johnson and Meeks (1994) have noted in their study of Fort Payne chert, color is the least reliable of the attributes as there can be much overlap between materials. Materials with grayish colors (e.g., Fort Payne chert, Kosciusko quartzite, novaculite, and Coastal Plain/Tallahatta agate) proved the most complex to assign to types in this study. A further complicating factor relating to color is the presence of thermal alteration, which has been discussed specifically for Fort Payne chert (e.g., Johnson and Morrow 1981). Whenever questionable materials were encountered, comparisons were made to flakes derived from known materials (both thermally altered and nonaltered samples) in a comparative collection. Characteristics such as opacity, grain size, texture, and inclusions were used to make distinctions. An indeterminate class was used for flakes that could not confidently be assigned to a raw material type.

Results

The results of the debitage analysis are presented in Table 11.1. In total, nine raw material types were identified in this study. The locally available (100 km or less) materials were Tuscaloosa gravel chert, sandstone, siltstone, and Kosciusko quartzite. The exotics (from sources more than 100 km away) were Fort Payne chert, Tallahatta quartzite/sandstone, novaculite, quartz crystal, and Coastal Plain/Tallahatta agate. In all 18 samples, across both macrodebitage and microdebitage scales, locally available Tuscaloosa gravel chert dominates (see Table 11.1). Blue-gray Fort Payne cherts (Lumsden 1988) likely from the Tennessee River valley are the second most common material across all samples, though

Table 11.1. Results of the macrodebitage and microdebitage analysis

Raw Material	No. of pieces			Percent			
	6.35 mm	1.58 mm	n	6.35 mm	6.35 mm West Blocks 1 & 2	6.35 mm East Blocks 1 & 2	6.35 mm East Block 3
Tuscaloosa gravel	662	2,012	2,674	.25	.20	.21	.43
Fort Payne chert	110	278	388	.28	.12	.29	.32
Tallahatta quartzite	12	32	44	.27	.00	.21	.63
Kosciusko quartzite	1	3	4	.25	.00	.00	1.00
Sandstone	3	8	10	.30	.13	.20	.00
Siltstone	1	0	1	1.00	.00	.00	1.00
Quartz crystal	1	12	13	.08	.00	.09	.00
Novaculite	2	23	25	.08	.00	.12	.00
Tallahatta agate	0	4	4	.00	.00	.00	.00
Indeterminate	17	55	72	.24	.43	.22	.20

present in more samples at the microartifact scale. Tallahatta quartzite (Curren 1982; Dunning 1964; Maudsely 1998), from east-central Mississippi and southwest Alabama, represents the third most common raw material and was also present in more microartifact than macroartifact samples. Novaculite and quartz crystal, both presumably from the Ouachita Mountains of Arkansas, were present in only one macroartifact sample but were present in 12 and 6 microartifact samples, respectively. Locally available sandstone had similar representation in both the microartifact and macroartifact samples, while siltstone was present in only one of the macroartifact samples. Local Kosciusko quartzite was present in only one macroartifact sample and in only three microartifact samples. Lastly, the nonlocal Coastal Plain/Tallahatta agate, which is known to co-occur within the Tallahatta formation (Dunning 1964), was found in small percentages in only the microartifact sample.

Twenty fragments of bifaces were also present in the quarter-inch sample. No tool fragments were found in the sixteenth-inch sample. A majority of the bifaces (n = 14) were made from locally available Tuscaloosa gravel cherts, and six of these were diagnostic proximal fragments of projectile points. All six date to the Woodland period and can be classified as the type Tombigbee Stemmed (McGahey 2000). Five of these projectile-point fragments had unmodified bases, either cortex or a remnant striking platform, which has been demonstrated to be a diagnostic Middle Woodland trait in the area (Edmonds 2009; Rafferty 1994). Of three diagnostic proximal projectile-point fragments made of Fort Payne chert, two can be typed as Tombigbee Stemmed (with one having an unmodified base), and the third can be classified as a Woodland period Wilson point (McGahey 2000).

Discussion

For the consideration of the Cork site data, the term *explanation* is preferred here over *interpretation,* not merely as a purely semantic argument but because interpretation connotes an inductive approach to studying artifacts. While this is certainly not the case with every instance in which the term is used, it can allow a certain kind of bias to encroach upon research. Inductive and deductive reasoning both have important roles to play within scientific study, but explanations should be derived from theory rather than directly from artifacts themselves.

Not all explanations are scientific: many are based on common-sense approaches to understanding observed patterns (Dunnell 1982). Common-sense explanations also tend to rely on human intent or cognition as a means of generating explanations. While it is obvious such behaviors existed and human intent and cognitive abilities do have effects on behavior at a certain scale, these behaviors are essentially only different ways of introducing variability. They are not, in and of themselves, the forces that condition the differential persistence of that variability.

Nor should proposed explanations be merely descriptive. True explanations require the observance of change within form through time or across space or the observance of disparity within different scales of artifacts. While both a lack of change and an absence of disjunction between artifact scales are important to note, only the observance of difference provides the basis for testing implications of what conditions factored in the observed patterns. This point is important to note specifically for microartifacts. Microartifact research has often been pursued, as is the case with this study, for evidence of cultural behavior not found in higher artifact scales. It is this potential for microartifacts to add to our understanding of the past that lends import to the continued and increased recovery of such samples.

Evolutionary explanations are not easily deduced from such a limited study as this. However, an evolutionary approach does consider how the variability within the archaeological record is viewed, collected, assessed, and, ultimately, explained. Various analytical methods are not central to the arguments outlined in this chapter as any particular method may be useful in any number of situations and within different schools of thought. Conceptualizations of the record are important distinctions, and in the case of lithic materials, functional aspects are the primary, if not the exclusive, focus of evolutionary explanations.

Function (following Dunnell 1978) relates to a tool or attribute of a tool that has some selective value, either positive or negative. Those with positive values will tend to rise in prominence over time, so long as the selective forces remain consistent. Because most lithic tools such as projectile points are largely, if not exclusively, functional (Dunnell 2005), the physical properties of a particular raw material will affect tool function and, by extension, its selective value. Such factors are difficult to assess with current data, but quantification of material properties (see Yonekura et al. 2008) shows great promise in providing the framework to address such issues at the occupation level. Explanations relating to the modes by which materials were acquired will necessarily rest at higher spatial and temporal scales and may include other factors beyond tool function as primary elements.

The predominance of locally available gravel cherts in both size samples is not unexpected but suggests that factors other than need for lithic raw material are responsible for the presence of the nonlocal materials, Fort Payne chert, Tallahatta quartzite, novaculite, quartz crystal, and Coastal Plain/Tallahatta agate, at the Cork site. The relative absence of local Kosciusko quartzite also suggests that a generalized need for raw material is not responsible for the observed patterns.

The scale of this study, both spatially and temporally, does not allow for direct testing of whether these materials represent direct acquisition by the population of the Cork site or whether the presence of these materials represents trade, either directly with populations in the source areas or indirectly via intermediaries. Additional information would be required from sites within the region, including both contemporaneous occupations to determine the spatial extent of similar patterns and non-contemporaneous occupations to determine the temporal extent of such patterns. Such studies would be interesting and would provide new avenues of research as most studies on the mechanism by which exotic materials may enter into an assemblage have tended to focus on highly mobile populations (Eerkens et al. 2007; Meltzer 1989) rather than sedentary populations such as the Middle Woodland populations in Mississippi. Carr and Stewart's (2004) work with exotic lithics at Poverty Point is an exception, as the residents of the site are increasingly recognized to have been sedentary. Further, it should not be assumed at this scale that the presence of exotic lithics represents some behavior selected for increased access to exotic materials as a supplement to local materials, as not all behaviors can be expected to be efficient, particularly in the short term (Dunnell 1989, 1999).

Despite the limitations imposed upon testable implications by this study's focus on a single occupation, some interesting patterns and possible directions for further investigation can be drawn from this analysis. Although it cannot be definitively settled as to the way in which exotic materials arrived at the site, some conclusions can be drawn as to the factors that conditioned their representation once they arrived at the site and became a part of the available material. Similar to results in the study that influenced this undertaking (Eerkens et al. 2007), exotics are more heavily, albeit still at small proportions, represented in the microartifact sample (see Table 11.1). This suggests that primarily late-stage biface reduction, use wear, or tool rejuvenation were the activities responsible for the more prominent proportional representation within individual raw material types of exotics in the microartifact sample. This further suggests that those materials most likely arrived at the Cork site as either late-stage bifacial blanks/preforms or formalized tools. Further technological-functional analysis could prove useful in clarifying and assessing these potential factors.

This pattern does not occur at the same proportion for all nonlocal materials, however. As can be seen from Table 11.1, Fort Payne chert is present in relatively high numbers in both the microartifact and macroartifact samples, at levels lower than but in a pattern very similar to that of the locally available gravel cherts. Fort Payne chert is also the only raw material other than locally available gravel chert to be represented in the bifaces included in this study sample. While it is argued that other nonlocal materials entered the site as bifaces, the lack of bifaces made of those materials may suggest that only a relatively small number of such bifaces were imported to the site. Thus, sampling error may be responsible for a lack of representation of other exotics. These other bifaces, however, may also have been curated and reduced to a higher degree than those made of local gravels and Fort Payne chert.

Although direct tests of material acquisition or explanations of why such behaviors may have emerged and persisted are not possible with a study at this scale, the comparison of patterns within raw material classes may provide some insight into this aspect of Middle Woodland Cork site activities. Taking the microdebitage versus macrodebitage in the local gravels as indicative of direct acquisition, the observed patterns of Fort Payne chert suggest that this material was treated similarly, which in turn suggests that this material may have been acquired directly by the inhabitants of the Cork site on a regular basis. Trade in unmodified nodules, however, may be another possibility. Similar factors may have been conditioning the presence of Tallahatta quartzite in the record, as its representation may also be considered more like that of local gravels rather than some of the more distant exotics (novaculite and quartz crystal).

Statistical analysis was used to confirm these patterns. Chi-square tests for both size grades of local gravels/Fort Payne ($\chi^2 = 2.32$; $df = 1$; $p = .128$), local gravels/Tallahatta quartzite ($\chi^2 = .147$; $df = 1$; $p = .929$), and local gravels/quartz ($\chi^2 = 2.03$; $df = 1$; $p = .155$) are likely problematic due to the influence of the large local gravels sample size and the relatively small sample sizes for Tallahatta quartzite and quartz. Phi-square tests can potentially help control for sample size. The result for local gravels/Fort Payne (.000758) indicates that no association exists between material type and size grade (Shennan 1988:78–81). However, the percentages of total flakes that fall within the large size grade from the three most prominent materials (see Table 11.1) suggest that these materials are not dissimilar. While the sample sizes for the other materials are too small to be useful in statistical analysis, these data indicate that both Fort Payne chert and Tallahatta quartzite were treated similarly to local gravels, in terms of reduction, by the inhabitants of the Cork site. In this case, the macrodebitage is just as informative as the microdebitage for these three materials. The higher percentage of quarter-inch flakes suggests that these materials were subject to earlier-stage reduction than other materials and thus likely arrived at the site as larger nodules.

Little more can be said about Kosciusko quartzite. However, the lack of this material, which is available relatively close to the Cork site (Figure 11.1), is curious. Research by McGahey (1999) suggests that this material was only exploited during the latter portion of the Early Archaic subperiod and in the

Late Woodland through Mississippian periods. The relative lack of Kosciusko quartzite at the Cork site is in line with these conclusions and lends further credence to the conclusion that some factor other than immediate need for lithic raw material conditioned the presence of some artifacts at this site.

Novaculite and quartz crystal are almost exclusively represented in the microartifact sample. This indicates that tools made from these materials may have been more highly curated and thus reused, rejuvenated, and reduced to a greater extent than those made from other materials. While it may be tempting to offer individualistic explanations for this pattern, such as the recognition of some aesthetic quality of the raw material by a prehistoric toolmaker, such explanations, as has been discussed previously, likely rely largely on common sense rather than scientific explanations drawn from theory (Dunnell 1982). Further, if such behaviors did in fact condition what we see archaeologically, it is unlikely that exotic materials would have been reduced to the point of only being represented at the microartifact scale. It is far more likely that some functional (i.e., selective) aspect of the material factored in its curation and reuse as a tool. These functional aspects may include the mechanics of reduction, the resilience of the material, or some other characteristic that suits a specific or specialized tool form. With regard to the use of quartz at the Cork site in this regard, Johnson (1993b) reports on the use of quartz crystals as drills at an Archaic lapidary site in the Mississippi Delta. However, the quartz drills in that case appear to have been quartz crystals that were unmodified aside from use wear as drill bits. Given that the only quartz present in the Cork site sample is in the form of flake debris, and given the lack of evidence for a lapidary industry at this site, it is unlikely that quartz was used in a similar fashion. This does not preclude, however, explanation of material representation as a result of function. Indeed, what is most likely causing the pattern seen at the occupational level is selection operating on the materials once they arrived at the Cork site. These materials became incorporated into the available lithic assemblage and were subsequently reduced through use and/or rejuvenation. At this scale, similar patterns may represent similar functional aspects of the materials or dissimilar functions that result in similar patterns of reduction. As noted above, data on the functional qualities of material types that could clarify this ambiguity are not currently available and require quantification.

Temporal and spatial variability in the representation of exotic materials at the Cork site are difficult to access based on this study, most likely due to the method of sampling used. However, all of the samples contain Fort Payne chert, again suggesting that this material was continuously, and possibly directly, acquired over the temporal extent of the occupation. One of the two samples that contained no exotic materials other than Fort Payne chert is from the westernmost group, with the other from the central group. Again, sample size is likely problematic, but this may suggest an increase in the use of exotics over the span of the occupation at the Cork site.

Summary and Conclusions

The theoretical considerations of scale, classification, and explanation have been applied to a small study of lithic materials from the Cork site with interesting results. Many of the conclusions summarized below are not explanations in and of themselves. While the patterns outlined by this study are informative, taken on their own they are not explanatory. A pattern, as used here, is essentially just the data gleaned from an organization and comparison of archaeological material. The data are not self-explanatory, and although some inferences may be drawn from them, those inferences also require explanation in a scientifically testable way. If a pattern suggests a raw material was probably acquired directly from its source, the true explanation for that pattern will rest on addressing why direct acquisition predominated.

Primarily, it is suggested that some nonlocal raw materials likely arrived at the site as either late-stage bifacial blanks/preforms or as completed formalized tools. While no direct assessment of the means by which the materials arrived at this site can be made due to the scale and scope of this study, some broader implications are suggested for future research.

Some of the nonlocal raw materials, particularly Fort Payne chert and possibly Tallahatta quartzite, appear to be present in patterns similar to those of local gravel cherts, suggesting a recurrent, perhaps direct, mode of acquisition of those materials. Diagnostic similarity in projectile-point base fragments between artifacts made of Fort Payne chert and of local gravel cherts also may support this inference. If materials were acquired as late-stage blanks/preforms or formalized tools via trade, the diagnostic characteristics of the projectile points might differ from those in the local area as they were not manufactured by members of the same cultural lineage. That is to say, contemporaneous projectile points from the Tennessee River valley likely differ from those manufactured in the region surrounding the Cork site as a result of historical relatedness. Additionally, if nonlocal materials were reduced to bifacial blanks or late-stage bifaces as trade goods by inhabitants of the procurement region, they may have had different tool trajectories and different final tool forms. Thus, these knappers may have made different decisions along the reductive pathway than would the inhabitants of the Cork site if they acquired and reduced the material directly at its source before transport. It is interesting to note that while all of the projectile points of local gravel chert are typed as Tombigbee Stemmed, one of the three Fort Payne chert projectile points is dissimilar. This may suggest some smaller degree of trade in material underlying the possible predominance of direct acquisition. However, tool function must also be considered. It is likely not reasonable to assume that the inhabitants of the Cork site only made one kind of projectile point or biface. Different tools may have performed different functions, and the dissimilar biface may represent a functionally different tool within the same toolkit.

Although this study did not address ceramic artifacts, ceramic styles have been used to tackle the question of possible interaction spheres within the lower Mississippi River valley (Lipo et al. 1997). By altering the level of classification, Lipo and colleagues were able to tease out information based on the sharing of stylistic traits across space to determine possible areas of interaction. Operating under the assumption that cultural ideas are more likely to be exchanged with high levels of interaction, high degrees of stylistic similarity (representing shared cultural ideas) in ceramic forms, ordered via seriation, across space were taken to indicate high degrees of interaction. It would be interesting to judge how patterns of lithic raw material distribution would compare to distributions of ceramic styles, and such comparisons could potentially help answer questions of direct acquisition or exchange networks, particularly if the possible interaction spheres overlap sources of what might otherwise be considered nonlocal material.

The relative lack of Kosciusko quartzite in the study sample is also interesting and possibly informative. As noted previously, this material is the most closely available of all of the nonlocal materials found in this analysis. Its presence at the site suggests that it was a known lithic material source, but it was apparently not exploited as readily as more distant materials. This in turn may indicate, particularly when coupled with the dominance of local Tuscaloosa gravel in all of the study samples, that there was no pressing shortage of raw material. Future research into what other possible factors, such as the functional aspects of the raw materials, may have been shaping such behaviors could prove to be both interesting and informative.

At the smaller scale of the occupation, explanations concerning micro/macroartifact proportions within raw materials are suggested to rest on the functional aspects of those materials. Thus the similar patterns in Tuscaloosa gravel chert, Fort Payne chert, and Tallahatta quartzite may suggest similar functional aspects relating to the kind of tools made from them or similar reduction strategies for dissimilar tool functions. The same statement applies to the roughly similar patterns observed in novaculite and quartz. Quantification of the functional properties of raw materials would likely show great promise in refining functional explanations.

This study also highlights the fact that methods of recovery have effects on the kinds of data that are represented in assemblages. Archaeologists should carefully consider the ways in which we treat the archaeological record, particularly because most of our methods of investigation are destructive. As Dunnell and Stein (1989) point out, artifacts at different scales do not merely represent different-sized versions of the same artifacts, but each contain their own kind of information. By simply failing to collect certain artifacts, bias is introduced into the record and our eventual understanding of the past diminished.

That different kinds of patterns can be observed from a relatively quick, small sample-based analysis in only one class of artifacts has also been demonstrated by this undertaking. Initial sorting of materials and analysis were completed within a month and yielded information that was not obtainable via the quarter-inch sample alone. While nonlocal materials were present in the larger-sized sample, only one flake each of both quartz and novaculite was present. One flake does not make a pattern, and no possible explanations other than some nebulous interaction with the region from which they derived could be proposed. The patterns in the microdebitage samples in comparison with the macrodebitage provided the basis for determining possible behavioral inferences and testable implications of material use and acquisition, not only for the nonlocal but also for the local materials as well. The differences between the two size grades for each material are what indicated the proposed primacy of biface reduction, maintenance, and use within the lithic assemblage from the Cork site.

The microartifact samples used in this study required little additional effort for recovery in the field. A one-sixteenth-inch mesh screen was simply placed beneath the quarter-inch mesh screen during water screening. Essentially the only additional effort required was in bagging the artifacts after screening was completed. This may differ, however, depending on the clay content of the soils at a site. If screening through such small mesh presents a problem, the collection of soil samples for later processing would likely be the best alternative. Such methods can be easily incorporated into most excavation projects. The recovered samples do not necessarily need to be processed or analyzed as part of the research design, but some samples of smaller artifacts should be recovered for other potential research questions and the possibility of future developments and refinements of archaeological methods and techniques. Curation and storage of such samples may incur increased cost to the budget of a project but may be beneficial to limit the extent of the excavation as a whole to adjust for such costs. Excavating a site without any regard to microartifact recovery may allow a greater percentage of the site to be dug, but one must balance the data that are lost through recovery bias against the data that would not be recovered from a more extensive excavation.

There are undoubtedly many other interesting and important findings that can be drawn from any number of artifact classes and scales. In an evolutionary approach, the point to be taken is not that analytical methods and techniques are somehow different or unique. What is different from this perspective is the conceptualization of culture and the variation within the archaeological record. Thus it is not important to recover microartifacts simply because there are so many of them. It is important, however, to either recover or preserve a representative sample of all manner of artifacts. These different artifacts contain different kinds of information on the variability of past behaviors and are our only means, though indirect, of observing the variability of the past. It is this variability and its differential persistence over time that an evolutionary approach attempts to explain. These concepts have broader implications, such as those related to assessments of site significance, and archaeologists should take care to bear in mind that our handling of the record we study in many ways affects our ability to study it.

Acknowledgments

I would like to thank Janet Rafferty for her suggestion and encouragement to undertake this study. Thanks are also due to her and Evan Peacock for their comments on an early draft of this chapter. And, finally, my thanks to the editors and reviewers of this volume for their comments and suggestions that improved the final result.

12

Raising the Bar

Lithic Analysis and Archaeological Research in the Southeast

William Andrefsky Jr.

When I was asked to provide comments on the collection of lithic analysis papers presented at the Southeastern Archaeological Conference (included within this volume), I did not realize the extent to which lithic tools and debitage had been overlooked in the region as a medium for interpreting past aboriginal practices and behaviors. According to the session abstract, the goal of the lithic symposium and this volume is to highlight contemporary methods and theory in lithic analysis to encourage researchers in the Southeast to integrate lithic data into their site interpretations. After a quick perusal of the literature for the region, it was apparent that very few Southeast lithics-related publications have appeared in the national peer-reviewed literature (Daniel 2001; Shott and Ballenger 2007); slightly more lithic research occurs in regional journal venues (Carr and Bradbury 2000; Franklin and Simek 2008; Peacock 2004); and other contributions are found in edited volumes not necessarily focused specifically on lithics in the region (Anderson and Sassaman 1996; Carr 1994a; Henry and Odell 1989; Johnson and Morrow 1987). Similar to the case of Mesoamerica and the American Southwest, there is a relatively low proportion of lithics-based research relative to ceramics and architecture.

Such a trend comes as a surprise to me. However, I have been hooked on stone tool technology since the sixth grade when I first began looking at Louis Leakey's Oldowan pebble tools and wondering whether the broken cobbles in my local creek could have been made by *Australopithecus*. I have since come to believe that all of those boyhood "pebble tools" were made by rushing water during spring floods. However, I also think that many of them look exactly like Leakey's Oldowan tools and that stone context and composition are just as important as stone condition and configuration when studying stone tool technology. In other words, where the raw material comes from and its flaking properties are just as important for interpreting stone tools as the shape and wear found on the specimen.

The goal of this collection of essays is to stimulate researchers in the Southeast to recognize stone tools and debitage as important research data that can be used in parallel with more popular archaeological materials. With that goal in mind, I provide comments on this collection of lithic research framed around some of the issues the authors have chosen to address in their particular studies, while at the same time recognizing context, composition, condition, and configuration.

Lithic Technological Organization and *Chaîne Opératoire*

Several chapters in this volume emphasize an approach toward understanding lithic data using what is called Lithic Technological Organization (LTO). The concept of LTO has been used in archaeological investigations for more than 30 years since its introduction by Binford (1973, 1977) in the 1970s. It has been variously defined by practitioners (Kelly 1988; Koldehoff 1987; Nelson 1991; Shott 1986; Torrence 1983), but all generally agree that it refers to the manner in which humans organize themselves with regard to lithic technology in the context of social, economic, and environmental contexts (Carr et al. this volume). I consider LTO a strategy that deals with the way lithic technology (the acquisition, production, maintenance, reconfiguration, and ultimately discard of stone artifacts) is entwined within the daily lives and adaptive choices and decisions of tool makers and users.

A classic example of the use of LTO is found in the contribution of Thacker, Hardison, and Conklin in this collection. Here they explain how a major shift in settlement practices between the Early and Middle Archaic in the Uwharrie Mountains of central North Carolina can be understood by looking at stone tool provisioning tactics. They adopted a model of LTO developed by Kuhn (1994) that examines the manner in which toolmakers provision themselves with stone tools. They show that Early Archaic populations tended to provision individuals and that Middle Archaic populations shifted to the provisioning of places and that these differences were required as a result of how the two populations used the landscape. Early Archaic populations were more mobile, choosing to move from location to location more frequently, and the later populations tended to stay longer in one place. Such differences in residential mobility were reflected in stone tools and debitage found during each time period at their investigation site (31MG328).

Tentatively, Thacker and colleagues suggest that the change in settlement strategy is linked to environmental change, but that remains to be assessed.

However, this is a classic example of how LTO can be employed to more effectively interpret past aboriginal activities and adaptive strategies.

The Potts chapter emphasizes methodological and interpretive problems between individual flake analysis and size grade data when dealing with a raw material such as quartz with poor chipping quality. However, I think this chapter brings up another important issue related to LTO that is often overlooked. It demonstrates that stone tool technological choices are not predetermined by some kind of mental template or by cognitive intents of prehistoric toolmakers as is often argued by proponents of *chaîne opératoire* (Audouze 1999; Boëda 1995). Some researchers who advocate *chaîne opératoire* as a method of conducting lithic analysis believe it is possible to link specific operational chains of tool production with different cultures of the past and that human thought patterns are intelligible from stone tool technology: "It is felt by many today that technopsychology in particular provides a pathway to the cognitive minds of prehistoric knappers and that it is one of the most informative and meaningful ways of conducting lithic analysis" (Bar-Yosef and Van Peer 2009:105). Many feel this view of *chaîne opératoire* is the primary difference between the concepts of lithic reduction sequences and *chaîne opératoire.* Of course, lithic reduction sequences and LTO are not the same things so I will not dwell upon this debate (see Shott 2003). However, in my opinion this view of *chaîne opératoire* is contradictory to an understanding of LTO.

LTO embraces the possibility that aboriginal toolmakers adjust, adapt, and respond technologically to their social, economic, and environmental contexts. Past aboriginal cultures may strive to produce stone tools in uniform mental images, but contextual factors such as raw material package size, abundance, and quality (Andrefsky et al. 1999; Ashton and White 2003; Dibble 1995; Kuhn 1991), as well as circumstances of production such as unanticipated tasks, will play a significant role in tool production and consumption processes (Tomka 2001; Wurz 2002). The cognitive or technopsychological linkages to tool production expressed in that view of *chaîne opératoire* (note that Bar-Yosef and Van Peer do not accept technopsychology either) act to limit our ability to understand the contexts and situations that can be so important for understanding the conditions under which stone tools are made, used, modified, and discarded. The Potts chapter is a great example of how regional contexts of lithic raw material can influence stone tool technology. The majority of cores and debitage recovered from the Madison Park site (1MT318) were from locally available raw materials (quartz). However, the majority of unhafted bifaces (69.1 percent) and hafted bifaces (80.5 percent) were made from nonquartz material. The data are not displayed to determine whether such trends are significant, but it is probable that raw material differences in tool type relate to tool function and perhaps to the context of site use. The main thrust of this contribution emphasizes a comparison of methodological approaches, but the overall results show the importance of contexts in a study of LTO.

Chaîne opératoire as used by Franklin and colleagues in their chapter is very much in agreement with my use of LTO as reviewed here. They view *chaîne opératoire* as a holistic approach toward understanding stone tools. Nothing in their analysis suggests to me that they are advocating a technopsychological interpretation of their data. They advocate an approach that uses multiple lines of data and analysis. Such approaches usually increase the reliability of interpretations. It is surprising that their different lines of analysis produced so many analytical contradictions. We do not know whether the contradictions in data analysis are the result of bias in one technique over another, or whether there is something underlying the trends that actually relate to prehistoric behavior. I think their analysis could have explored this in more depth. Unexpected or contradictory results are really interesting and they help us to better understand how we might interpret and analyze data. Such results require us to ask additional questions of our data, and they open new areas of inquiry to help account for initial contradictions.

The Bradbury and Carr chapter also advocates an approach that uses LTO. In this study the authors suggest that the prevalence of blade technology in Paleoindian times and its absence in Early Archaic times along with the prevalence of bipolar technology in Early Archaic times might best be understood by examining these trends through an LTO lens. Of course, they begin their thesis with an appropriate review of the terminological and identification problems archaeologists have had with these kinds of technologies and suggest that some of the patterning in these two technologies may relate to such problems. However, they advocate bipolar technology as a strategy used to conserve lithic raw materials based upon preliminary data associated with raw material sources and the occurrence of this technology on Early Archaic sites. They further suggest that blade technology better fits the Paleoindian mobile pattern of adaptive strategy and may not be present in Early Archaic sites because of a change in this strategy.

I think that Bradbury and Carr may be on to something here with regard to looking at such technologies using perspectives associated with LTO. Their opinion about use of bipolar technology and limited quantities or limited actual sizes of raw materials makes sense and others have said similar kinds of things about adoption of bipolar technology (Andrefsky 1994b; Goodyear 1993). Table 12.1 provides an example comparing sizes of bipolar and freehand artifacts. The six Washington state sites (45PO) show significantly smaller bipolar cores as compared to freehand cores from the same sites. The Vail, Debert, and Shoop site data include unnamed bipolar objects that may be flakes taken from bipolar cores; however, they are shown to be much smaller (3.7, 3.6, and 5.1 cm,

Table 12.1. Size of bipolar and freehand artifacts

Site	Mean Size of Bipolar Cores (cm^3)	Mean Size of Freehand Cores (cm^3)
45PO137	38	165
45PO138	29	1,519
45PO139	46	1,320
45PO140		3,003
45PO141	59	180
45PO144		2,544

respectively; Shott 1989) than the listed bipolar cores and much smaller than the freehand cores. These data conform to Bradbury and Carr's listed data.

Related to this topic is the Sain and Goodyear chapter that explores Clovis blade technology at the Topper and Big Pine Tree sites. They show that Clovis blade technology from the South Carolina Coastal Plain looks different from Clovis blade technology from the Mid-South and from the Southern Plains. They also suggest that there may be differences in the two sites based upon use and retouch found on Clovis blades and based upon raw material package size.

Given our experimental work with blade and bifacial flake cutting edges (Rasic and Andrefsky 2001) and other experimental studies (Prascimunas 2007), blade technology is no more conservative than bifacial technology with regard to providing cutting edge amount. Some may argue that Clovis blade technology is centered in the Southeast (including Texas in this region), given the high numbers of Clovis blades and blade cores at sites from this region (see Beck and Jones 2010; Faught 2006, 2008; Yahnig 2004) relative to other regions of North and South America. In fact, Clovis technology may have originated in the Southeast and spread throughout the continent from here. This is an interesting topic related to human colonization of the Western Hemisphere and the nature of human colonization in general, and it may perhaps only be definitively addressed by lithic analysis.

Lithic Raw Materials and Human Organization

Another topic that intersected many of the contributions in this volume deals with lithic raw material provenance, abundance, size, and shape as these relate to human land-use strategies and technological practices. I have been interested in the relationship of lithic raw materials and human organization for the past several decades (Ammerman and Andrefsky 1982; Andrefsky 1994a, 2009) and still believe that it is one of the most important factors related to technological variability in stone tools and debitage. Many of the factors we often recognize as diagnostic for reduction stages or sequences in debitage are directly related to raw material size, shape, and configuration. For instance, cortex amount is often used to assess reduction stage (more cortex = earlier stages, and less cortex = later stage). However, cortex amount is directly related to the kind of raw material harvested by toolmakers. Chippable raw material in the form of angular talus debris may have little or no cortex on it and debitage produced from reduction of these materials will have little or no cortex on it regardless of the stage of reduction. Similarly, debitage size may have more to do with the size of the raw material nodule than with the stage of reduction. This was effectively demonstrated by Kuhn (1991), who showed that centripetal and platformed core technologies were selected on the basis of available nodule size. Archaeological studies of lithic raw material have been effective for helping researchers understand artifact functional effectiveness (Bamforth 2003; Brantingham et al. 2000; Hofman 2003; Terry et al. 2009), retouch intensity on tools (Andrefsky 2008b; Bradbury et al. 2008; Milliken and Peresani 1998), aspects of risk management (Beck et al. 2002; Braun 2005; Soressi and Hays 2003), and core technological strategies (Ashton and White 2003; Brantingham and Kuhn 2001; Roth and Dibble 1998).

Contributors to this volume have not neglected the importance of lithic raw materials in contemporary research in the Southeast. Many of the chapters just discussed under the topic of LTO certainly fall within the lithic raw material arena. The contribution by Cooper focuses upon the shift in chert source location use from the Late Archaic to Fort Ancient times at a site in eastern Kentucky. He shows that both temporal occupations used broadly the same technology, but the change in procurement patterns emphasized a shift in other aspects of their adaptive strategies. Edmonds (this volume) studied differences in debitage size categories to show that nonlocal lithic raw materials were often found in only microdebitage sizes. Based upon this patterning he notes that nonlocal lithic raw materials were probably more often brought onto his study site (Cork site) in the form of finished or late-stage tools. The Potts chapter also emphasizes differences in lithic raw material type and relates such differences to technological variability associated with raw material differences. All of these examples are important contributions toward an understanding of past aboriginal land use in the Southeast and move forward the original goal of this collection of lithic studies.

One of the areas that lithic researchers really need to make some progress on relates to establishing diagnostic signatures for chert locations. As Cooper notes in his chapter, "Kentucky cherts have a wide range of variation, even within the same geologic formation." He further concludes, "In an area with as much raw material diversity as Kentucky, and in the Southeast in general, further development of chert type collections and chert type definitions can add finer resolution to our view of settlement patterns, social networks, and migration patterns, as well as changes in these systems through time." I could not agree more with his assessment. This is not just an issue with chert sources in the Southeast; it is a global problem. In their study of Scandinavian chert Högberg and Olausson (2007) note that there is as much within-source heterogeneity as there is between-source homogeneity with regard to characteristics such as color, structure, translucency, and cortex condition, among other characteristics. They also found that Scandinavian chert had the same kinds of problems with geochemical characterization as most other cherts found throughout the world—geochemical signatures were not diagnostic to location. This is not surprising since most cherts form in ancient submarine contexts that cover thousands of square miles and undergo multiple phases of genesis over thousands of years (see Luedtke 1992). However, not all cherts form in these kinds of contexts. Geochemical methods may be helpful in determining chert provenance on materials that have undergone relatively isolated genesis due to silica precipitation from unique sources such as volcanic vents truncating sedimentary deposits. Figure 12.1 shows scatter plots of three separately collected chert sources in southern Oregon roughly 50 km distant from each other. Even though two of the chert sources are macroscopically identical, they are geochemically diagnostic due to differential local formation processes (Andrefsky et al. 2010). Figure 12.1a shows the separation of the three chert sources via discriminant function analysis. Figure 12.1b is a scatter plot of the first function accounting for 82 percent of the variance and listing the three most diagnostic elements for the separation of sources. These geochemical differences were obtained using an x-ray fluorescence analyzer that explored multiple trace elements before discovery of vanadium, rubidium, and titanium as locationally diagnostic indicators.

The Southeast, like most other areas of the world, needs to begin assessing its chert source locational issues before making sweeping statements about human land use, migration, and tool-stone associations with exotic and local proximities. In many cases, regional lithic researchers can probably effectively identify chert by macroscopic characteristics. However, to my knowledge, this has seldom been evaluated with a blind test, nor have such descriptions been uniformly stated and published for use by others working in the same region. Finally, some chert sources may be so large and cover such an enormous region that source designation to that region is meaningless with regard to migration of people and transport of tools from one site to another, since in many cases the distances between sites are less than the potential distance encompassed by the chert source area. As noted above for the Scandinavian study, it is almost impossible for lithic researchers to effectively identify chert from

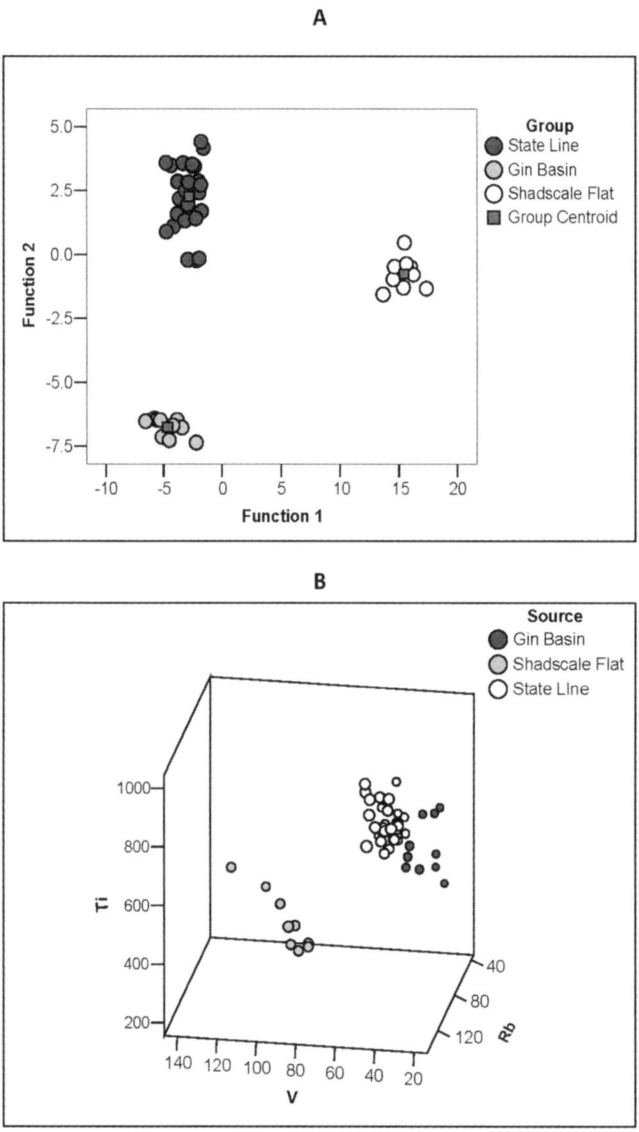

Figure 12.1. Geochemical separation of primary chert sources based upon x-ray fluorescence analysis: a) discriminant function analysis of the three chert sources; b) three primary elements in function 1 responsible for 82 percent of the variance.

various sources using macroscopic, microscopic, or geochemical techniques. Such identification difficulties must almost certainly be compounded when examining archaeological specimens with no cortex and perhaps no mineral inclusions. Such identification challenges are probably even more difficult with microdebitage.

Methodological Considerations

Several of the contributions within this volume focused on issues with implications beyond lithic analysis in the Southeast. These might be characterized as methodological or analytical studies that certainly apply to lithic studies from the region, but they have significance for all lithic analysis even if they were framed from examples taken in the southeastern region.

Certainly the Price chapter falls into this category. Here a case is being made to consider the kinds of information being lost or the kinds of misinformation being created as a result of artifact collection techniques that disregard small artifacts as a result of large mesh sizes being used to collect data. Price persuasively builds a case that most archaeological investigations in the Southeast are biased by using 6.35-mm (.25-inch) mesh to sift site deposits. She shows that minimally 60 percent of artifact inventories falls below the 6.35-mm mesh size and is seldom recovered. Price's examples not only include debitage vital for flake debris aggregate analysis, but also small hafted bifaces, drill tips used for bead making, raw material diversity, and microdebitage studies. This 60-percent loss of data is increased to over 90 percent when considering the very small fraction often lost in 3.17-mm (.125-inch) mesh but recovered in 1.58-mm (.0625-inch) mesh.

Other areas of the United States already require recovery of artifacts via 3.17-mm screen and many investigators go beyond this and recover a constant volume sample from each stratum that is later screened through nested geologic mesh sizes to recover materials partitioned into extremely tiny individual sizes such as grass seeds and insect body parts. One way investigators can increase systematic recovery of the small fraction without increasing costs by 60–90 percent is to effectively sample their materials and then extrapolate from that sample to the larger collection. As researchers begin "thinking bigger" by "collecting smaller" materials, such as DNA samples, residues on tools, and microliths, our ability to understand past activities and behaviors shall become better informed and more believable. Price's essay is a wake-up call for all archaeologists. We deal with a nonrenewable resource that is destroyed every day by land development, erosion, and probably most frequently by archaeologists who are neglecting a large proportion of this resource.

Recent investigations at sites with very early components such as "pre-Clovis" have led many archaeologists to ask rather elementary questions about lithic artifacts such as, What defines a stone tool? or, Has this rock been intentionally modified by a person living long ago? or, What does evidence for stone tool use look like? In many regards the Pevny chapter begins the process of dissecting these questions and looking at the empirical evidence to help address such questions. Pevny emphasizes the potential effects of taphonomic processes on lithic artifacts. She explores the characteristics found on stone artifacts that relate to geochemical weathering, soil sheen, heat exposure, trampling wear, and other postdepositional processes. Such taphonomic processes are not new to lithic analysts (Ackerman 1964; Gifford-Gonzalez et al. 1985; McBrearty et al. 1998; Rasic 2004), but it is surprising that many do not consider such processes when assessing tool use or even tool definition. Her contribution makes us think about how we should look for these kinds of wear and eliminate such "noise" from intentional retouch and use damage found on such artifacts. Her study also reminds lithic researchers that there are many other kinds of wear that we need to be cognizant of such as screen damage, baggage and transport wear, and human contamination from washing and handling of ancient artifacts.

Many of the chapters presented in the volume allude to tool production stages or sequences. For instance, Potts discusses various production trajectories for biface reduction, bipolar core reduction, and freehand core reduction among others. She uses debitage size grades assessed through aggregate analysis in an effort to recognize these production trajectories composed primarily of assemblages of low-quality quartz. Franklin and colleagues also attempt to recognize reduction stages using mass analysis of debitage sizes, even though they advocate and demonstrate multiple approaches to assemblage analysis. Cooper's study also uses multiple lines of evidence, but one of his techniques is to determine reduction stages via mass analysis. Interestingly, the Miller and Smallwood chapter actually explores the concept of biface production as a staged process versus a continuum; however, these authors do not examine debitage size or debitage at all. Even though the focus of their chapter is an assessment of stage versus continuum in the production of Clovis bifaces (incidentally, they find that both may be applicable), I find a different aspect of their contribution more relevant to the goals of the conference symposium and this volume. For the authors to effectively evaluate stage versus continuum they have had to develop a new index for assessing degree of biface production (flaking index). The degree of biface production is intimately linked to artifact curation and the manner in which artifact curation is used within LTO. Other lithic studies have focused on curation indices as measures of tool use (Andrefsky 2006; Clarkson 2002; Quinn, Andrefsky, et al. 2008), but Miller and Smallwood have developed the index for tool production (not use). This certainly will be a useful technique that can be used in a longitudinal manner with debitage studies that seek to understand production or reduction sequencing. I cannot wait to apply their flaking index to my control samples of bifaces from experimental studies (Williams and Andrefsky 2009; Wilson and Andrefsky 2008) and to assess this against independent measures of aggregate and individual flake analytical procedures.

Summary

This collection is a good cross section of contemporary lithic research. It will encourage those archaeologists currently sympathetic to the potential contributions of lithic analysis to explore their data in more detail. It may even stimulate those researchers who think very little about the value of lithic data to begin more systematic studies. I certainly hope it does both.

However, for many archaeologists, lithic data sets represent extremely limited packages of information that can contribute toward a greater understanding of human behaviors, lifeways, and past adaptive strategies used by different social systems. To motivate such researchers toward a more enlightened view of lithic analysis, it will take extremely interesting questions framed in parsimonious models, with reliable and believable analysis. We cannot expect researchers to embrace interpretations of lithic data that simply imply mechanical relationships about broken rocks. For instance, many archaeologists will not become excited about statements such as "this debitage assemblage indicates that early-stage core reduction probably occurred at this site" or "early-stage or late-stage or perhaps both stages of reduction were conducted at the site." Of course, there are researchers out there like myself who find such statements fascinating, and such statements stimulate me to attempt to eliminate the uncertainty within those statements. However, my guess is that most archaeologists and even more non-archaeologists would find such research conclusions somewhat lame.

Lithic analysts need to recognize that lithic artifacts (tools and debitage) are simply tools to help us better understand the people and communities that made and used those artifacts. We need to emphasize the broader archaeological issues that we wish to address and understand, and then systematically demonstrate how lithic analysis can help investigators arrive at such understanding. Yes, we need to do the nitty-gritty complicated research to better understand aspects of stone tool technology (such as taphonomic processes, breakage patterns, wear analysis, debitage shape characteristics, flake pattern analysis), but we must also make sure to connect these investigations to the broader questions that we are also interested in understanding. If we do not lose sight of these larger questions, then we shall certainly stimulate researchers in the Southeast to integrate lithic data into their site interpretations.

Several of the chapters in this volume have done an excellent job in stating how their investigations relate to such broader goals. All of the contributions in this volume have emphasized the potential importance of lithic analysis for a more comprehensive understanding of past aboriginal lifeways and behaviors in the Southeast and within a larger arena. This volume makes an exciting statement about Southeast archaeological research. I am pleased and honored to have been asked to participate with the original group of scholars in Mobile, Alabama. I am confident that this volume will help lift the research bar for lithic analysis in the Southeast and beyond.

Acknowledgments

I have presented here some data on chert source location analysis. I thank my colleagues Jennifer Ferris, Nathan Goodale, Justin Williams, and George Jones for helping me collect, x-ray, and analyze the chert presented here. I wish to thank Phil Carr, Andrew Bradbury, and Sarah Price for inviting me to participate in the conference and for allowing me to contribute my opinions to this volume. All three were great hosts and I learned much from our conversations and exchanges during my visit to the Southeast.

13

The Organization of Technology Approach in the Southeast

A Call to Arms or a Requiem?

George H. Odell

Andrew Bradbury and Philip Carr, along with Sarah Price, have once again (Carr and Bradbury 2000) issued a call to lithic analysts in the American Southeast for more frequent employment of an "organization of technology" approach to the study of stone artifacts. A useful definition of this concept was provided by Koldehoff (1987:154): "The way in which a culture or society designs its tools and structures tool production, use, and maintenance, so that the tools can respond effectively to the demands placed upon them by the society in its daily interactions with the environment (both biophysical and social), is considered the organization of technology." As described by Carr (1994a:1) from the standpoint of the lithic analyst, "The key to studies of technological organization is relating artifacts, such as chipped stone tools and debitage, to a variety of economic and social parameters that allow sound inferences concerning the dynamics of past cultures" (see also Kelly 1988:717; Nelson 1991:57).

Expressed another way, the organization of technology approach examines the ways that technology is manipulated to promote the successful adaptation of human groups. Manipulation is considered broadly and, with regard to stone tools, includes all endeavors of which these objects formed a conceptual or material part, from procurement to discard. This is little different from what is regarded as behavioral archaeology (Schiffer 1976), with an emphasis on the dynamic interchange with prehistoric cultural systems. It is also almost identical to the French *chaîne opératoire* as conceived most broadly (Franklin et al. this volume; Geneste and Maury 1997; Odell 2001; Sellet 1993).

In this collection, Carr and colleagues have decried the paucity of lithic studies in the Southeast employing an organization of technology approach, despite a strong start in this region (Amick 1987; Carr 1991). How is this initiative to be interpreted? As a nudge to awaken slumbering minions, who will forthwith don their armor and proceed to the battlements? Or as a pathetic dirge to mourn the passing of missed opportunities? Perhaps these chapters provide clues to the state of lithic research in the Southeast and the likelihood that integrative approaches to archaeological remains, such as the organization of technology, will be embraced in the near future. Taking as a premise the idea that this collection is at least minimally representative of lithic research in the Southeast, I will discuss the contribution from an organization of technology perspective.

Procurement and Use of Raw Material

The choice of raw material for tools is crucial to the prehistoric organization of technology because it conditions all other decisions regarding the technology. Thus one could ask, What do people do when the only tool stone available is of poor quality? This was an issue that Randall Cooper (this volume) confronted when analyzing tools from the Elk Fork site in eastern Kentucky. As if to highlight the power of raw material constraints to influence other parts of the technological system, Cooper found that cultural responses were similar in both the Late Archaic and Fort Ancient occupations. That is, faced with relatively low-quality local material in the form of Newman chert, occupants in both periods made an effort to conserve tools brought with them from other regions. Worn-out tools they discarded, while the abundance at the site of small sharpening flakes of these substances suggests that tool users maintained still-usable implements for transport to another locale. The paucity of cores in both components is to be expected in this situation, as bipolar nodule-bashing would destroy the very characteristics that enable their identification as cores. This behavior might occur less frequently in the Fort Ancient occupation if these people were stockpiling their chert.

None of these comments are meant to suggest that responses to tool resource adversity will always be uniform or easy for an archaeologist to ascertain. Neither is the case, as Tara Potts' study shows. Her archaeological results demonstrate that one cannot assume that local or subpar tool stone (in this case, quartz) will always be made into expedient tools or fashioned through bipolar techniques (see Andrefsky 1994b). But in attempting to understand the dimensions of the problem through experimental means, she noted several anomalies that will have to be ironed out through additional experimentation. This is an excellent beginning in what one hopes might turn into an ongoing experimental program.

Sometimes the problem for an analyst is in accumulating the data necessary for evaluating the types of stone present in an assemblage. Working at a Middle

Woodland settlement in Mississippi, Edmonds took samples of debitage at two different screen sizes (6.35 mm and 1.58 mm; .25 inch and .0625 inch, respectively), which he refers to as macroartifact and microartifact samples. As expected, local gravel cherts dominate both size grades. What is not expected is the greatly increased proportion of nonlocal materials in the 1.58-mm over the 6.35-mm screen. While still not particularly abundant in absolute quantities, exotic materials such as quartz crystal, Fort Payne chert, novaculite, Tallahatta quartzite, and Kosciusko quartzite are much more abundant in the smaller-size mesh samples. Thus, tools of these substances must have entered the site at a late stage of reduction, either as finished tools or as preforms. This kind of information is difficult to acquire without the use of smaller-mesh screens, but the principal reason one would employ such screens in the first place would be to approach behavioral, and not simple cultural historical, questions. Therefore, an archaeologist must come to this sort of analysis with behavioral questions in mind, rather than simply making do with field techniques more suitable for other analytical inquiries, then trying to plug the questions in later.

This is an issue that the study by Sarah Price has hammered home from the perspective of field technique. Time and time again, she shows different results depending on the screen size used. Use of a mesh size that is too large can make an entire raw material or knapping technique invisible just like those small rodents and bats that were being missed on Middle Eastern sites before archaeologists started employing techniques suitable for their recovery (Payne 1972).

Technological Attributes

If one is asking questions concerning chronology or cultural affiliation, then the most useful unit of analysis is an aggregate one, such as tool type. Although the attributes that make up a tool type are complex, so is human culture and sets of attributes, defining types, can be shown to vary along temporal and spatial axes. Questions that go beyond the identification of time and space—e.g., how a tool was made, used, or hafted; how it fit into other cultural systems—are not so easily approached through typological systems. These behavioral kinds of questions usually vary along trajectories that are not easily recognizable but may be studied by isolating individual attributes or small subsets of attributes.

No wonder, then, that several of the chapters in this volume are deeply concerned with the interaction of variables or attributes with themselves or with other elements in the cultural repertoire. In fact, Sain and Goodyear's approach is almost totally attribute based. Their blade score analysis—a measure of bladeness derived from scores on six attributes—is an innovative and potentially useful set of criteria by which to assess the nature of this technique in an assemblage.

The most outspokenly integrative approach in this volume, in the sense of pursuing different lines of evidence to support a claim, has been taken by Franklin and colleagues. Some of their analyses produce contradictory results, which is a little off-putting to those who demand that science give them order. But, one must consider that the questions being asked are as complex as the human culture in which they are rooted and often depend on nonmaterial variables that remain unknown to present-day analysts. If we are uncertain of the parameters of the cultural systems that articulate with our questions, then should we be surprised if some of the answers we get do not jibe with what we expect? The more deeply we delve into a cultural issue, the more contradictions we must confront because of all the things we do not know that impinge upon the questions we ask. In our line of work, this is what science looks like. The only reasonable solution is to compare the separate lines of evidence to one another and choose the path that makes the most sense—which is exactly what Franklin and colleagues have done.

Within lithic analysis, the employment of attributes has been particularly important in the area of debitage studies. Here, two distinct methods have developed: individual flake analysis and size grade analysis. Although they have occasionally been perceived as competing, they are not really competitors but different ways of analyzing flakes. It is from this perspective that Potts conducted experiments to determine which method works best with the low-grade quartz flakes in her assemblage. Size grade analysis turned out to be the more reliable in this case, though these results should not be automatically extended to other material classes without additional experimentation.

Critiques of individual flake analysis (Ahler 1989b; Bradbury and Carr 1995, 1999; Morrow 1997; Shott 1994) have been frequent and are undeniable, but it seems to me that the interpretive aspects of size grade analysis could also use a little help (an idea that is not foreign to most of the practitioners who have applied the technique). This point can be extrapolated from Price's work comparing screen mesh sizes. For example, she reports experimental data on Bangor chert in which all flakes classed as late stage are smaller than 6.35 mm. On the other hand, she also cites Phase II testing in Florida in which 30 percent of the flakes from a quarry assemblage (and therefore early stage) were recovered in the 3.17-mm (.125-inch) screen, and 50 percent of the smaller size grade flakes (mostly shatter) were interpreted as indicative of early tool reduction. And these contradictions do not even factor in the probability that most archaeological sites are amalgams of different reduction stages and techniques. When it comes to debitage analysis, folks, we are all flying a little blind.

Attributes have also been invoked to set boundaries between contiguous stages in a bifacial reduction sequence (Callahan 1979). The problem is, Miller and Smallwood (and others before them; e.g., Shott 1996a) have made a strong case that bifacial reduction does not proceed in stages but is a continuum. So if bifacial stages do not exist, are the attributes used to define them valid for anything?

I would argue that they are (see also Bradbury and Carr 1999), if only to distinguish early and late episodes. The criteria that Callahan (1979:8–12) established are useful in a general sense, and I have employed his stages 2–4 to provide a general classification of bifaces. As this is a purely descriptive device, I do not consider it a denial that bifacial reduction is really a continuum and that stage construction is arbitrary.

Miller and Smallwood also point out that the concept of stages assumes an end target—usually a projectile point, drill, or refined biface. I do not deny that many archaeologists probably perceive them in this way, in which case Miller and Smallwood are correct. But if this accurately describes the prehistoric situation, then our ancestors were either imbeciles or incompetents. If the object of bifacial reduction was to knap every piece to completion (Callahan's stage 5), then the massive quantities of bifaces in North American assemblages left in the early and middle stages of reduction suggest that these guys really were not very good at their craft.

Now, none of us believe this scenario for a minute, so something else was clearly at work. First, bifacial axes are significantly different from projectile points, and there are bifacial chisels, adzes, wedges, hoes, butchering knives, and probably bludgeons in there to boot—all with different design requirements, and most of them not reduced to "completion." And second, several of the less-refined bifaces in most of the assemblages I have analyzed could not possibly have been on a lengthy bifacial trajectory that ended up in a projectile point—they are too thin, too thick, too poorly shaped, and so on. These were clearly never on such a reduction stream in the first place and can be placed in a separate category analytically (Odell 1996a).

Technological Strategies

As used here, an "attribute" is an element or quality of an object (say, the length of a flake) that was produced through human technology. Having been a part of the technological process, the element, if unique or characteristic of the technology, can be isolated and used as a surrogate to identify parts of the process itself. The attribute is pertinent to the analytical documentation of that technology, but not particularly to the prehistoric people's use of it. This latter can be termed a "strategy," meaning the dominant direction that a particular people took the technology.

Two chapters in this volume inspect prehistoric technological strategies. Bradbury and Carr take on a fascinating conundrum in the early prehistory of the North American continent, that of Clovis blade technology. Since a relatively large proportion of Clovis sites containing blades occur in the Southeast, this topic is of particular interest in this region. The conundrum is this: Given the advantages of a blade technology, why did it die out in the Early Archaic? My take on this problem is that it is difficult to understand why something died out when you do not really know why it existed in the first place. Our knowledge of the blade's purpose, use as a tool, and place within Clovis cultural systems remains largely unknown and little studied (Collins 1999).

I am not a big fan of the idea that the increase in cutting edge provided by a blade (Bar-Yosef and Kuhn 1999; Bordaz 1970:57; Sheets and Muto 1972) was specifically selected for, or seen as a great advantage, by any prehistoric tool user. However, blades do possess the advantage of having been knapped to standard shapes and sizes, which means that they were optimal as interchangeable cutting edges in composite tools. The European Mesolithic counts several examples of blades or microliths, usually made on blades, discovered in their original hafts. Blades or microliths were inserted into grooves in arrows (Becker 1945; Matthiassen 1937; Petersson 1951; Troels-Smith 1961), and were used in lances (Beck 1966), as a knife blade (Norling-Christensen and Bröste 1945), and in slotted bone points (Madsen 1868:pl. 40, nos. 1a and 1b, 5; Müller 1918:fig. 9; Westerby 1927:fig. 45).

It is reasonable to suppose that blades also served this range of purposes in the New World. However, only a straight blade (i.e., one that is not curved in lateral section) will fit in your garden-variety groove, which was usually straight. Recently, Boldurian and Hoffman (2009) considered the manufacture of Clovis blades and noted that they possess a distinct lateral curvature compared to Upper Paleolithic blades, which are straight. Not long after the Clovis pieces were knapped, the culture's blade industry died out.

It seems to me that, near the demise of this technology, Clovis blades were laterally curved because they could be, indicating that they were no longer being placed in grooves like their Upper Paleolithic counterparts were or, supposedly, as they themselves once were. By this time, blades probably served the same range of functions as flakes and, since flakes were considerably easier to produce, people ceased making blades. In this regard, Sain and Goodyear (this volume) report that the blades recovered from the Topper and Big Pine Tree sites in South Carolina exhibit little lateral curvature. Is it possible that this is a chronological indicator, placing these occupations in the earlier Paleoindian period?

Bradbury and Carr propose another conundrum for consideration: the genesis of bipolar or bipolar-type damage and flaking. One problem here is that it is difficult to recognize the existence of a bipolar technology from evidence on the resulting flakes and almost impossible to accurately distinguish any individual flake as bipolar (Jeske and Lurie 1993). Another problem concerns the specific type of activity that produced the damage or the flakes in question, an issue that has occasioned some controversy. One camp asserts that most of the products exhibiting this kind of damage result from bipolar techniques; the other invokes a function as wedges, which produces a similar kind of damage (Goodyear 1993; Hayden 1980; Honea 1965; LeBlanc 1992; Shott 1989, 1999).

I view the entire debate rather whimsically, as both activities were undoubtedly practiced in prehistory. An underrecognized analytical issue here is that it is difficult to tell the difference without observing each piece through a microscope. Wedging usually produces not only the characteristic battering, but also bright abrasive polish from the wood, bone, or other substance being split. The point is that you cannot just eyeball a collection of battered stones and pronounce how that battering got there. It takes observing each piece at an appropriate level of magnification, after which you might conclude that the piece had been subjected to both sources of damage.

The other contribution from this compendium that delves into the issue of prehistoric technological strategies involves Thacker and colleagues' project in the Uwharrie Mountains of North Carolina. Deriving interpretations from Kuhn's (1992, 1994) provisioning models, the authors produce evidence from their lithic data that people's reduction techniques, and ultimately their entire logistical program, changed during the early middle portion of the Middle Archaic of the region. As mobility decreased, reflected in a wider array of reduction alternatives in the later Middle Archaic, prehistoric inhabitants altered their provisioning strategies from the individual to the camp, according to the model. This constitutes a serious change in the people's logistical organization and demonstrates the relationship between planning and the nature of material remains. Obviously, this project is not completed and the model needs to be tested more thoroughly. I do find it exciting that data of this nature are being employed to address questions of significant cultural import in the lives of the former occupants of the region.

Tool Function

The organization of technology must incorporate tool function. Was utilization, after all, not the ultimate goal? Why go to all the trouble of procuring and manufacturing an implement if not to use it? So figuring out how tools were used is certainly a step toward understanding a cultural group's technological organization, though the latter requires considerably more than simply reporting tool motion and worked material.

But first, one must hone the craft such that one's sample contains only those objects pertinent to the study. Put another way, when dealing with any phenomenon, one must eliminate, at least conceptually, all phenomena that are irrelevant to the one under consideration (if you are studying birds in flight, then you had better factor out all the airplanes). This is the significance of Pevny's contribution, a thorough consideration of all postdepositional modifications that may have affected the appearance of the use wear being analyzed through a microscope. The paucity of use wear in her sample may relate to the casual nature of the tools themselves, as she suggests, but also to their location of discard: in a workshop where tools were manufactured and repaired and not necessarily an activity area where they were utilized.

On a more substantive level, Franklin and colleagues' work in bluff shelters of Tennessee demonstrates how functional analyses, combined with other types of studies, contribute to a more complete overall comprehension of prehistoric occupation than would otherwise be the case. For instance, analyses of reduction at the Eagle Drink Bluff Shelter show a wide range of levels of reduction. The small size of the shelter notwithstanding, this might be interpreted as indicative of an extensive or long-term occupation. However, the functional analysis indicates a more restricted array of activities, suggestive of a spring or summer hunting camp. This finding, in turn, forces the investigators to adjust their reasoning concerning the technological classes present at the site. Such is the strength of multiple lines of inquiry, which reinforces the worth of expending the considerable energy and time it takes to accumulate these disparate data sets.

Conclusion

Lithic analysis is about stones by definition and about people by choice. Much of what has been written about stones has not involved people very much, and the archaeological community has been the poorer for it; hence this renewed call for more behavioral approaches. The *nom du jour* for this flavor of behavioralism is organization of technology, a concept that is broad enough to include a wide range of topics yet conveys the idea that it is the *prehistoric people's* technology we are talking about, not the analyst's.

The authors of the chapters in this volume have understood this distinction pretty well and have managed to stay on target. I include in this statement chapters that superficially appear to be more about technique than about organization of technology: Price's on screen mesh sizes and Pevny's on postdepositional modification of artifacts. Price shows us that you cannot interpret stones very well if your data set does not contain the evidence that will allow you to know what people did with their stones, and Pevny illustrates that your interpretations will be skewed if the data set contains extraneous and irrelevant information. In other words, you cannot interpret what you do not acquire (Price), and your interpretations will be wrong if you have lousy data to start with (Pevny).

The contributions in this collection are, of course, self-selected and do not truly represent lithic analysis in the Southeast in any statistical sense. Yet, the authors are part of a young and influential subset of scholars who are bringing the study of archaeological stone tools to a new level. I would like to think that these individuals, and the ideas encapsulated in this volume, will breathe new life into lithic analysis in the Southeast and beyond.

Acknowledgments

I thank Phil Carr, Andrew Bradbury, and Sarah Price for organizing the session of SEAC in which the chapters in this volume were originally presented and for following the process through to its completion. This is an important initiative, and I appreciate being a part of it.

Works Cited

Abbott, L. E.

1996 Archaeological Testing of Five Upland Sites within the Uwharrie Ranger District, Uwharrie National Forest: Intersite Analysis in the Carolina Slate Belt, Montgomery County, North Carolina. New South Associates Technical Report 270 (Stone Mountain, Georgia). Submitted to the USDA—Forest Service Southeastern Forest Experiment Station, Asheville, North Carolina.

2003 Quarry Studies in North Carolina: What Have We Learned in the Last 30 Years? *Journal of Middle Atlantic Archaeology* 19:87–105.

Abrams, M. D., and G. J. Nowacki

2008 Native Americans as Active and Passive Promoters of Mast Fruit Trees in the Eastern USA. *The Holocene* 18:1123–1137.

Ackerman, R. E.

1964 Lichens and the Patination of Chert in Alaska. *American Antiquity* 29:386–387.

Ahler, S. A.

1971 Projectile Point Form and Function at Rodgers Shelter, Missouri. Missouri Archaeological Society Research Series No. 8. Missouri Archaeological Society, Columbia.

1975 *Pattern and Variety in Extended Coalescent Lithic Technology.* Ph.D. dissertation, University of Missouri, Columbia. University Microfilms, Ann Arbor.

1989a Experimental Knapping with KRF and Midcontinental Cherts: Overview and Applications. In *Experiments in Lithic Technology,* edited by D. S. Amick and R. P. Mauldin, pp. 199–234. BAR International Series 528. British Archaeological Reports, Oxford.

1989b Mass Analysis of Flaking Debris: Studying the Forest Rather than the Trees. In *Alternative Approaches to Lithic Analysis,* edited by D. O. Henry and G. H. Odell, pp. 85–118. Archeological Papers of the American Anthropological Association No. 1. American Anthropological Association, Arlington, Virginia.

Ahler, S. A., and R. C. Christensen

1983 *A Pilot Study of Knife River Flint Procurement and Reduction at Site 32DU508, a Quarry and Workshop Location in Dunn County, North Dakota.* Department of Anthropology and Archeology, University of North Dakota, Grand Forks. Submitted to State Historical Society of North Dakota, Bismarck, Contract No. YA553-CT1-1089. Copies available from State Historical Society of North Dakota, Bismarck.

Amick, D. S.

1985 Late Archaic Fort Payne Biface Manufacture at the Topsy Site (40WY204), Buffalo River Basin, Tennessee. *Southeastern Archaeology* 4:134–151.

1987 *Lithic Raw Material Variability in the Central Duck River Basin: Reflections of Middle and Late Archaic Organizational Strategies.* Publications in Anthropology No. 50. Tennessee Valley Authority, Chattanooga. Report of Investigations No. 46. Department of Anthropology, University of Tennessee, Knoxville.

1999 Raw Material Variation in Folsom Stone Tool Assemblages and the Division of Labor in Hunter-Gatherer Societies. In *Folsom Lithic Technology: Explorations in Structure and Variation,* edited by D. S. Amick, pp. 169–187. Archaeological Series No. 12. International Monographs in Prehistory, Ann Arbor.

2007 Behavioral Causes and Archaeological Effects of Lithic Artifact Recycling. In *Tools Versus Cores: Alternative Approaches to Stone Tool Analysis,* edited by S. McPherron, pp. 223–252. Cambridge Scholars Publications, Newcastle, U.K.

Amick, D. S., and R. P. Mauldin

1997 Effects of Raw Material on Flake Breakage Patterns. *Lithic Technology* 22(1):18–32.

Amick, D. S., and R. P. Mauldin (editors)

1989 *Experiments in Lithic Technology.* BAR International Series 528. British Archaeological Reports, Oxford.

Amick, D. S., R. P. Mauldin, and L. R. Binford

1989 The Potential of Experiments in Lithic Technology. In *Experiments in Lithic Technology,* edited by D. S. Amick and R. P. Mauldin, pp. 1–14. BAR International Series 528. British Archaeological Reports, Oxford.

Ammerman, A. J., and W. Andrefsky Jr.

1982 Reduction Sequences and the Exchange of Obsidian in Neolithic Calabria. In *Contexts for Prehistoric Exchange,* edited by J. Ericson and T. Earle, pp. 149–172. Academic Press, New York.

Anderson, D. G.

1990 Paleoindian Colonization of Eastern North America: A View from the Southeastern United States. In *Early Paleoindian Economies of Eastern North America,* edited by K. B. Tankersley and B. L. Isaac, pp. 163–216. *Research in Economic Anthropology* Suppl. 5.

1996 Models of Paleoindian and Early Archaic Settlement in the Lower Southeast. In *The Paleoindian and Early Archaic Southeast: A Historical Perspective,* edited by D. G. Anderson and K. E. Sassaman, pp. 29–57. The University of Alabama Press, Tuscaloosa.

2004 Paleoindian Occupations in the Southeastern United States. In *New Perspectives on the First Americans,* edited by B. T. Lepper and R. Bonnichsen, pp. 119–128. Texas A&M University Press, College Station.

2005 Pleistocene Human Occupation of the Southeastern United States: Research Directions for the Early Twenty-First Century. In *Paleoamerican Origins: Beyond Clovis,* edited by R. Bonnichsen, B. T. Lepper, D. Stanford, and M. R. Waters, pp. 29–42. Center for the Study of the First Americans, Texas A&M University, College Station.

Anderson, D. G., and G. T. Hanson

1988 Early Archaic Settlement in the Southeastern United States: A Case Study from the Savannah River Valley. *American Antiquity* 53:262–286.

Anderson, D. G., L. D. O'Steen, and K. E. Sassaman

1996 Environmental and Chronological Considerations. In *The Paleoindian and Early Archaic Southeast,* edited by D. G. Anderson and K. E. Sassaman, pp. 3–15. The University of Alabama Press, Tuscaloosa.

Anderson, D. G., and K. E. Sassaman (editors)

1996 *The Paleoindian and Early Archaic Southeast.* The University of Alabama Press, Tuscaloosa.

Anderson, D. G., and J. Schuldenrein

1983 Early Archaic Settlement on the Southeastern Atlantic Slope: A View from Rucker's Bottom Site, Elbert County, Georgia. *North American Archaeologist* 3:177–210.

Anderson-Gerfaud, P.

1981 *Contribution méthodologique à l'analyse des microtraces d'utilisation sur les outils préhistoriques.* Thèse de Troisième Cycle, Bordeaux University, Bordeaux, France.

Andrefsky, W., Jr.

1986 A Consideration of Blade and Flake Curvature. *Lithic Technology* 15:48–54.

1994a Raw Material Availability and the Organization of Technology. *American Antiquity* 59:21–35.

1994b The Geological Occurrence of Lithic Material and Stone Tool Production Strategies. *Geoarchaeology: An International Journal* 9(5):345–391.

1998 *Lithics: Macroscopic Approaches to Analysis.* Cambridge University Press, Cambridge.

2001 Emerging Directions in Debitage Analysis. In *Lithic Debitage: Context, Form, Meaning,* edited by W. Andrefsky Jr., pp. 2–14. University of Utah Press, Salt Lake City.

2004 Partitioning the Aggregate: Mass Analysis and Debitage Assemblages. In *Aggregate Analysis in Chipped Stone,* edited by C. T. Hall and M. L. Larson, pp. 201–210. University of Utah Press, Salt Lake City.

2006 Experimental and Archaeological Verification of an Index of Retouch for Hafted Bifaces. *American Antiquity* 71:743–759.

2007 The Application and Misapplication of Mass Analysis in Lithic Debitage Studies. *Journal of Archaeological Science* 34.392–402.

2008a An Introduction to Stone Tool Life History and Technological Organization. In *Lithic Technology: Measures of Production, Use, and Curation,* edited by W. Andrefsky Jr., pp. 3–22. Cambridge University Press, Cambridge.

2008b Projectile Point Provisioning Strategies and Human Land-Use. In *Lithic Tech-*

nology: Measures of Production, Use, and Curation, edited by W. Andrefsky Jr., pp. 195–214. Cambridge University Press, Cambridge.

2009 The Analysis of Stone Tool Procurement, Production, and Maintenance. *Journal of Archaeological Research* 17:65–103.

Andrefsky, W., Jr. (editor)

2001 *Lithic Debitage: Context, Form, Meaning.* University of Utah Press, Salt Lake City.

2008 *Lithic Technology: Measures of Production, Use, and Curation.* Cambridge University Press, Cambridge.

Andrefsky, W., Jr., J. Ferris, J. Williams, N. Goodale, and G. T. Jones

2010 Geologic Context and Diagnostic Provenance of Cherts. Paper presented at the 2010 Annual Meeting of the Society for American Archaeology, St. Louis.

Andrefsky, W., Jr., S. Van Galder, and K. Presler

1999 *Archaeological Investigations at Birch Creek (35ML181): 1998 Season Interim Report.* Contributions in Cultural Resource Management No. 64. Center for Northwest Anthropology, Washington State University, Pullman.

Ashton, N., and M. White

2003 Bifaces and Raw Materials: Flexible Flaking in the British Early Paleolithic. In *Multiple Approaches to the Study of Bifacial Technologies,* edited by M. Soressi and H. L. Dibble, pp. 109–124. University Museum Monograph 115. University of Pennsylvania Museum of Archaeology and Anthropology, Philadelphia.

Audouze, F.

1999 New Advances in French Prehistory. *Antiquity* 73:167–175.

2002 Leroi-Gourhan, a Philosopher of Technique and Evolution. *Journal of Archaeological Science* 10:277–306.

Austin, R. J.

2001 Beyond Technology and Functions: Evaluating the Research Significance of Lithic Scatters. In *Thinking About Significance,* edited by R. J. Austin, K. S. Hoffman, and G. R. Ballo. Papers and Proceedings of the Florida Archaeological Council, Inc. Professional Development Workshop, St. Augustine, Florida. Special Publication Series No. 1. Florida Archaeological Council, Inc., Riverview.

Bailey, G.

2007 Time Perspectives, Palimpsests, and the Archaeology of Time. *Journal of Anthropological Archaeology* 26:198–223.

Bamforth, D. B.

1986 Technological Efficiency and Tool Curation. *American Antiquity* 51:38–50.

2003 Rethinking the Role of Bifacial Technology in Paleoindian Adaptations on the Great Plains. In *Multiple Approaches to the Study of Bifacial Technologies,* edited by M. Soressi and H. L. Dibble, pp. 209–228. University Museum Monograph 115. University of Pennsylvania Museum of Archaeology and Anthropology, Philadelphia.

Bamforth, D. B., and M. Becker

2006 The Allen Site Lithic Assemblage. In *The Allen Site: A Paleoindian Camp in Southwestern Nebraska,* edited by D. B. Bamforth, pp. 148–183. University of New Mexico Press, Albuquerque.

Bamforth, D. B., and K. Hicks
2008 Production Skill and Paleoindian Workgroup Organization in the Medicine Creek Drainage, Southwestern Nebraska. *Journal Archaeological Method and Theory* 15:132–153.
Banning, E. B.
2002 *Archaeological Survey.* Kluwer Academic/Plenum, New York.
Barham, L. S.
1987 The Bipolar Technique in Southern Africa: A Replication Experiment. *South African Archaeological Bulletin* 42:45–50.
Bar-Yosef, O., and S. L. Kuhn
1999 The Big Deal about Blades: Laminar Technologies and Human Evolution. *American Anthropologist* 101(2):322–338.
Bar-Yosef, O., and P. Van Peer
2009 The Chaîne Opératoire Approach in Middle Paleolithic Archaeology. *Current Anthropology* 50:103–131.
Baumler, M. F., and L. B. Davis
2004 The Role of Small-Sized Debitage in Aggregate Lithic Analysis. In *Aggregate Analysis in Chipped Stone,* edited by C. T. Hall and M. L. Larson, pp. 45–64. University of Utah Press, Salt Lake City.
Baumler, M. F., and C. E. Downum
1989 Between Micro and Macro: A Study of the Interpretation of Small-Sized Lithic Debitage. In *Experiments in Lithic Technology,* edited by D. S. Amick and R. P. Mauldin, pp. 101–116. BAR International Series 528. British Archaeological Reports, Oxford.
Beck, C., and G. T. Jones
1989 Bias and Archaeological Classification. *American Antiquity* 54:244–262.
2010 Clovis and Western Stemmed: Population Migration and the Meeting of Two Technologies in the Intermountain West. *American Antiquity* 75:81–116.
Beck, C., A. K. Taylor, G. T. Jones, C. M. Fadem, C. R. Cook, and S. A. Millward
2002 Rocks Are Heavy: Transport Costs and PaleoArchaic Quarry Behavior in the Great Basin. *Journal of Anthropological Archaeology* 21:481–507.
Beck, J.
1966 En boplads et enkeltfund fra Fyns Maglemosetid. *Fynske Minder,* pp. 161–172.
Becker, C. F.
1945 En 8000-aarig stenalderboplads i Holmegaards Mose. *Fra Nationalmuseets Arbejdsmark,* pp. 61–72.
Behm, J. A.
1983 Flake Concentrations: Distinguishing Between Flintworking Areas and Secondary Deposits. *Lithic Technology* 12(1):9–16.
Bense, J. A.
1994 *Archaeology of the Southeastern United States: Paleoindian to World War I.* Academic Press, San Diego.
Binford, L. R.
1962 Archaeology as Anthropology. *American Antiquity* 28:217–225.

1973 Interassemblage Variability: The Mousterian and the "Functional" Argument. In *The Explanation of Culture Change: Models in Prehistory,* edited by C. Renfrew, pp. 227–254. Duckworth, London.

1977 Forty-seven Trips: A Case Study in the Character of Archaeological Formation Processes. In *Stone Tools as Cultural Markers,* edited by R. S. V. Wright, pp. 24–36. Australian Institute of Aboriginal Studies, Canberra.

1978 Dimensional Analysis of Behavior and Site Structure: Learning from an Eskimo Hunting Stand. *American Antiquity* 43:330.

1979 Organization and Formation Processes: Looking at Curated Technologies. *Journal of Anthropological Research* 35:255–272.

1980 Willow Smoke and Dogs' Tails: Hunter-Gatherer Settlement Systems and Archaeological Site Formation. *American Antiquity* 45:1–17.

1981 Behavioral Archaeology and the "Pompeii Promise." *Journal of Anthropological Research* 37:195–208.

1982 The Archaeology of Place. *Journal of Anthropological Archaeology* 1:1–31.

Blasco, R., J. Rosell, J. Fernández Peris, I. Cáceres, and J. María Vergés

2008 A New Element of Trampling: An Experimental Application on the Level XII Faunal Record of Bolomor Cave (Valencia, Spain). *Journal of Archaeological Science* 35:1605–1618.

Bleed, P. F.

1986 The Optimal Design of Hunting Weapons: Maintainability or Reliability. *American Antiquity* 51:737–747.

2001 Trees or Chains, Links or Branches: Conceptual Alternatives for Consideration of Stone Tool Production and Other Sequential Activities. *Journal of Archaeological Method and Theory* 8(1):101–127.

2002 Obviously Sequential, but Continuous or Staged? Refits and Cognition in Three Late Paleolithic Assemblages from Japan. *Journal of Anthropological Archaeology* 21:329–343.

Bleed, P., and M. Meier

1980 An Objective Test of the Effects of Heat Treatment of Flakeable Stone. *American Antiquity* 45:502–507.

Blitz, J. H.

1988 Adoption of the Bow in Prehistoric North America. *North American Archaeologist* 9(2):123–145.

Boëda, E.

1995 Levallois: A Volumetric Construction, Methods, a Technique. In *The Definition and Interpretation of Levallois Technology,* edited by H. L. Dibble and O. Bar-Yosef, pp. 41–68. University of Pennsylvania Press, Philadelphia.

Boisvert, R. A.

1986 Late Archaic Settlement Models in the Middle Ohio Valley: A Perspective from Big Bone Lick, Kentucky. Ph.D. dissertation, Department of Anthropology, University of Kentucky, Lexington.

Boldurian, A. T., and E. E. Hoffman

2009 Clovis Blade Manufacture: Analytical Procedure to Infer "Technique." *North American Archaeologist* 30:167–194.

Booth, R. K., S. T. Jackson, S. L. Forman, J. E. Kutzbach, I. E. A. Bettis, J. Kreig, and D. K. Wright
2005 A Severe Centennial-Scale Drought in Mid-continental North America 4200 Years Ago and Apparent Global Linkages. *The Holocene* 15:321–328.

Bordaz, J.
1970 *Tools of the Old and New Stone Age.* Natural History Press, Garden City, N.Y.

Bordes, F.
1961 *Typologie du Paleolithique: Ancient et Moyen.* Delmas, Bordeaux, France.

Boyd, R., and P. J. Richerson
1985 *Culture and the Evolutionary Process.* University of Chicago Press, Chicago.

Bradbury, A. P.
1997 The Bow and Arrow in the Eastern Woodlands: Evidence for an Archaic Origin. *North American Archaeologist* 18(3):207–234.
1998 The Examination of Lithic Artifacts from an Early Archaic Assemblage: Strengthening Inferences Through Multiple Lines of Evidence. *Midcontinental Journal of Archaeology* 23:263–288.
2006 The Organization of Lithic Technology and the Bifurcate Occupation of the Hart Site (15La183), Lawrence County, Kentucky. *North American Archaeologist* 27(1):1–24.
2007 Lithic Analysis of an Early Archaic Knapping Area. *Midcontinental Journal of Archaeology* 32:47–70.
2010 Bipolar Reduction Experiments and the Examination of Middle Archaic Bipolar Technologies in West-Central Illinois. *North American Archaeologist* 31(1):67–116.

Bradbury, A. P., and P. J. Carr
1995 Flake Typologies and Alternative Approaches: An Experimental Assessment. *Lithic Technology* 20(2):100–116.
1999 Examining Stage and Continuum Models of Flake Debris Analysis: An Experimental Approach. *Journal of Archaeological Science* 26:105–116.
2004a Exploring Mass Analysis, Screens, and Attributes. In *Aggregate Analyses in Chipped Stone,* edited by C. T. Hall and M. L. Larson, pp. 21–44. University of Utah Press, Salt Lake City.
2004b Combining Aggregate and Individual Methods of Flake Debris Analysis: Aggregate Trend Analysis. *North American Archaeologist* 25(1):65–90.
2009 Hits and Misses when Throwing Stones at Mass Analysis. *Journal of Archaeological Science* 36:2788–2796.

Bradbury, A. P., P. J. Carr, and D. R. Cooper
2008 Raw Material and Retouched Flakes. In *Lithic Technology: Measures of Production, Use, and Curation,* edited by W. Andrefsky Jr., pp. 233–256. Cambridge University Press, Cambridge.

Bradbury, A. P., and J. D. Franklin
2000 Raw Material Variability, Package Size, and Mass Analysis. *Lithic Technology* 25(1):42–78.

Bradley, B. A.
1974 Comments on the Lithic Technology of the Casper Site Materials. In *Casper Site: A Hell Gap Bison Kill on the High Plains,* edited by G. C. Frison, pp. 191–197. Academic Press, New York.

1982 Flaked Stone Technology and Typology. In *The Agate Basin Site,* edited by G. C. Frison and D. J. Stanford, pp. 181–208. Academic Press, New York.

1991 Flaked Stone Technology and Typology in the Northern High Plains. In *Prehistoric Hunters of the High Plains,* 2nd ed., edited by G. C. Frison, pp. 369–395. Academic Press, New York.

1993 Paleo-Indian Flaked Stone Technology in the North American High Plains. In *From Kostenki to Clovis: Upper Paleolithic–Paleo-Indian Adaptations,* edited by O. Soffer and N. D. Praslov, pp. 251–262. Plenum Press, New York.

Brantingham, P. J.

2003 A Neutral Model of Stone Raw Material Procurement. *American Antiquity* 68:487–510.

Brantingham, P. J., and S. L. Kuhn

2001 Constraints on Levallois Core Technology: A Mathematical Model. *Journal of Archaeological Science* 28:747–761.

Brantingham, P. J., J. W. Olsen, J. A. Rech, and A. I. Krivoshapkin

2000 Raw Material Quality and Prepared Core Technologies in Northeastern Asia. *Journal of Archaeological Science* 27:255–271.

Braun, D. R.

2005 Examining Flake Production Strategies: Examples from the Middle Paleolithic of Southwest Asia. *Lithic Technology* 30:107–125.

Brookes, S. O.

1979 *The Hester Site: An Early Archaic Occupation in Monroe County, Mississippi.* Archaeological Report No. 5. Mississippi Department of Archives and History, Jackson.

Brooks, P. B., R. L. Brooks, and M. B. Collins

1979 *The Bluestone Archeological Project: Excavations at the 15RO35–36 Site Complex.* Special Report No. 1. Archaeological Services of Kentucky, Lexington.

Brooms, B. M.

1992 Archaeological/Historical Report for Widening of U.S. 431 North of Pittsview to Seale, Alabama. Highway Department Project F-433(21), Russell County. Report submitted to Alabama Department of Transportation by Troy State University, Troy, Alabama.

Broster, J. B., and M. R. Norton

1993 The Carson-Conn-Short Site (40BN190): An Extensive Clovis Habitation in Benton County, Tennessee. *Current Research in the Pleistocene* 10:3–5.

1996 Recent Paleoindian Research in Tennessee. In *The Paleoindian and Early Archaic Southeast,* edited by D. G. Anderson and K. E. Sassaman, pp. 288–297. The University of Alabama Press, Tuscaloosa.

Brown, C. T.

2001 The Fractal Dimensions of Lithic Reduction. *Journal of Archaeological Science* 28:619–631.

Brown, J., and R. Vierra

1983 What Happened in the Middle Archaic? Introduction to an Ecological Approach to Koster Site Archaeology. In *Archaic Hunters and Gatherers in the American*

Midwest, edited by J. L. Phillips and J. A. Brown, pp. 165–196. Academic Press, New York.

Bruce, K. L.

2001 All Rocks Are Not Alike. *Southeastern Archaeology* 20:78–92.

Bullock, P., N. Fedoroff, A. Jongerius, G. J. Stoops, and T. Tursina

1985 *Handbook for Soil Thin Section Description.* Waine Research Publishers, Wolverhampton, U.K.

Burris, A.

2006 Defining an Alternate Typology for Early Holocene Projectile Points from the Hester Site (22MO569), Northeast Mississippi: A Systematic Approach. Unpublished Master's thesis, Department of Sociology, Anthropology, and Social Work, Mississippi State University.

Burroni, D., R. E. Donahue, A. M. Pollard, and M. Mussi

2002 The Surface Alteration Features of Flint Artefacts as a Record of Environmental Processes. *Journal of Archaeological Science* 29:1277–1287.

Butzer, K.

1982 *Archaeology as Human Ecology: Method and Theory for a Contextual Approach.* Cambridge University Press, Cambridge.

Cable, J. S.

1996 Haw River Revisited: Implications for Modeling Terminal Late Glacial and Early Holocene Hunter-Gatherer Settlement Systems in the Southeast. In *The Paleoindian and Early Archaic Southeast,* edited by D. G. Anderson and K. E. Sassaman, pp. 107–148. The University of Alabama Press, Tuscaloosa.

Cahen, D., L. H. Keeley, and F. L. Van Noten

1979 Stone Tools, Toolkits, and Human Behavior in Prehistory. *Current Anthropology* 20:661–683.

Callahan, E.

1979 The Basics of Biface Knapping in the Eastern Fluted Point Tradition: A Manual for Flintknappers and Lithic Analysts. *Archaeology of Eastern North America* 7:1–180.

1991 Out of Theory and into Reality: A Comment on Nami's Comment. *Plains Anthropologist* 36:367–368.

Carr, Kurt W., Christopher Bergman, and Crista M. Haag

2010 Some Comments on Blade Technology and Eastern Clovis Lithic Reduction Strategies. *Lithic Technology* 25(2):91–125.

Carr, P. J.

1991 Organization of Technology and Lithic Analysis: Prehistoric Hunter-Gatherer Occupation of the Hayes Site (40ML139). Unpublished Master's thesis, Department of Anthropology, University of Tennessee, Knoxville.

1994a The Organization of Technology: Impact and Potential. In *The Organization of North American Prehistoric Chipped Stone Tool Technologies,* edited by P. J. Carr, pp. 1–8. Archaeological Series No. 7. International Monographs in Prehistory, Ann Arbor, Michigan.

1994b Technological Organization and Prehistoric Hunter-Gatherer Mobility: Examination of the Hayes Site. In *The Organization of North American Prehistoric Chipped Stone Tool Technologies,* edited by P. J. Carr, pp. 35–44. Archaeological Series No. 7. International Monographs in Prehistory, Ann Arbor, Michigan.

1995 Hunter-Gatherers, Mobility, and Technological Organization: The Early Archaic of East Tennessee. Unpublished Ph.D. dissertation, Department of Anthropology, University of Tennessee, Knoxville.

2004 Phase II Archaeological Testing at Site 1RU142, for Widening of US Highway 431, Russell County, Alabama. Report submitted to Alabama Department of Transportation. Center for Archaeological Studies, University of South Alabama, Mobile.

2008 Through the Lens of the Lithic Analyst: The Organization of Mississippi Delta Chipped-Stone Technologies. In *Time's River: Archaeological Syntheses from the Lower Mississippi River Valley,* edited by J. Rafferty and E. Peacock, pp. 201–222. The University of Alabama Press, Tuscaloosa.

Carr, P. J. (editor)

1994 *The Organization of North American Prehistoric Chipped Stone Tool Technologies.* Archaeological Series No. 7. International Monographs in Prehistory, Ann Arbor, Michigan.

Carr, P. J., and A. P. Bradbury

2000 Contemporary Lithic Analysis and Southeastern Archaeology. *Southeastern Archaeology* 19:120–134.

2001 Flake Debris Analysis, Levels of Production, and the Organization of Technology. In *Lithic Debitage: Context, Form, Meaning,* edited by W. Andrefsky Jr., pp. 126–146. University of Utah Press, Salt Lake City.

2004 Exploring Mass Analysis, Screens, and Attributes. In *Aggregate Analysis in Chipped Stone,* edited by C. T. Hall and M. L. Larson, pp. 21–44. University of Utah Press, Salt Lake City.

2010 Learning from Lithics: A Perspective on the Foundation and Future of the Organization of Technology. Submitted for publication in *Reduction Sequence, Chaîne Opératoire, and Other Methods: The Epistemologies of Different Approaches to Lithic Analysis,* edited by G. Tostevin. Interdisciplinary Contributions to Archaeology Series, Springer Press.

Carr, P. J., and B. Koldehoff

1994 A Preliminary Analysis of Mississippian Lithic Technology at Wickliffe Mounds (15BA4), Ballard County, Kentucky. *Tennessee Anthropologist* 19:46–65.

Carr, P. J., and T. L. Potts

2008 Lithic Analysis. In *Archaeology at Madison Park: Phase III Data Recovery at 1MT318, the Madison Park Site, Associated with the Bridge Replacement over the Western RR Overpass/Sevenmile Creek, ALDOT Project BRF-153(11) & NHF-507(4), Montgomery County, Alabama (AHC 98-1029),* by T. L. Potts. Center for Archaeological Studies, University of South Alabama, Mobile.

Carr, P. J., and L. H. Stewart

2004 Poverty Point Chipped-Stone Tool Raw Materials: Inferring Social and Economic Strategies. In *Signs of Power: The Rise of Cultural Complexity in the South-*

east, edited by J. L. Gibson and P. J. Carr, pp. 129–145. The University of Alabama Press, Tuscaloosa.

Chapman, J.

1973 *The Icehouse Bottom Site (40MR23).* Report of Investigations 13. Department of Anthropology, University of Tennessee, Knoxville.

1975 *The Rose Island Site and the Bifurcate Point Tradition.* Report of Investigations 14. Department of Anthropology, University of Tennessee, Knoxville.

1981 *The Bacon Bend and Iddins Sites.* Publications in Anthropology No. 25, Tennessee Valley Authority, and Report of Investigations No. 31. Department of Anthropology, University of Tennessee, Knoxville.

Chase, D. W.

1966 A Stratified Archaic Site in Lowndes County, Alabama. *Florida Anthropologist* 19(2):91–114.

Claggett, S. R., and J. S. Cable (assemblers)

1982 *The Haw River Sites: Archaeological Investigations at Two Stratified Sites in the North Carolina Piedmont.* Report No. 2386. Commonwealth Associates, Jackson, Michigan.

Clark, J. D., and H. Kurashina

1981 A Study of the Work of a Modern Tanner in Ethiopia and Its Relevance for Archaeological Interpretation. In *Modern Material Culture: The Archaeology of Us,* edited by R. A. Gould and M. B. Schiller, pp. 303–343. Academic Press, New York.

Clark, J. E.

1999 On *Stone Tools: Theoretical Insights into Human Prehistory* by George H. Odell. *Lithic Technology* 24(2):126–135.

Clarkson, C.

2002 An Index of Invasiveness for the Measurement of Unifacial and Bifacial Retouch: A Theoretical, Experimental and Archaeological Verification. *Journal of Archaeological Science* 29:65–75.

Cobb, C. R.

2000 *From Quarry to Cornfield: The Political Economy of Mississippian Hoe Production.* The University of Alabama Press, Tuscaloosa.

Cohen, M. N.

1985 Prehistoric Hunter-Gatherers: The Meaning of Social Complexity. In *Prehistoric Hunter-Gatherers: The Emergence of Cultural Complexity,* edited by T. D. Price and J. A. Brown, pp. 99–122. Academic Press, San Diego.

Collins, M. B.

1999 *Clovis Blade Technology: A Comparative Study of the Keven Davis Cache, Texas.* University of Texas Press, Austin.

2002 The Gault Site, Texas, and Clovis Research. *Athena Review* 3(2):24–36.

2007 Discerning Clovis Subsistence from Stone Artifacts and Site Distributions on the Southern Plains Periphery. In *Foragers of the Terminal Pleistocene in North America,* edited by R. B. Walker and B. N. Driskell, pp. 59–87. University of Nebraska Press, Lincoln.

Collins, M. B., and C. A. Hemmings
2005 Lesser-Known Clovis Diagnostic Artifacts: I. The Bifaces. *La Tierra* 32(2):9–20.
Conklin, C.
2008 Leave No Stone Unturned: Investigating Changes in Subsistence and Settlement Through Lithic Analysis at Site 31MG328 in the Uwharrie Mountains. B.A. honors thesis, Wake Forest University, Winston-Salem, North Carolina.
Cooper, D. R.
2005 Technological Analysis of the Lithic Assemblage. In *Phase III Investigations at the Elk Fork Site (15MO140), Morgan County, Kentucky,* by R. L. Herndon, pp. 149–212. Contract Publication No. 03-217. Cultural Resource Analysts, Inc., Lexington, Kentucky.
Cooper, P., and C. Norville
1979 Historic and Prehistoric Archaeological Resources Survey of a Certain 4875 Acres of the Uwharrie National Forest. Catawba College, Salisbury, North Carolina.
Cooper, P., and S. L. Smith
1981 An Historic and Prehistoric Archaeological Resources Survey of a Certain 4190 Acres of the Uwharrie National Forest, Davidson and Montgomery Counties, North Carolina. Catawba College, Salisbury, North Carolina.
Cotterell, B., and J. Kamminga
1979 The Mechanics of Flaking. In *Lithic Use-Wear Analysis,* edited by B. Hayden, pp. 97–112. Academic Press, New York.
1987 The Formation of Flakes. *American Antiquity* 52:675–708.
Courty, M.-A., P. Goldberg, and R. I. Macphail
1989 *Soils and Micromorphology in Archaeology.* Cambridge University Press, Cambridge.
Cowan, C. W.
1985 Understanding the Evolution of Plant Husbandry in Eastern North America: Lessons from Botany, Ethnography, and Archeology. In *Prehistoric Food Production in North America,* edited by R. I. Ford, pp. 205–243. Anthropological Papers No. 75. Museum of Anthropology, University of Michigan, Ann Arbor.
Cowan, C. W., H. E. Jackson, K. Moore, A. Nickelhoff, and T. L. Smart
1981 The Cloudsplitter Rockshelter, Menifee County, Kentucky: A Preliminary Report. *Bulletin of the Southeastern Archaeological Conference* 24:60–76.
Crabtree, D. E.
1972 *An Introduction to Flintworking.* Occasional Papers No. 28. Idaho State University Museum, Pocatello, Idaho.
Curren, C.
1982 Middle and Late Archaic Utilization of Tallahatta Quartzite in Southwestern Alabama. In *Archaeology in Southwest Alabama: A Collection of Papers,* edited by C. Curren, pp. 31–41. Alabama Tombigbee Regional Commission, Camden.
Curwen, E. C.
1930 Prehistoric Flint Sickles. *Antiquity* 4:179–186.
Daniel, I. R.
1998 *Hardaway Revisited: Early Archaic Settlement in the Southeast.* The University of Alabama Press, Tuscaloosa.

2001 Stone Raw Material Availability and Early Archaic Settlement in the Southeastern United States. *American Antiquity* 66:237–265.

Daniel, I. R., and J. R. Butler

1996 An Archaeological Survey and Petrographic Description of Rhyolite Sources in the Uwharrie Mountains, North Carolina. *Southern Indian Studies* 45:1–37.

Daniel, I. R., and R. P. S. Davis

1996 *The Projectile Point Classification Project: A Classification of Projectile Points in Existing Archaeological Collections from North Carolina (Phase II).* Technical Report No. 26. Research Laboratories of Anthropology, University of North Carolina, Chapel Hill.

Dean, W. E., T. S. Ahlbrandt, R. Y. Anderson, and J. P. Bradbury

1996 Regional Aridity in North America During the Middle Holocene. *The Holocene* 6(2):145–155.

Del Bene, T. A.

1979 Once upon a Striation: Current Models of Striation and Polish Formation. In *Lithic Use-Wear Analysis,* edited by B. Hayden, pp. 167–177. Academic Press, New York.

Deller, D. B., and C. J. Ellis

2001 Evidence for Post-Clovis Paleoindian Ritual from the Caradoc Site (AfHj-104), Southwestern Ontario, Canada. *American Antiquity* 66:267–284.

Des Jean, T., and J. L. Benthall

1994 A Lithic Based Prehistoric Cultural Chronology of the Upper Cumberland Plateau. *Tennessee Anthropologist* 19(2):115–147.

Diamond, G.

1979 The Nature of So-Called Polished Surfaces on Stone Artifacts. In *Lithic Use-Wear Analysis,* edited by B. Hayden, pp. 159–166. Academic Press, New York.

Dibble, H. L.

1995 Middle Paleolithic Scraper Reduction: Background, Clarification, and Review of the Evidence to Date. *Journal of Archaeological Method and Theory* 2:299–368.

1997 Platform Variability and Flake Morphology: A Comparison of Experimental and Archaeological Data and Implication for Interpreting Prehistoric Lithic Technological Strategies. *Lithic Technology* 22:150–170.

Dibble, H. L., T. P. Raczek, and S. P. McPherron

2005 Excavator Bias at the Site of Pech de l'Aze IV, France. *Journal of Field Archaeology* 30(3):317–328.

Dickens, W. A.

2005 Biface Reduction and Blade Manufacture at the Gault Site (41BL323): A Clovis Occupation in Bell County, Texas. Unpublished Ph.D. dissertation, Department of Anthropology, Texas A&M University, College Station.

Dockall, J.

1997 Wear Traces and Projectile Impact: A Review of the Experimental and Archaeological Evidence. *Journal of Field Archaeology* 24:321–331.

Donahue, R. E.

1994 The Current State of Lithic Microwear Research. In *Stories in Stone,* edited by N. Ashton and A. David, pp. 156–168. Lithic Studies Society, London.

Donahue, R. E., and D. B. Burroni
2004 Lithic Microwear Analysis and the Formation of Archaeological Assemblages. In *Lithics in Action,* edited by E. A. Walker, F. Wenban-Smith, and F. Healy, pp. 140–148. Oxbow Books, Oxford.

Dragoo, D. W.
1973 Wells Creek: An Early Man Site in Stewart County, Tennessee. *Archaeology of Eastern North America* 1:1–56.

Driese, S. G., Z.-H. Li, and L. D. McKay
2008 Evidence for Multiple, Episodic, Mid-Holocene Hypsithermal Recorded in Two Soil Profiles Along an Alluvial Floodplain Catena, Southeastern Tennessee, USA. *Quaternary Research* 69:276–291.

Driskell, B. N.
1996 Stratified Late Pleistocene and Early Holocene Deposits at Dust Cave, Northwestern Alabama. In *The Paleoindian and Early Archaic Southeast,* edited by D. G. Anderson and K. E. Sassaman, pp. 315–330. The University of Alabama Press, Tuscaloosa.
1998 An Assessment of Use-Wear Traces on Chipped Stone Artifacts. In *Wilson-Leonard: An 11,000-Year Archaeology Record of Hunter-Gatherers in Central Texas: III. Artifacts and Special Artifacts Studies,* edited by M. B. Collins, pp. 732–743. Studies in Archeology 31. Texas Archeological Research Laboratory, University of Texas, Austin.

Drye, C. M.
1998 An Analysis and Interpretation of the Archaic Projectile Point Sequence from Lowder's Ferry, Stanly County, North Carolina. *North Carolina Archaeology* 47:34–65.

Dunnell, R. C.
1971 *Systematics in Prehistory.* Free Press, New York.
1978 Style and Function: A Fundamental Dichotomy. *American Antiquity* 43:192–202.
1982 Science, Social Science and Common Sense. *Journal of Anthropological Research* 38:1–25.
1989 Aspects of the Application of Evolutionary Theory in Archaeology. In *Archaeological Thought in America,* edited by C. C. Lamberg-Karlovsky, pp. 35–49. Cambridge University Press, Cambridge.
1999 The Concept of Waste in an Evolutionary Archaeology. *Journal of Anthropological Archaeology* 18:243–250.
2005 Measuring Relatedness. In *Mapping Our Ancestors: Phylogenetic Approaches in Anthropology and Prehistory,* edited by C. P. Lipo, M. J. O'Brien, M. Collard, and S. J. Shennan, pp. 109–118. Transaction, New Brunswick, New Jersey.

Dunnell, R. C., and J. K. Stein
1989 Theoretical Issues in the Interpretation of Microartifacts. *Geoarchaeology: An International Journal* 4:31–42.

Dunning, A. B.
1964 The Tallahatta Formation in Clarke County, Alabama. *Journal of Alabama Archaeology* 10(2):50–60.

Edmonds, J. L.
2009 Mobility and Population Change in Northeast Mississippi: An Object-Based Seriation of Projectile Points as a Relative Paleodemographic Indicator. Unpublished Master's thesis, Department of Anthropology and Middle Eastern Cultures, Mississippi State University.

Eerkens, J. W., J. R. Ferguson, M. D. Glascock, C. E. Skinner, and S. A. Waechter
2007 Reduction Strategies and Geochemical Characterization of Lithic Assemblages: A Comparison of Three Case Studies from Western North America. *American Antiquity* 72:585–597.

Ellerbusch, E. C.
2004 Paleoamerican Prismatic Blade Economy from the Nuckolls Site (40Hs60), Lower Tennessee River Valley, Tennessee. *Current Research in the Pleistocene* 21:35–38.

Ellis, C., A. C. Goodyear III, D. F. Morse, and K. B. Tankersley
1998 Archaeology of the Pleistocene-Holocene Transition in Eastern North America. *Quaternary International* 49/50:151–160.

Emerson, T. E., and D. L. McElrath
2009 The Eastern Woodlands Archaic and the Tyranny of Theory. In *Archaic Societies: Diversity and Complexity across the Midcontinent,* edited by T. E. Emerson, D. L. McElrath, and A. C. Fortier, pp. 23–38. State University of New York Press, Albany.

Eren, M. I.
2005 Northeastern North American Paleoindian Uniface Types: Techno-Typological Analyses of Unifacial Stone Tools from Paleo Crossing (33ME274), Ohio. Unpublished undergraduate honors thesis, Harvard College, Cambridge, Massachusetts.

Eren, M. I., M. Dominguez-Rodrigo, S. L. Kuhn, D. S. Adler, I. Le, and O. Bar-Yosef
2005 Defining and Measuring Reduction in Unifacial Stone Tools. *Journal of Archaeological Science* 32:1190–1201.

Eren, M. I., A. Greenspan, and C. G. Sampson
2008 Are Upper Paleolithic Blade Cores More Productive than Middle Paleolithic Discoidal Cores? A Replication Experiment. *Journal of Human Evolution* 55(6):952–961.

Evans, A. A., and R. E. Donahue
2005 The Elemental Chemistry of Lithic Microwear: An Experiment. *Journal of Archaeological Science* 32:1733–1740.

Faught, M. K.
2006 Paleoindian Archaeology in Florida and Panama. In *Paleoindian Archaeology: A Hemispheric Perspective,* edited by J. E. Morrow and C. Gnecco, pp. 164–183. University Press of Florida, Tallahassee.
2008 Archaeological Roots of Human Diversity in the New World: A Compilation of Accurate and Precise Radiocarbon Ages from Earliest Sites. *American Antiquity* 73:670–698.

Ferring, C. R. (editor)
2001 *The Archaeology and Paleoecology of the Aubrey Clovis Site (41DN479), Denton*

County, Texas. Center for Environmental Archaeology, University of North Texas, Denton. Submitted to U.S. Army Corps of Engineers, Fort Worth District, Contract No. DACW63-86-C-0098. Copies available from www.StormingMedia.us.

Fisher, A., P. V. Hansen, and P. Rasmussen

1984 Macro and Micro Wear Traces on Lithic Projectile Points: Experimental Results and Prehistoric Examples. *Journal of Field Archaeology* 3:19–46.

Fladmark, K. R.

1982 Microdebitage Analysis: Initial Considerations. *Journal of Archaeological Science* 9:205–220.

Flannery, K. V.

1968 Archaeological Systems Theory and Early Mesoamerica. In *Anthropological Archaeology in the Americas,* edited by B. J. Meggars, pp. 67–87. Anthropological Society of America, Washington, D.C.

Flenniken, J. J.

1981 *Replicative Systems Analysis: A Model Applied to the Vein Quartz Artifacts from the Hoko River Site.* Reports of Investigation No. 59. Washington State University, Laboratory of Anthropology, Pullman.

Flenniken, J. J., and E. G. Garrison

1975 Thermally Altered Novaculite and Stone Tool Manufacturing Techniques. *Journal of Field Archaeology* 2:125–131.

Flenniken, J. J., and J. C. Haggerty

1979 Trampling as an Agency in the Formation of Edge Damage: An Experiment in Lithic Technology. *Northwest Anthropological Research Notes* 13:208–214.

Franklin, J. D.

1999 The Rime of the Ancient Miners. Unpublished Master's thesis, Department of Anthropology, University of Tennessee, Knoxville.

2001 Excavating and Analyzing Prehistoric Lithic Quarries: An Example from 3rd Unnamed Cave, Tennessee. *Midcontinental Journal of Archaeology* 26:199–217.

2002 The Prehistory of Fentress County, Tennessee: An Archaeological Survey. Ph.D. dissertation, Department of Anthropology, University of Tennessee, Knoxville. University Microfilms, Ann Arbor.

2008 Luminescence Dates and Woodland Ceramics from Rock Shelters on the Upper Cumberland Plateau of Tennessee. *Tennessee Archaeology* 3(1):87–100.

Franklin, J. D., M. A. Hays, L. M. Langston, and J. N. Godsey

2008 A Diachronic Perspective on Lithic Technology and Function at Eagle Drink Bluff Shelter, Upper Cumberland Plateau, Tennessee. Paper presented at the 73rd Annual Meeting of the Society for American Archaeology, Vancouver.

Franklin, J. D., and J. F. Simek

2008 Core Refitting and the Accuracy of Techniques for Aggregate Lithic Analyses: The Case of 3rd Unnamed Cave, Tennessee. *Southeastern Archaeology* 27:108–121.

Freeman, A. K. L., E. E. Smith Jr., and K. B. Tankersley

1996 A Stone's Throw from Kimmswick: Clovis Period Research in Kentucky. In *The Paleoindian and Early Archaic Southeast,* edited by D. G. Anderson and K. E. Sassaman, pp. 384–403. The University of Alabama Press, Tuscaloosa.

Frison, G. C., and B. A. Bradley

1980 *Folsom Tools and Technology at the Hanson Site, Wyoming.* University of New Mexico Press, Albuquerque.

Futato, E. M.

1996 A Synopsis of Paleoindian and Early Archaic Research in Alabama. In *The Paleoindian and Early Archaic Southeast,* edited by D. G. Anderson and K. E. Sassaman, pp. 299–314. The University of Alabama Press, Tuscaloosa.

Gatus, T.

1980 Appendix C: Chert Descriptions. In *Taylorsville Lake, Kentucky, Archaeological Resources Survey and Evaluation, Season II,* by J. H. Sorensen, M. B. Collins, T. W. Gatus, S. Grant, R. Levy, C. R. Norville, N. O'Malley, J. Riesenweber, and M. Stafford, pp. 571–593. Archaeological Report 24. University of Kentucky, Department of Anthropology, Lexington.

1981 The Hall Shelter: A Multi-component Site in Southeastern Kentucky. Unpublished Master's thesis, Department of Anthropology, University of Kentucky, Lexington.

1985 Appendix D: Chert Resource Utilization. In *Prehistoric and Historic Sites Archaeology in the Proposed Yatesville Reservoir, Lawrence County, Kentucky,* by C. M. Niquette and T. K. Donham, pp. 420–431. Contract Publication Series 85-13. Cultural Resource Analysts, Inc., Lexington, Kentucky.

1987 Chert Type Descriptions. In *A Phase I Archaeological Examination of the Danville Tank Site (15BO16), Boyle County, Kentucky,* by R. D. Boedy and C. M. Niquette, pp. 153–159. Contract Publication Series 87-07. Cultural Resource Analysts, Inc., Lexington, Kentucky.

Geneste, J. M.

1985 *Analyse lithique d'industries Moustériennes du Périgord: Une approche technologique du comportement des groupes humains au Paléolithique Moyen.* Thèse de Doctorat, Université de Bordeaux I, Bordeaux, France.

1991 Systèmes techniques de production lithique: Variations techno-économiques dans les processus de réalisation des outillages paléolithiques. *Techniques et Culture* 17-18:1–35.

Geneste, J. M., and S. Maury

1997 Contributions of Multidisciplinary Experimentation to the Study of Upper Paleolithic Projectile Points. In *Projectile Technology,* edited by H. Knecht, pp. 165–189. Plenum Press, New York.

Gibson, J. L.

1994 Empirical Characterization of Exchange Systems in Lower Mississippi Valley Prehistory. In *Prehistoric Exchange Systems in North America,* edited by T. G. Baugh and J. E. Ericson, pp. 127–175. Plenum Press, New York.

2006 Navels of the Earth: Sedentism in the Early Mound Building Cultures in the Lower Mississippi Valley. *World Archaeology* 38:311–329.

Gifford-Gonzalez, D. P., D. B. Damrosch, D. R. Damrosch, J. Pryor, and R. L. Thunen

1985 The Third Dimension in Site Structure: An Experiment in Trampling and Vertical Dispersal. *American Antiquity* 50:803–818.

Giliberti, J. A.
1995 San Patrice and Related Early Tool Assemblage from the Beaumont Gravel Pit Site (22-PE-504): A Late Paleoindian Site in South Mississippi. Unpublished Master's thesis, Department of Anthropology and Sociology, University of Southern Mississippi, Hattiesburg.

Goldberg, P., and S. C. Sherwood
2006 Deciphering Human Prehistory Through the Geoarchaeological Study of Cave Sediments. *Evolutionary Anthropology* 15:20–36.

Goodyear, A. C., III
1974 *The Brand Site: A Techno-functional Study of a Dalton Site in Northeast Arkansas.* Research Series 7. Arkansas Archeological Society, Fayetteville.
1979 *A Hypothesis for the Use of Cryptocrystalline Raw Materials among Paleoindian Groups of North America.* Research Manuscript 156. South Carolina Institute of Archaeology and Anthropology, Columbia.
1993 Tool Kit Entropy and Bipolar Reduction: A Study of Inter-assemblage Lithic Variability among Paleo-Indian Sites in the Northeastern United States. *North American Archaeologist* 14:1–23.
1997 Update: Savannah River Quarry Site. *Mammoth Trumpet* 12(2). Center for the Study of The First Americans, Oregon State University, Corvallis.
1999 The Early Holocene Occupation of the Southeastern United States: A Geoarchaeological Summary. In *Ice Age Peoples of North America,* edited by R. Bonnichsen and K. L. Turnmire, pp. 432–481. Oregon State University Press, Corvallis.
2005 Evidence of Pre-Clovis Sites in the Eastern United States. In *Paleoamerican Origins: Beyond Clovis,* edited by R. Bonnichsen, B. T. Lepper, D. Stanford, and M. R. Waters, pp. 103–112. Center for the Study of the First Americans, Texas A&M University, College Station.

Goodyear, A. C., III, and T. Charles
1984 *An Archaeological Survey of Chert Quarries in Western Allendale County, South Carolina.* Research Manuscript Series 195. South Carolina Institute of Archaeology and Anthropology, Columbia.

Goodyear, A. C., III, and J. E. Foss
1993 The Stratigraphic Significance of Paleosols at Smith Lake Creek (38AL135) for the Study of the Pleistocene-Holocene Transition in the Savannah River Valley. In *Proceedings of the First International Conference on Pedo-Archaeology,* edited by J. E. Foss, M. E. Timpson, and M. W. Morris, pp. 27–40. Special Publication 93-03, University of Tennessee, Knoxville.

Goodyear, A. C., III, D. S. Miller, and A. M. Smallwood
2007 Introducing Clovis at the Topper Site, 38AL23, Allendale County, South Carolina. Paper presented at the 72nd Annual Meeting of the Society for American Archaeology, Austin.

Goodyear, A. C., III, and K. Steffy
2003 Evidence of a Clovis Occupation at the Topper Site, 38AL23, Allendale County, South Carolina. *Current Research in the Pleistocene* 20:23–25.

Gorman, M., and D. S. Leigh
2004 Wet Early to Middle Holocene Conditions on the Upper Coastal Plain of North Carolina, USA. *Quaternary Research* 61:256–264.

Goryacheva, I. G.
1998 *Contact Mechanics in Tribology.* Kluwer Academic, Dordrecht, Netherlands.

Grace, R.
1989 *Interpreting the Function of Stone Tools: The Quantification and Computerisation of Microwear Analysis.* BAR International Series 474. Archaeopress, Oxford.

Graham, C. D. R.
1990 Geology. In *Archaeological Site Distributions on the Cumberland Plateau of Eastern Kentucky,* edited by T. Sussenbach, pp. 13–24. Program for Cultural Resource Assessment, University of Kentucky, Lexington.

Granger, J. E., E. E. Hardesty, and A. T. Bader
1992 *Phase III Data Recovery Archaeology at Habich Site (15JF550) and Associated Manifestations at Guthrie Beach, Jefferson County, Kentucky: I. The Excavations.* Report of Investigations 90-2. Archaeological Resources Consultant Services, Louisville.

Green, F. E.
1963 The Clovis Blades: An Important Addition to the Llano Complex. *American Antiquity* 29:145–165.

Greiser, S. T.
1977 Micro-Analysis of Wear Patterns on Projectile Points and Knives from the Jurgens Site, Kersey, Colorado. *Plains Anthropologist* 22:107–116.

Gremillion, K. J.
1998 Three Thousand Years of Human Activity at the Cold Oak Shelter. In *Current Archaeological Research in Kentucky,* Vol. 5, edited by C. D. Hockensmith, K. C. Carstens, C. Stout, and S. J. Rivers, pp. 1–14. Kentucky Heritage Council, Frankfort.

Hall, C. L., and W. E. Klippel
1988 A Polythetic-Satisficer Approach to Prehistoric Natural Shelter Selection in Middle Tennessee. *Midcontinental Journal of Archaeology* 13:159–186.

Hall, C. T., and M. L. Larson (editors)
2004 *Aggregate Analysis in Chipped Stone.* University of Utah Press, Salt Lake City.

Hardison, J.
2007 *31MG328 Site Excavation Research Design and Guide.* USDA North Carolina National Forests, Troy.

Harmon, M. A., and R. J. Snedeker
1993 *Heritage Resources Survey for the Badin Lake Recreation Development, Montgomery County, North Carolina.* USDA National Forests, Asheville, North Carolina.

Hassan, F. A.
1978 Sediments in Archaeology: Methods and Implications for Paleoenvironmental and Cultural Analysis. *Journal of Field Archaeology* 5:197–213.

Hayden, B.
1980 Confusion in the Bipolar World: Bashed Pebbles and Splintered Pieces. *Lithic Technology* 9:2–7.
Hayden, B. (editor)
1979 *Lithic Use-Wear Analysis.* Academic Press, New York.
Hayden, B., N. Franco, and J. Spafford
1996 Evaluating Lithic Strategies and Design Criteria. In *Stone Tools: Theoretical Insights into Human Prehistory,* edited by G. H. Odell, pp. 9–45. Plenum Press, New York.
Hayden, B., and J. Kamminga
1979 An Introduction to Use-Wear: The First Conference on Lithic Use-Wear. In *Lithic Use-Wear Analysis,* edited by B. Hayden, pp. 1–13. Academic Press, New York.
Haynes, G.
2002 *The Early Settlement of North America: The Clovis Era.* Cambridge University Press, Cambridge.
Hays, M.
1998 A Functional Analysis of the Magdalenian Assemblage from Grotte XVI Dordogne, France. Unpublished Ph.D. dissertation, Department of Anthropology, University of Tennessee, Knoxville.
Hays, M., and G. Lucas
2001 Experimental Investigations of Aurignacian Dufour Bladelets. In *Questioning the Answers: Resolving Fundamental Problems of the Early Upper Paleolithic,* edited by M. Hays and P. Thacker, pp. 109–116. BAR International Series 1005. British Archaeological Reports, Oxford.
Healdan, D. M.
1995 Identifying Lithic Reduction Loci with Size-Graded Macrodebitage: A Multivariate Approach. *American Antiquity* 60:689–699.
Hemmings, E. T.
1987 The Horner Site Debitage. In *The Horner Site: The Type Site of the Cody Cultural Complex,* edited by G. C. Frison and L. C. Todd, pp. 435–442. Academic Press, Orlando, Florida.
Henderson, A. G.
2008 Fort Ancient Period. In *The Archaeology of Kentucky: An Update,* edited by D. Pollack, pp. 739–902. Kentucky Heritage Council, Frankfort.
Henry, D. O., and G. H. Odell (editors)
1989 *Alternative Approaches to Lithic Analysis.* Archeological Papers of the American Anthropological Association No. 1. American Anthropological Association, Arlington, Virginia.
Herndon, R. L.
2005 *Phase III Investigations at the Elk Fork Site (15MO140), Morgan County, Kentucky.* Contract Publication No. 03-217. Cultural Resource Analysts, Inc., Lexington, Kentucky.
Hofman, J. L.
2003 Tethered to Stone or Freedom to Move: Folsom Biface Technology in Regional

Perspective. In *Multiple Approaches to the Study of Bifacial Technologies,* edited by M. Soressi and H. L. Dibble, pp. 229–250. University Museum Monograph 115. University of Pennsylvania Museum of Archaeology and Anthropology, Philadelphia.

Högberg, A., and D. Olausson

2007 *Scandinavian Flint: An Archaeological Perspective.* Aarhus University Press, Aarhus, Denmark.

Holmes, W. H.

1894 Natural History of Flaked Stone Implements. In *Memoirs of the International Congress of Anthropology,* edited by C. S. Wake, pp. 120–139. Schulte, Chicago.

Honea, K. H.

1965 The Bipolar Flaking Technique in Texas and New Mexico. *Texas Archeological Society Bulletin* 36:259–267.

Howard, C. D.

1990 The Clovis Point: Characteristics and Type Description. *Plains Anthropologist* 35:255–262.

Huckell, B. B.

2007 Clovis Lithic Technology: A View from the Upper San Pedro Valley. In *Murray Springs: A Clovis Site with Multiple Activity Areas in the San Pedro Valley, Arizona,* edited by C. V. Haynes Jr. and B. B. Huckell, pp. 170–213. Anthropological Papers of the University of Arizona No. 71. University of Arizona Press, Tucson.

Hudler, D. B.

2003 Use-Wear Analysis of Selected Pavo Real Artifacts. In *Pavo Real (41BX52): A Paleoindian and Archaic Camp and Workshop on the Balcones Escarpment, South-Central Texas,* edited by M. B. Collins, D. B. Hudler, and S. L. Black, pp. 253–266. Studies in Archeology 41, Texas Archeological Research Laboratory, University of Texas at Austin, and Archeological Studies Program Report 50, Environmental Affairs Division, Texas Department of Transportation.

Hull, K.

1987 Identification of Cultural Site Formation Processes Through Microdebitage Analysis. *American Antiquity* 52:772–783.

Ingbar, E. E., M. L. Larson, and B. A. Bradley

1989 A Non-typological Approach to Debitage Analysis. In *Experiments in Lithic Technology,* edited by D. S. Amick and R. P. Mauldin, pp. 67–99. BAR International Series 528. British Archaeological Reports, Oxford.

Inizian, M., H. Roche, and J. Tixier

1992 *Technology of Knapped Stone.* Cercle de Recherches et d'Études Préhistoriques, Meudon, France.

Irwin, H. T., and H. M. Wormington

1970 Paleo-Indian Tool Types in the Great Plains. *American Antiquity* 35:24–34.

Ison, C.

1988 The Cold Oak Shelter: Providing a Better Understanding of the Terminal Archaic. In *Paleoindian and Archaic Research in Kentucky,* edited by C. D. Hockensmith, D. Pollack, and T. N. Sanders, pp. 125–138. Kentucky Heritage Council, Frankfort.

Jackson, H. E., and S. L. Scott

1992 The G.W.O. Site (22-Jo-568), An Early Archaic Site in Jones County, Mississippi. *Mississippi Archaeology* 27(2):56–75.

Janzen, D. E.

1977 An Examination of Late Archaic Development in the Falls of the Ohio Area. In *For the Director: Research Essays in Honor of James B. Griffin*, edited by C. E. Cleland, pp. 123–143. Anthropological Papers No. 61. University of Michigan, Ann Arbor.

Jefferies, R. W.

1996 Hunters and Gatherers after the Ice Age. In *Kentucky Archaeology*, edited by R. B. Lewis, pp. 39–77. University Press of Kentucky, Lexington.

1997 Middle Archaic Bone Pins: Evidence of Mid-Holocene Regional-Scale Social Groups in the Southern Midwest. *American Antiquity* 62:464–487.

2008a *Holocene Hunter-Gatherers of the Lower Ohio River Valley*. The University of Alabama Press, Tuscaloosa.

2008b Archaic Period. In *The Archaeology of Kentucky: An Update*, edited by D. Pollack, pp. 193–338. Kentucky Heritage Council, Frankfort.

2009 Archaic Cultures of Western Kentucky. In *Archaic Societies: Diversity and Complexity across the Midcontinent*, edited by T. E. Emerson, D. L. McElrath, and A. C. Fortier, pp. 635–666. State University of New York Press, Albany.

Jennings, T. A.

2008 *San Patrice Technology and Mobility across the Plains-Woodland Border*. Memoir 12, Oklahoma Anthropological Society; R. E. Bell Monographs in Anthropology No. 5, Sam Noble Oklahoma Museum of Natural History, Norman.

Jennings, T. A., C. D. Pevny, and W. A. Dickens

2010 A Biface and Blade Core Efficiency Experiment: Implications for Early Paleoindian Technological Organization. *Journal of Archaeological Science* 37:2155–2164.

Jeske, R. J.

1992 Energetic Efficiency and Lithic Technology: An Upper Mississippian Example. *American Antiquity* 57:467–481.

Jeske, R. J., and R. Lurie

1993 The Archaeological Visibility of Bipolar Technology: An Example from the Koster Site. *Midcontinental Journal of Archaeology* 18:131–160.

Jodry, M.

1998 The Possible Design of Folsom Ultrathin Bifaces as Filet Knives for Jerky Production. *Current Research in the Pleistocene* 15:75–77.

Johnson, G. A.

1977 Aspects of Regional Analysis in Archeology. *Annual Review of Anthropology* 6:479–508.

Johnson, H. B., and S. C. Meeks

1994 Source Areas and Prehistoric Use of Fort Payne Chert. *Journal of Alabama Archaeology* 40:66–78.

Johnson, J. K.

1983 Poverty Point Period Blade Technology in the Yazoo Basin, Mississippi. *Lithic Technology* 12(3):49–56.

1984 Measuring Prehistoric Quarry Site Activity in Northeastern Mississippi. In *Prehistoric Chert Exploitation: Studies from the Midcontinent,* edited by B. M. Butler and E. E. May, pp. 225–236. Occasional Paper No. 2. Center for Archaeological Investigations, Southern Illinois University, Carbondale.

1989 The Utility of Production Trajectory Modeling as a Framework for Regional Analysis. In *Alternative Approaches to Lithic Analysis,* edited by D. O. Henry and G. H. Odell, pp. 119–138. Archeological Papers of the American Anthropological Association No. 1. American Anthropological Association, Arlington, Virginia.

1993a Lithics. In *The Development of Southeastern Archaeology,* edited by J. K. Johnson, pp. 36–52. The University of Alabama Press, Tuscaloosa.

1993b Poverty Point Period Crystal Drill Bits, Microliths, and Social Organization in the Yazoo Basin, Mississippi. *Southeastern Archaeology* 12:59–64.

2000 Beads, Microdrills, Bifaces, and Blades from Watson Brake. *Southeastern Archaeology* 19:95–104.

Johnson, J. K., and S. O. Brookes

1988 Rocks from the Northeast: Archaic Exchange in North Mississippi. *Mississippi Archaeology* 23:53–63.

Johnson, J. K., and C. A. Morrow

1981 Thermal Alteration and Fort Payne Chert. *Journal of Alabama Archaeology* 27:141–149.

Johnson, J. K., and C. A. Morrow (editors)

1987 *The Organization of Core Technology.* Westview Press, Boulder, Colorado.

Justice, N. D.

1987 *Stone Age Spear and Arrow Points of the Midcontinental and Eastern United States.* Indiana University Press, Bloomington.

Kalin, J.

1981 Stem Point Manufacture and Debitage Recovery. *Archaeology of Eastern North America* 9:134–175.

Kantner, J.

2005 Regional Analysis in Archaeology. In *Handbook of Archaeological Methods,* edited by C. Chippindale and H. D. G. Maschner, pp. 1179–1223. AltaMira, Walnut Creek, California.

Kay, M.

1996 Microwear Analysis of Some Clovis and Experimental Stone Tools. In *Stone Tools: Theoretical Insights into Human Prehistory,* edited by G. H. Odell, pp. 315–344. Plenum Press, New York.

1998 Scratchin' the Surface: Stone Artifact Microwear Evaluation. In *Wilson-Leonard: An 11,000-Year Archaeology Record of Hunter-Gatherers in Central Texas: III. Artifacts and Special Artifacts Studies,* edited by M. B. Collins, pp. 743–794. Studies

in Archeology 31. Texas Archeological Research Laboratory, University of Texas, Austin.
1999 Microscopic Attributes of the Keven Davis Blades. In *Clovis Blade Technology: A Comparative Study of the Keven Davis Cache, Texas,* edited by M. B. Collins, pp. 126–143. University of Texas Press, Austin.

Keeley, L.
1974 Technique and Methodology in Microwear Studies: A Critical Review. *World Archaeology* 5:323–336.
1980 *Experimental Determination of Stone Tool Uses: A Microwear Analysis.* University of Chicago Press, Chicago.
1982 Hafting and Retooling: Effects on the Archaeological Record. *American Antiquity* 47:798–809.
1988 Hunter-Gatherer Economic Complexity and "Population Pressure": A Cross Cultural Analysis. *Journal of Anthropological Archaeology* 7:373–411.

Keeley, L. H., and M. Newcomer
1977 Microwear Analysis of Experimental Flint Tools: A Test Case. *Journal of Archaeological Science* 4:29–62.

Kelly, R. L.
1988 The Three Sides of a Biface. *American Antiquity* 53:717–734.
1994 Some Thoughts on Future Directions in the Study of Stone Tool Technological Organization. In *The Organization of North American Prehistoric Chipped Stone Tool Technologies,* edited by P. J. Carr, pp. 132–136. Archaeological Series No. 7. International Monographs in Prehistory, Ann Arbor, Michigan.

Kelly, R. L., and L. C. Todd
1988 Coming into the Country: Early Paleoindian Hunting and Mobility. *American Antiquity* 53:231–244.

Kidder, T. R., and K. E. Sassaman
2009 The View from the Southeast. In *Archaic Societies: Diversity and Complexity across the Midcontinent,* edited by T. E. Emerson, D. L. McElrath, and A. C. Fortier, pp. 667–694. State University of New York Press, Albany.

Kimball, L. R.
1994 Microwear Analysis of Late and Terminal Archaic Projectile Points from the Padula Site (36NM15), Pennsylvania. *Journal of Middle Atlantic Archaeology* 10:169–179.
1996 Early Archaic Settlement and Technology: Lesson from Tellico. In *The Paleoindian and Early Archaic Southeast,* edited by D. G. Anderson and K. E. Sassaman, pp. 149–186. The University of Alabama Press, Tuscaloosa.

Knudson, R.
1979 Inference and Imposition in Lithic Analysis. In *Lithic Use-Wear Analysis,* edited by B. Hayden, pp. 269–281. Academic Press, New York.

Koldehoff, B.
1987 The Cahokia Flake Tool Industry: Socio-Economic Implications for Late Prehistory in the Central Mississippi Valley. In *The Organization of Core Tech-*

nology, edited by J. K. Johnson and C. A. Morrow, pp. 151–186. Westview Press, Boulder, Colorado.

Kruskal, W. H., and W. A. Wallis

1952 Use of Ranks in One-Criterion Variance Analysis. *Journal of the American Statistical Association* 47:583–621.

Kuhn, S. L.

1991 "Unpacking" Reduction: Lithic Raw Material Economy in the Mousterian of West-Central Italy. *Journal of Anthropological Archaeology* 10:76–106.

1992 On Planning and Curated Technologies in the Middle Paleolithic. *Journal of Anthropological Research* 48:185–214.

1994 A Formal Approach to the Design and Assembly of Mobile Toolkits. *American Antiquity* 59:426–442.

1995 *Mousterian Lithic Technology: An Ecological Perspective.* Princeton University Press, Princeton, New Jersey.

2004 Upper Paleolithic Raw Material Economics at Ucagizli Cave, Turkey. *Journal of Anthropological Archaeology* 23:431–448.

Kuijt, I., W. C. Prentiss, and D. L. Pokotylo

1995 Bipolar Reduction: An Experimental Study of Debitage Variability. *Lithic Technology* 20(2):116–127.

LaMoreaux, H. K., G. A. Brook, and J. A. Knox

2009 Late Pleistocene and Holocene Environments of the Southern United States from the Stratigraphy and Pollen Content of a Peat Deposit on the Georgia Plain. *Palaeogeography, Palaeoclimatology, Palaeoecology* 280(3-4):300–312.

Larson, M., and M. Kornfeld

1997 Chipped Stone Nodules: Theory, Method, and Examples. *Lithic Technology* 22:4–18

Lawrence, R. A.

1979 Experimental Evidence for the Significance of Attributes Used in Edge Damage Analysis. In *Lithic Use-Wear Analysis,* edited by B. Hayden, pp. 113–122. Academic Press, New York.

LeBlanc, R.

1992 Wedges, Pieces Esquillées, Bipolar Cores, and Other Things: An Alternative to Shott's View of Bipolar Industries. *North American Archaeologist* 13:1–14.

Ledbetter, R. J., D. G. Anderson, L. D. O'Steen, and D. T. Elliott

1996 Paleoindian and Early Archaic Research in Georgia. In *The Paleoindian and Early Archaic Southeast,* edited by D. G. Anderson and K. E. Sassaman, pp. 270–287. The University of Alabama Press, Tuscaloosa.

Leigh, D. S.

2008 Late Quaternary Climates and River Channels of the Atlantic Coastal Plain, Southeastern USA. *Geomorphology* 101:90–108.

Leroi-Gourhan, A.

1993 [1964] *Gesture and Speech.* Translated by A. B. Berger. MIT Press, Cambridge, Massachusetts.

Levi-Sala, I.
1986 Use-Wear and Post-Depositional Surface Modification: A Word of Caution. *Journal of Archaeological Science* 13:229–244.
1996 *A Study of Microscopic Polish on Flint Implements.* BAR International Series 629. Archaeopress, Oxford.

Lipo, C. P., M. E. Madsen, R. C. Dunnell, and T. Hunt
1997 Population Structure, Cultural Transmission, and Frequency Seriation. *Journal of Anthropological Archaeology* 16:301–333.

Liu, K. B., and M. L. Fearn
2000 Reconstruction of Prehistoric Landfall Frequencies of Catastrophic Hurricanes in Northwestern Florida from Lake Sediment Records. *Quaternary Research* 54:238–245.

Lopinot, N. H., and J. H. Ray
2007 Trampling Experiments in the Search for the Earliest Americans. *American Antiquity* 72:771–782.

Luchsinger, H. M.
2002 Micromorphological Analysis of the Sediments and Soils from the Gault Site, A Paleoindian Site in Central Texas. Unpublished Master's thesis, Department of Anthropology, Texas A&M University, College Station.

Luedtke, B. E.
1992 *An Archaeologist's Guide to Chert and Flint.* Archaeological Research Tools 7. Institute of Archaeology, University of California, Los Angeles.

Lumsden, D. N.
1988 Origin of the Fort Payne Formation (Lower Mississippian), Tennessee. *Southeastern Geology* 28:167–180.

MacDonald, G. F.
1968 *Debert: A Paleo-Indian Site in Central Nova Scotia.* Archeological Papers 16. National Museum of Canada, Ottawa.

Madsen, A. P.
1868 *Afbildninger af Danske Oldsager.* Copenhagen.

Magne, M. P. R.
1985 *Lithics and Livelihood: Stone Tool Technologies of Central and Southern Interior B.C.* Mercury Series No. 133. Archaeology Survey of Canada, Ottawa.
1989 Lithic Reduction Stages and Assemblage Formation Processes. In *Experiments in Lithic Technology,* edited by D. S. Amick and R. P. Mauldin, pp. 15–31. BAR International Series 528. British Archaeological Reports, Oxford.
2001 Debitage Analysis as a Scientific Tool for Archaeological Knowledge. In *Lithic Debitage: Context, Form, Meaning,* edited by W. Andrefsky Jr., pp. 21–31. University of Utah Press, Salt Lake City.

Mallouf, R. J.
1981 *A Case Study of Plow Damage to Chert Artifacts: The Brookeen Creek Cache, Hill County, Texas.* Report 33. Office of the State Archeologist, Texas Historical Commission, Austin.

Mandeville, M. D.
1973 A Consideration of the Thermal Pretreatment of Chert. *Plains Anthropologist* 18:177–202.

Mann, H. B., and D. R. Whitney
1947 On a Test of Whether One of Two Random Variables Is Stochastically Larger than the Other. *Annals of Mathematical Statistics* 18:50–60.

Marshall, S. B.
1985 Paleoindian Artifact Form and Function at Shawnee Minisink. In *Shawnee Minisink: A Stratified Paleoindian–Archaic Site in the Upper Delaware Valley of Pennsylvania,* edited by C. W. McNett Jr., pp. 165–209. Academic Press, London.

Masson, M.
1998 Analysis of Debitage. In *Wilson-Leonard: An 11,000-Year Archaeology Record of Hunter-Gatherers in Central Texas: III. Artifacts and Special Artifacts Studies,* edited by M. B. Collins, pp. 683–702. Studies in Archeology 31. Texas Archeological Research Laboratory, University of Texas, Austin.

Mate, C. M.
2008 *Tribology on the Small Scale: A Bottom Up Approach to Friction, Lubrication, and Wear.* Oxford University Press, Oxford.

Matthiassen, Th.
1937 Gudenaa-Kulturen. En Mesolitisk Inlands-bebyggelse i Jylland. *Aarböger,* pp. 1–186.

Maudlin, R. P., and D. S. Amick
1989 Investigation Patterning in Debitage from Experimental Bifacial Core Reduction. In *Experiments in Lithic Technology,* edited by D. S. Amick and R. P. Mauldin, pp. 189–200. BAR International Series 528. British Archaeological Reports, Oxford.

Maudsely, J. R.
1998 What's Your TQ (Tallahatta Quartzite) IQ? *Central States Archaeological Journal* 45:166–170.

McAvoy, J. M.
1992 *Nottoway River Survey: Part I. Clovis Settlement Patterns: The 30 Year Study of a Late Ice Age Hunting Culture on the Southern Interior Coastal Plain of Virginia.* Archaeological Society of Virginia Special Publication No. 28. Dietz Press, Richmond.

McBrearty, S., L. C. Bishop, T. Plummer, R. Dewar, and N. Conrad
1998 Tools Underfoot: Human Trampling as an Agent of Lithic Artifact Edge Modification. *American Antiquity* 63:108–129.

McElrath, D. L., A. C. Fortier, B. Koldehoff, and T. E. Emerson
2009 The American Bottom: An Archaic Cultural Crossroads. In *Archaic Societies: Diversity and Complexity across the Midcontinent,* edited by T. E. Emerson, D. L. McElrath, and A. C. Fortier, pp. 317–376. State University of New York Press, Albany.

McGahey, S. O.
1999 Use and Avoidance of Kosciusko Quartzite in Prehistoric Mississippi Flaked

Stone Assemblages. In *Raw Materials and Exchange in the Mid-South: Proceedings of the 16th Annual Mid-South Archaeological Conference, Jackson, Mississippi—June 3 and 4, 1995,* edited by E. Peacock and S. O. Brookes, pp. 1–11. Mississippi Department of Archives and History, Jackson.

2000 *Mississippi Projectile Point Guide.* Archaeological Report No. 31. Mississippi Department of Archives and History, Jackson.

McReynolds, T. E.

2005 Spatial and Temporal Patterning in the Distribution of North Carolina Projectile Points. *North Carolina Archaeology* 54:1–33.

Meeks, S. C.

2000 *The Use and Function of Late Middle Archaic Projectile Points in the Midsouth.* Report of Investigations 77. Office of Archaeological Services, Moundville, Alabama.

Meltzer, D. J.

1989 Was Stone Exchanged among Eastern North American Paleoindians? In *Eastern Paleoindian Lithic Resource Use,* edited by C. J. Ellis and J. C. Lothrop, pp. 11–39. Westview Press, New York.

Meltzer, D. J., and D. Cooper

2006 On Morphometric Differentiation of Clovis and Non-Clovis Blades. *Current Research in the Pleistocene* 23:143–145.

Merrill, R. K., D. E. Gann, and S. P. Jennings

1988 *Tishomingo County Geology and Mineral Resources.* Bulletin 127. Mississippi Department of Natural Resources, Bureau of Geology, Jackson.

Metcalfe, D., and K. R. Barlow

1992 A Model for Exploring the Optimal Trade-off Between Field Processing and Transport. *American Anthropologist* 94:340–356.

Metcalfe, D., and K. M. Heath

1990 Microrefuse and Site Structure: The Hearths and Floors of the Heartbreak Hotel. *American Antiquity* 55:781–796.

Michie, J. L.

1996 The Taylor Site: An Early Occupation in Central South Carolina. In *The Paleoindian and Early Archaic Southeast,* edited by D. G. Anderson and K. E. Sassaman, pp. 238–269. The University of Alabama Press, Tuscaloosa.

Miller, D. S.

2007 Site Formation Processes in an Upland Paleoindian Site: The 2005–2007 Topper Firebreak Excavations. Unpublished Master's thesis, Department of Anthropology, University of Tennessee, Knoxville.

Milliken, S., and M. Peresani

1998 *Lithic Technology: From Raw Material Procurement to Tool Production.* Proceedings of the Workshop No. 12 of the XIII International Congress of Prehistoric and Protohistoric Sciences, September 8–14, 1996, Forli, Italy.

Milne, S. B.

2009 Debitage Sample Size and Its Implications for Understanding Lithic Assemblage Variability. *Canadian Journal of Archaeology* 33:40–64.

Minchak, S. A.
2007 A Microwear Study of Clovis Blades from the Gault Site, Bell County, Texas. Unpublished Master's thesis, Department of Anthropology, Texas A&M University, College Station.

Moore, C., J. Irwin, and W. Covington
2004 Pine Barrens and Possum's Rations Revisited: Late Paleoindian and Early Archaic Settlement in the Carolina Sandhills. Paper presented at the 61st Annual Meeting of the Southeastern Archaeological Conference, St. Louis.

Morrow, J. E.
1995 Clovis Projectile Point Manufacture: A Perspective from the Ready Lincoln Hills Site, llJY46, Jersey County, Illinois. *Midcontinental Journal of Archaeology* 20:167–191.
1996 The Organization of Early Paleoindian Lithic Technology in the Confluence Region of the Mississippi, Illinois, and Missouri Rivers. Unpublished Ph.D. dissertation, Department of Anthropology, Washington University, St. Louis.

Morrow, T. A.
1997 A Chip off the Old Block: Alternative Approaches to Debitage Analysis. *Lithic Technology* 22:51–69.

Morse, D. F.
1973 Dalton Culture in Northeast Arkansas. *Florida Anthropologist* 26(1):23–38.

Müller, S.
1918 *Oldtidens Kunst i Danmark: 1. Stenalderens Kunst.* C. A. Reitzel, Copenhagen.

Nadel, D.
2001 Indoor/Outdoor Flint Knapping and Minute Debitage Remains: The Evidence from Ohalo II Submerged Camp (19.5 KY, Jordan Valley). *Lithic Technology* 26:118–137.

Nash, S. E.
1996 Is Curation a Useful Heuristic? In *Stone Tools: Theoretical Insights into Human Prehistory,* edited by G. H. Odell, pp. 81–100. Plenum Press, New York.

Nelson, Margaret C.
1991 The Study of Technological Organization. In *Archaeological Method and Theory,* Vol. 3, edited by M. B. Schiffer, pp. 57–100. University of Arizona Press, Tucson.

Nicholson, B. A.
1983 A Comparative Evaluation of Four Sampling Techniques and of the Reliability of Microdebitage as a Cultural Indicator in Regional Surveys. *Plains Anthropologist* 28:273–281.

Nielsen, A. E.
1991 Trampling the Archaeological Record: An Experimental Study. *American Antiquity* 56:483–503.

Norling-Christensen, H., and K. Bröste
1945 *Skeletgraven fra Korsør Nor et Menneskefund fra aeldre Stenalder.* Fra Nationalmuseets Arbejdsmark.

Odell, G. H.
1975 Micro-Wear in Perspective: A Sympathetic Response to Lawrence H. Keeley. *World Archaeology* 7:226–240.

1977 The Application of Micro-Wear Analysis to the Lithic Component of an Entire Prehistoric Settlement: Methods, Problems, and Functional Reconstructions. Unpublished Ph.D. dissertation, Department of Anthropology, Harvard University, Cambridge.

1981 The Mechanics of Use-Breakage of Stone Tools: Some Testable Hypotheses. *Journal of Field Archaeology* 8:197–209.

1989 Experiments in Lithic Reduction. In *Experiments in Lithic Technology,* edited by D. S. Amick and R. P. Mauldin, pp. 163–198. BAR International Series 528. British Archaeological Reports, Oxford.

1996a *Stone Tools and Mobility in the Illinois Valley: From Hunter-Gatherer Camps to Agricultural Villages.* Archaeological Series No. 10. International Monographs in Prehistory, Ann Arbor, Michigan.

1996b Economizing Behavior and the Concept of "Curation." In *Stone Tools: Theoretical Insights into Human Prehistory,* edited by G. H. Odell, pp. 51–80. Plenum Press, New York.

1998 Investigating Correlates of Sedentism and Domestication in Prehistoric North America. *American Antiquity* 63:553–571.

2000 Stone Tool Research at the End of the Millennium: Procurement and Technology. *Journal of Archaeological Research* 8:269–331.

2001 Stone Tool Research at the End of the Millennium: Classification, Function, and Behavior. *Journal of Archaeological Research* 9:45–100.

2003 *Lithic Analysis.* Kluwer Academic/Plenum, New York.

Odell, G. H. (editor)

1996 *Stone Tools: Theoretical Insights into Human Prehistory.* Plenum Press, New York.

Odell, G. H., and F. Cowan

1986 Experiments with Spears and Arrows on Animal Targets. *Journal of Field Archaeology* 3:195–212.

Odell, G. H., and F. Odell-Vereecken

1980 Verifying the Reliability of Lithic Use-Wear Assessments by "Blind Tests": The Low Power Approach. *Journal of Field Archaeology* 7:87–120.

Oliver, B. L.

1999 *Uwharrie Lithics Conference Projectile Point Chronology Workbook.* North Carolina Office of State Archaeology and State Historic Preservation Office, Raleigh.

Otvos, E. G.

2005 Holocene Aridity and Storm Phases, Gulf and Atlantic Coasts, USA. *Quaternary Research* 63:368–373.

Parry, W. J.

1994 Prismatic Blade Technologies in North America. In *The Organization of North American Prehistoric Chipped Stone Tool Technologies,* edited by P. J. Carr, pp. 87–98. Archaeological Series No. 7. International Monographs in Prehistory, Ann Arbor, Michigan.

Parry, W. J., and R. L. Kelly

1987 Expedient Core Technology and Sedentism. In *The Organization of Core Technology,* edited by J. K. Johnson and C. A. Morrow, pp. 285–305. Westview Press, Boulder, Colorado.

Patterson, L. W.
1990 Characteristics of Bifacial-Reduction Flake-Size Distribution. *American Antiquity* 55:550–558.
Payne, S.
1972 Partial Recovery and Sample Bias: The Results of Some Sieving Experiments. In *Papers in Economic Prehistory,* edited by E. Higgs, pp. 49–64. Cambridge University Press, Cambridge.
Peacock, E.
1989 Microdebitage from Cached Pitted Stones. *Mississippi Archaeology* 24:17–27.
2004 Using Macro- and Microartifacts to Investigate the Function and Duration of Short-Term Prehistoric Sites: An Example from North Mississippi. *Mississippi Archaeology* 39:3–24.
Peacock, E., P. J. Carr, S. E. Price, J. R. Underwood, W. L. Kingery, and M. Lilly
2010 Confirmation of an Archaic Period Mound in Southwest Mississippi. *Southeastern Archaeology* 29:355–368.
Peacock, E., and D. W. Fant
2002 Biomantle Formation and Artifact Translocation in Upland Sandy Soils: An Example from the Holly Springs National Forest, North-Central Mississippi, U.S.A. *Geoarchaeology* 17(1):91–114.
Pecora, A. M., III
1995 Technological Analysis of the Main Site Lithic Assemblage. In *Upper Cumberland Archaic and Woodland Period Archaeology at the Main Site (15BL35), Bell County, Kentucky,* Vol. II, by S. D. Creasman, pp. D-1–D-85. Contract Publication Series 94-56. Cultural Resource Analysts, Lexington, Kentucky.
Petersson, M.
1951 Mikrolithen als Pfeilspitzen: Ein Fund aus dem Lille Loshult Moor Ksp. Loshult, Skane. *Meddelanden fran Lunds Universitets Historiska Museum* 4:123–137.
Pevny, C. D.
2009 Clovis Debitage from Excavation Area 8 at the Gault Site (41BL323), Texas: Form and Function. Unpublished Ph.D. dissertation, Department of Anthropology, Texas A&M University, College Station.
Pineda, C. A., R. T. Martin, D. K. Hallbauer, L. Jacobson, V. M. Prozesky, and W. J. Przybylowicz
1997 Geochemical Microanalysis of Patina Layers on Rock Artefacts from the Central Karoo and Southern Free State, South Africa. *Nuclear Instruments and Methods in Physics Research* 130:628–635.
Plackett, R. L.
1983 Karl Pearson and the Chi-Square Test. *International Statistical Review* 51(1):59–72.
Plisson, H., and M. Mauger
1988 Chemical and Mechanical Alteration of Microwear Polishes: An Experimental Approach. *Helinium* 28:3–16.
Pollack, D. (editor)
2008 *The Archaeology of Kentucky: An Update.* Kentucky Heritage Council, Frankfort.
Potts, T. L.
2008 *Archaeology at Madison Park: Phase III Data Recovery at 1MT318, the Madison*

Park Site, Associated with the Bridge Replacement over the Western RR Overpass/ Sevenmile Creek, ALDOT Project BRF-153(11) & NHF-507(4), Montgomery County, Alabama (AHC 98-1029). Center for Archaeological Studies, University of South Alabama, Mobile.

2010 *Phase III Data Recovery at 1EE639, Wetumpka, Elmore County, AL. ALDOT Project No. STPOA-8834(600),* Vol. I. Center for Archaeological Studies, University of South Alabama, Mobile.

Prascimunas, M. M.

2007 Bifacial Cores and Flake Production Efficiency: An Experimental Test of Technological Assumptions. *American Antiquity* 72:334–348.

Price, S. E.

2008 *Phase III Archaeology at Plash Island, Archaeological Site 1BA134, in Baldwin County, Alabama.* Report submitted to the U.S. Army Corps of Engineers, Mobile District. Center for Archaeological Studies, Mobile, Alabama.

2009 *Archaeology at Orange Beach: Phase III Data Recovery at 1BA21, the Bayou St. John Site, Orange Beach, Baldwin County, Alabama: Vol. I. Report.* Report submitted to the U.S. Army Corps of Engineers, Mobile District. Center for Archaeological Studies, Mobile, Alabama.

2010 *Archaeology on the Tombigbee River: Phase III Data Recovery at 1CK56, the Corps Site, Clark County, Alabama.* Report submitted to the U.S. Army Corps of Engineers, Mobile District. Contract No. W91278-06-D-0066, Task Order 0016.

Price, T. D., and J. A. Brown

1985 Aspects of Hunter-Gatherer Complexity. In *Prehistoric Hunter-Gatherers: The Emergence of Cultural Complexity,* edited by T. D. Price and J. A. Brown, pp. 3–20. Academic Press, San Diego.

Pryor, J. H.

1988 The Effect of Human Trample Damage on Lithics: A Consideration of Crucial Variables. *Lithic Technology* 17:45–50.

Purdy, B. A.

1974 Investigations Concerning the Thermal Alteration of Silica Materials: An Archaeological Approach. *Tebiwa* 17:37–66.

1975 Fractures for the Archaeologist. In *Lithic Technology: Making and Using Stone Tools,* edited by E. Swanson, pp. 133–141. Mouton, The Hague.

Purdy, B. A., and H. K. Brooks

1971 Thermal Alteration of Silica Materials: An Archaeological Approach. *Science* 173:322–325.

Quinn, C. P., W. Andrefsky Jr., I. Kuijt, and B. Finlayson

2008 Stone Tool Perforating and Retouch Intensity: A Neolithic Case Study. In *Lithic Technology: Measures of Production, Use, and Curation,* edited by W. Andrefsky Jr., pp. 150–174. Cambridge University Press, Cambridge.

Quinn, R. L., B. D. Tucker, and J. Krigbaum

2008 Diet and Mobility in Middle Archaic Florida: Stable Isotopic and Faunal Evidence from the Harris Creek Archaeological Site (8V024), Tick Island. *Journal of Archaeological Science* 35:2346–2356.

Rabinowicz, E.
1995 *Friction and Wear of Materials,* 2nd ed. John Wiley and Sons, New York.

Rafferty, J.
1994 Gradual or Step-Wise Change: The Development of Sedentary Settlement Patterns in Northeast Mississippi. *American Antiquity* 59:405–425.

Rafferty, J., and M. Galaty
2002 Point-Counting, Petrography, and Context: Analysis of Ceramics from a Middle Woodland Site in Eastern Mississippi. *La Tinaja: A Newsletter of Archaeological Ceramics* 14:2–7.

Rasic, J. C.
2004 Debitage Taphonomy. In *Aggregate Analysis in Chipped Stone,* edited by C. T. Hall and M. L. Larson, pp. 112–138. University of Utah Press, Salt Lake City.

Rasic, J. C., and W. Andrefsky Jr.
2001 Alaskan Blade Cores as Specialized Components of Mobile Toolkits. Assessing Design Parameters and Toolkit Organization Through Debitage Analysis. In *Lithic Debitage: Context, Form, Meaning,* edited by W. Andrefsky Jr., pp. 61–79. University of Utah Press, Salt Lake City.

Rieth, C. B. (editor)
2008 *Current Approaches to the Analysis and Interpretation of Small Lithic Sites in the Northeast.* New York State Education Department, Albany.

Root, M. J., J. D. William, M. Kay, and L. K. Shifrin
1999 Folsom Ultrathin Biface and Radial Break Tools in the Knife River Flint Quarry Area. In *Folsom Lithic Technology: Explorations in Structure and Variation,* edited by D. S. Amick, pp. 144–168. Archaeological Series No. 12. International Monographs in Prehistory, Ann Arbor.

Rosen, A. M.
1993 Microartifacts as a Reflection of Cultural Factors in Site Formation. In *Formation Processes in Archaeological Context,* edited by P. Goldberg, D. T. Nash, pp. 141–148. Monographs in World Archaeology 17. Prehistory Press, Madison, Wisconsin.

Roth, B.
2009 An Evaluation of Lithic Debitage Sampling Strategies at an Archaic Site in Southern Arizona. *Lithic Technology* 34:11–26.

Roth, B., and H. Dibble
1998 The Production and Transport of Blanks and Tools at the French Middle Paleolithic Site of Combe-Capelle Bas. *American Antiquity* 63:47–62.

Rottländer, R.
1975 The Formation of Patina on Flint. *Archaeometry* 17:106–110.

Rule, P., and J. Evans
1985 The Relationship of Morphological Variation to Hafting Techniques among Paleoindian Endscrapers at the Shawnee Minisink Site. In *Shawnee Minisink: A Stratified Paleoindian–Archaic Site in the Upper Delaware Valley of Pennsylvania,* edited by C. W. McNett Jr., pp. 211–220. Academic Press, London.

Sagan, C.
1996 *The Demon-Haunted World: Science as a Candle in the Dark.* Random House, New York.

Sanders, T. N.
1990 *Adams: The Manufacturing of Flaked Stone Tools at a Paleoindian Site in Western Kentucky.* Persimmon Press Monographs in Archaeology, Buffalo, New York.

Sassaman, K. E.
1994 Changing Strategies of Biface Production in the South Carolina Coastal Plain. In *The Organization of North American Prehistoric Chipped Stone Tool Technologies,* edited by P. J. Carr, pp. 99–117. Archaeological Series No. 7. International Monographs in Prehistory, Ann Arbor, Michigan.
2001 Articulating Hidden Histories of the Mid-Holocene in the Southern Appalachians. In *Archaeology of the Appalachian Highlands,* edited by L. P. Sullivan and S. C. Prezzano, pp. 103–133. University of Tennessee Press, Knoxville.
2005 Structure and Practice in the Archaic Southeast. In *North American Archaeology,* edited by T. Pauketat and D. D. Loren, pp. 79–107. Blackwell, Oxford.

Sassaman, K. E., and D. G. Anderson
1995 *Middle and Late Archaic Archaeological Records of South Carolina: A Synthesis for Research and Resource Management.* Savannah River Archaeological Research Papers 6. Occasional Papers of the Savannah River Archaeological Research Program. South Carolina Institute of Archaeology and Anthropology, University of South Carolina, Columbia.

Saunders, J. W., R. D. Mandel, C. G. Sampson, C. M. Allen, E. T. Allen, D. A. Bush, J. K. Feathers, K. J. Gremillion, C. T. Hallmark, H. E. Jackson, J. K. Johnson, R. Jones, R. T. Saucier, G. L. Stringer, and M. F. Vidrine
2005 Watson Brake, a Middle Archaic Mound Complex in Northeast Louisiana. *American Antiquity* 70:631–668.

Schiffer, M. B.
1976 *Behavioral Archaeology.* Academic Press, New York.
1988 The Structure of Archaeological Theory. *American Antiquity* 53:461–485.
1996 *Formation Processes of the Archaeological Record.* University of Utah Press, Salt Lake City.

Schmalz, R. F.
1960 Chert and the Patination of Chert Artifacts. *Proceedings of the Prehistoric Society* 26:44–49.

Schnurrenberger, D., and A. L. Bryan
1985 A Contribution to the Study of the Naturefact/Artifact Controversy. In *Stone Tool Analysis,* edited by M. G. Plew, J. C. Woods, and M. G. Pavesic, pp. 133–159. University of New Mexico Press, Albuquerque.

Seibel, S. K.
2009 The Two Dogs Site (31PR92): A Middle Archaic and Woodland Period Lithic Quarry in Person County, North Carolina. *North Carolina Archaeology* 58:88–121.

Sellet, F.
1993 Chaîne Opératoire: The Concept and Its Applications. *Lithic Technology* 18(1-2): 106–112.
2004 Beyond the Point: Projectile Manufacture and Behavioral Inference. *Journal of Archaeological Science* 31:1553–1566.

2006 Two Steps Forward, One Step Back: The Inference of Mobility Patterns from Stone Tools. In *Archaeology and Ethnoarchaeology of Mobility,* edited by F. Sellet, R. Greaves, and P.-L. Yu, pp. 221–239. University Press of Florida, Gainesville.

Semenov, S. A.

1964 *Prehistoric Technology.* Translated by M. W. Thompson. Adams and Dart, Bath, England.

Shea, J. J.

1987 On Accuracy and Relevance in Lithic Usewear. *Lithic Technology* 16:44–50.

1999 Artifact Abrasion, Fluvial Processes, and "Living Floors" at the Early Paleolithic site of 'Ubeidiya (Jordan Valley, Israel). *Geoarchaeology* 14:191–207.

Shea, J. J., and J. D. Klenck

1993 An Experimental Investigation of the Effects of Trampling on the Results of Lithic Microwear Analysis. *Journal of Archaeological Science* 20:175–194.

Sheehan, M. S.

2002 Dietary Responses to Mid-Holocene Climatic Change. *North American Archaeologist* 23:117–143.

Sheets, P. D., and G. R. Muto

1972 Pressure Blades and Total Cutting Edge: An Experiment in Lithic Technology. *Science* 175:632–634.

Shen, C.

1999 Were "Utilized Flakes" Utilized? An Issue of Lithic Classification in Ontario Archaeology. *Ontario Archaeology* 68:63–73.

Shennan, S.

1988 *Quantifying Archaeology.* Edinburgh University Press, Edinburgh.

2008 Evolution in Archaeology. *Annual Review of Anthropology* 37:75–91.

Sheppard, P. J., and L. A. Pavlish

1992 Weathering of Archaeological Cherts: A Case Study from the Solomon Islands. *Geoarchaeology* 7:41–53.

Shermer, M.

1999 *How We Believe: The Search for God in an Age of Science.* W. H. Freeman, New York.

2001 *The Borderlands of Science: Where Sense Meets Nonsense.* Oxford University Press, New York.

2002 *Why People Believe Weird Things: Pseudoscience, Superstition, and Other Confusions of Our Time.* Henry Holt, New York.

2005 *Science Friction: Where the Known Meets the Unknown.* Times Books, New York.

Sherwood, S. C.

2001 Microartifacts. In *Earth Sciences and Archaeology,* edited by P. Goldberg, V. T. Holliday, and C. R. Ferring, pp. 327–351. Kluwer, New York.

2010 *The Geoarchaeological Analysis of Eagle Drink Rockshelter, Fentress County, Tennessee.* Report submitted to the Department of Sociology and Anthropology, East Tennessee State University, Johnson City, Tennessee.

Sherwood, S. C., B. N. Driskell, A. R. Randall, and S. C. Meeks

2004 Chronology and Stratigraphy at Dust Cave, Alabama. *American Antiquity* 69:533–554.

Sherwood, S. C., J. F. Simek, and R. R. Polhemus
1995 Artifact Size and Spatial Process: Macro- and Microartifacts in a Mississippian House. *Geoarchaeology: An International Journal* 10:429–455.
Shoberg, M.
2007 *The Clovis Tool Chest at Gault: Blades To Go.* Paper presented at the 72nd Annual Meeting of the Society for American Archaeology, Austin, Texas.
Shott, M. J.
1986 Technological Organization and Settlement Mobility: An Ethnographic Examination. *Journal of Anthropological Research* 42:15–51.
1989 Bipolar Industries: Ethnographic Evidence and Archaeological Implications. *North American Archaeologist* 10:1–24.
1993 Spears, Darts, and Arrows: Late Woodland Hunting Techniques in the Upper Ohio Valley. *American Antiquity* 58:425–443.
1994 Size and Form in the Analysis of Flake Debris: Review and Recent Approaches. *Journal of Archaeological Method and Theory* 1:69–110.
1996a Stage Versus Continuum in the Debris Assemblage from Production of a Fluted Biface. *Lithic Technology* 21:6–22.
1996b An Exegesis of the Curation Concept. *Journal of Anthropological Research* 52:259–280.
1996c Innovation and Selection in Prehistory: A Case Study from the American Bottom. In *Stone Tools: Theoretical Insights into Human Prehistory,* edited by G. H. Odell, pp. 279–304. Plenum Press, New York.
1997 Stones and Shafts Redux: The Metric Discrimination of Chipped-Stone Dart and Arrow Points. *American Antiquity* 62:86–101.
1999 On Bipolar Reduction and Splintered Pieces. *North American Archaeologist* 20:217–238.
2000 The Quantification Problem in Stone-Tool Assemblages. *American Antiquity* 65:725–738.
2003 Chaîne Opératoire and Reduction Sequence. *Lithic Technology* 28:95–105.
Shott, M. J., and J. A. M. Ballenger
2007 Biface Reduction and the Measurement of Dalton Curation: A Southeastern Case Study. *American Antiquity* 72:153–175.
Shott, M. J., and M. C. Nelson
2008 Lithic Reduction, Its Measurement, and Implications: Comments on the Volume. In *Lithic Technology: Measures of Production, Use, and Curation,* edited by W. Andrefsky Jr., pp. 23–48. Cambridge University Press, Cambridge.
Simek, J. F.
1994 The Organization of Lithic Technology and Evolution: Notes from the Continent. In *The Organization of North American Prehistoric Chipped Stone Tool Technologies,* edited by P. J. Carr, pp. 118–122. Archaeological Series No. 7. International Monographs in Prehistory, Ann Arbor, Michigan.
Simek, J. F., J. D. Franklin, and S. C. Sherwood
1998 The Context of Early Southeastern Prehistoric Cave Art: A Report on the Archaeology of 3rd Unnamed Cave. *American Antiquity* 63:663–677.

Smallwood, A. M.
2006 Use-wear Analysis of the Clovis Biface Collection from the Gault Site in Central Texas. Unpublished Master's thesis, Department of Anthropology, Texas A&M University, College Station.

Smith, E. E., and N. Toth
1990 A Microwear Analysis of Paleoindian "Socketed" Endscrapers from South-central Indiana. *Current Research in the Pleistocene* 7:77–79.

Soffer, O., and N. D. Praslov (editors)
1993 *From Kostenki to Clovis: Upper Paleolithic–Paleo-Indian Adaptations.* Plenum Press, New York.

Solberger, J. B., and L. Patterson
1976 The Myth of Bipolar Flaking Industries. *Newsletter of Lithic Technology* 5(3): 40–42.

Solecki, R. S.
1955 Lamellar Flakes Versus Blades, a Reappraisal. *American Antiquity* 20:393–394.

Soressi, M., and M. A. Hays
2003 Manufacture, Transport, and Use of Mousterian Bifaces: A Case Study from the Perigord (France). In *Multiple Approaches to the Study of Bifacial Technologies,* edited by M. Soressi and H. L. Dibble, pp. 125–147. University Museum Monograph 115. University of Pennsylvania Museum of Archaeology and Anthropology, Philadelphia.

Stafford, C. R., R. L. Richards, and C. M. Anslinger
2000 The Bluegrass Fauna and Changes in Middle Holocene Hunter-Gatherer Foraging in the Southern Midwest. *American Antiquity* 65:317–336.

Stahle, D. W., and J. E. Dunn
1982 An Analysis and Application of the Size Distribution of Waste Flakes from the Manufacture of Bifacial Stone Tools. *World Archaeology* 14:84–97.

Stapert, D.
1976 Some Natural Surface Modifications on Flint in the Netherlands. *Paleohistoria* 18:7–41.

Stein, J. K.
1993 Scale in Archaeology, Geosciences, and Geoarchaeology. In *Effects of Scale on Archaeological and Geoscientific Perspectives,* edited by J. K. Stein and A. R. Linse, pp. 1–10. The Geological Society of America, Inc., Boulder, Colorado.

Steponaitis, V. P., J. D. Irwin, T. E. McReynolds, and C. Moore (editors)
2006 *Stone Quarries and Sourcing in the Carolina Slate Belt.* Research Report Number 25. University of North Carolina Research Laboratories of Archaeology, Chapel Hill.

Stevenson, M. G.
1985 The Formation of Artifact Assemblages at Workshops/Habitation Sites: Models from Peace Point in Northern Alberta. *American Antiquity* 50:63–81.
1991 Beyond the Formation of Hearth-Associated Artifact Assemblages. In *The Interpretation of Archaeological Spatial Patterning,* edited by E. M. Kroll and T. D. Price, pp. 269–300. Plenum Press, New York.

Sullivan, A. P., and K. C. Rozen

1985 Debitage Analysis and Archaeological Interpretation. *American Antiquity* 50:755–779.

Surovell, T. A.

2009 *Toward a Behavioral Ecology of Lithic Technology: Cases from Paleoindian Archaeology.* University of Arizona Press, Tucson.

Swanton, J. R.

1946 *Indians of the Southeastern United States.* Bureau of American Ethnology Bulletin No. 137. Smithsonian Institution, Washington, D.C.

Terry, K., W. Andrefsky Jr., M. V. Konstantinov

2009 Raw Material Durability, Function, and Retouch in the Upper Paleolithic of the Transbikal Region, Siberia. In *Lithic Materials and Paleolithic Societies,* edited by B. Adams and B. Blades, pp. 256–259. Wiley-Blackwell, West Sussex, U.K.

Thacker, P. T.

2006 Local Raw Material Exploitation and Prehistoric Hunter-Gatherer Mobility. In *Archaeology and Ethnoarchaeology of Mobility,* edited by F. Sellet, R. Greaves, and P.-L. Yu, pp. 240–261. University Press of Florida, Gainesville.

Thomas, D. H.

1969 Great Basin Hunting Patterns: A Quantitative Method for Treating Faunal Remains. *American Antiquity* 34:392–401.

Tomenchuk, J., and P. L. Stork

1997 Two Newly Recognized Paleoindian Tool Types: Single- and Double-Scribe Compass Gravers and Coring Gravers. *American Antiquity* 62:508–522.

Tomka, S. A.

2001 The Effect of Processing Requirements on Reduction Strategies and Tool Form: A New Perspective. In *Lithic Debitage: Context, Form, Meaning,* edited by W. Andrefsky Jr., pp. 207–225. University of Utah Press, Salt Lake City.

Torrence, R.

1983 Time Budgeting and Hunter-Gatherer Technology. In *Hunter-Gatherer Economy in Prehistory,* edited by G. Bailey, pp. 11–22. Cambridge University Press, Cambridge.

1994 Strategies for Moving on in Lithic Studies. In *The Organization of North American Prehistoric Chipped Stone Tool Technologies,* edited by P. J. Carr, pp. 123–131. Archaeological Series No. 7. International Monographs in Prehistory, Ann Arbor, Michigan.

Torrence, R. (editor)

1989 *Time, Energy, and Stone Tools.* Cambridge University Press, Cambridge.

Tostevin, G. B.

2006 Levels of Theory and Social Practice in the Reduction Sequence and Chaîne Opératoire Methods of Lithic Analysis. In Reduction Sequence, Chaîne Opératoire, and Other Methods: The Epistemologies of Different Approaches to Lithic Analysis. Electronic symposium held at the 71st Annual Meeting of the Society for American Archaeology, San Juan, Puerto Rico.

Towner, R. H.

1984 The Effects of Heat Treatment on Chert Tool Edge Damage. In *Lithic Resource Procurement: Proceedings from the Second Conference on Prehistoric Chert Ex-*

ploitation, edited by S. C. Vehik, pp. 199–208. Occasional Paper No. 4. Center for Archaeological Investigations, Southern Illinois University, Carbondale.

Towner, R. H., and M. Warburton
1990 Projectile Point Rejuvenation: A Technological Analysis. *Journal of Field Archaeology* 17:311–321.

Tringham, R., G. Cooper, G. Odell, B. Voytek, and A. Whitman
1974 Experimentation in the Formation of Edge Damage: A New Approach to Lithic Analysis. *Journal of Field Archaeology* 1:171–196.

Troels-Smith, J. J.
1961 Et Pileskaft fra Tidlig Maglemosetid. *Aarböger,* pp. 122–146.

Underwood, J. R., E. Peacock, S. E. Price, and P. J. Carr
2007 *A Synthesis of Archaeological Investigations at the Paxton Mound Site (22LI504), Lincoln County, Mississippi.* Draft Report. Mississippi Department of Transportation, Jackson.

Unger-Hamilton, R.
1984 The Formation of Use-wear Polish on Flint: Beyond the "Deposit Versus Abrasion" Controversy. *Journal Archaeological Science* 11:91–98.

Vallin, L., B. Masson, and J. Caspar
2001 Taphonomy at Hermies, France: A Mousterian Knapping Site in a Loessics Context. *Journal of Field Archaeology* 28:419–436.

Vaughan, P. C.
1985 *Use-Wear Analysis of Flaked Stone Tools.* University of Arizona Press, Tucson.

Vickery, K. D.
1976 An Approach to Inferring Archaeological Site Variability. Unpublished Ph.D. dissertation, Department of Anthropology, Indiana University, Bloomington.
1980 Preliminary Definition of Archaic "Study Units" in Southwestern Ohio. Ms. on file, Ohio Historic Preservation Office, Ohio Historical Society, Columbus.

Villa, P., and J. Courtin
1983 The Interpretation of Stratified Sites: A View from Underground. *Journal of Archaeological Science* 10:267–281.

Walsh, K.
2005 Risk and Marginality at High Altitudes: New Interpretations from Fieldwork on the Faravel Plateau, Hautes-Alpes. *Antiquity* 79:289–305.

Wandsnider, L.
1996 Describing and Comparing Archaeological Spatial Structures. *Journal of Archaeological Method and Theory* 3(4):319–384.

Ward, H. T., and R. P. S. Davis
1999 *Time Before History: The Archaeology of North Carolina.* University of North Carolina Press, Chapel Hill.

Waters, M. R., S. L. Forman, T. W. Stafford, and J. Foss
2009 Geoarchaeological Investigations at the Topper and Big Pine Tree Sites, Allendale County, South Carolina. *Journal of Archaeological Science* 36:1300–1311.

Waters, M. R., C. D. Pevny, and D. L. Carlson (editors)
2011 *A Clovis Workshop in Central Texas: Archaeological Investigations of Excavation Area 8 at the Gault Site.* Texas A&M University Press, College Station.

Watson, P. J.

2001 Ridges, Rises, and Rocks; Caves, Coves, Terraces, and Hollows: Appalachian Archaeology at the Millennium. In *Archaeology of the Appalachian Highlands,* edited by L. P. Sullivan and S. C. Prezzano, pp. 319–322. University of Tennessee Press, Knoxville.

Webb, C. H., J. L. Shiner, and E. W. Roberts

1971 The John Pearce Site (16CD56): A San Patrice Site in Caddo Parish, Louisiana. *Bulletin of the Texas Archeological Society* 42:1–49.

Westerby, E.

1927 *Stenalderbopladser ved Klampenborg.* Copenhagen.

White, A. M, L. R. Binford, and M. L. Papworth

1963 *Miscellaneous Studies in Typology and Classification.* Anthropological Papers No. 19. Museum of Anthropology, University of Michigan, Ann Arbor.

White, J. P.

1968 Fabricators, *Outils Escailles,* or Scalar Cores? *Mankind* 6:658–666.

Whittaker, J. C.

1994 *Flintknapping: Making and Understanding Stone Tools.* University of Texas Press, Austin.

Wholey, H. A.

2009 A Population Approach to the Middle Atlantic Archaic. *North American Archaeologist* 30:1–21.

Wiederhold, J. E.

2004 Toward the Standardization of Use-Wear Studies: Constructing an Analogue to Prehistoric Hide Work. Unpublished Master's thesis, Department of Anthropology, Texas A&M University, College Station.

Williams, J. P., and W. Andrefsky Jr.

2009 Technology, Style and Practice: An Examination of Debitage. Poster presented at the 74th Annual Meeting of the Society for American Archaeology, Atlanta.

Wilmsen, E. N.

1970 *Lithic Analysis and Cultural Inference: A Paleo-Indian Case.* Anthropological Papers No. 16. University of Arizona, Tucson.

Wilson, J. K., and W. Andrefsky Jr.

2008 Exploring Retouch on Bifaces: Unpacking Production, Resharpening, and Hammer Type. In *Lithic Technology: Measures of Production, Use, and Curation,* edited by W. Andrefsky Jr., pp. 86–105. Cambridge University Press, Cambridge.

Winters, H. D.

1969 *The Riverton Culture.* Monograph No. 1. Illinois Archaeological Survey, University of Illinois, Urbana.

Winton, V.

2004 *A Study of Paleolithic Artefacts from Selected Sites on Deposits Mapped as Clay-with-Flints of Southern England.* BAR British Series 360. British Archaeological Reports, Oxford.

Witthoft, J.

1967 Glazed Polish on Flint Tools. *American Antiquity* 32:383–388.

Wurz, S.
2002 Variability in the Middle Stone Age Lithic Sequence, 115,000–60,000 Years Ago at Klasies River, South Africa. *Journal of Archaeological Science* 29:1001–1015.

Yahnig, C.
2004 Lithic Technology of the Little River Clovis Complex, Christian County, Kentucky. In *New Perspectives on the First Americans,* edited by B. T. Lepper and R. Bonnichsen, pp. 111–117. Texas A&M University Press, College Station.

Yedlowski, J. L., and F. J. Vento
1992 Flaked Stone Raw Material. In *Prehistory of the Bay Springs Rockshelters, Tombigbee River Multi-R Resource District, Tishomingo County, Mississippi: Vol. 3. Lithic Artifacts,* edited by J. L. Yedlowski, pp. 387–410. Report on file at the Mississippi Department of Archives and History, Jackson.

Yonekura, K., H. Hasegawa, A. Hotta, and T. Suzuki
2008 A Novel Approach to Studies of Prehistoric Exploitation of Stone Tool Materials Using Material Composition, Surface Morphology, Microstructure and Mechanical Properties. *Archaeometry* 50:727–746.

Young, D., and D. B. Bamforth
1990 On the Macroscopic Identification of Used Flakes. *American Antiquity* 55:403–409.

Contributors

William Andrefsky Jr., Edward R. Meyer Distinguished Professor, Department of Anthropology, Washington State University.

Andrew P. Bradbury, Cultural Resource Analysts, Inc., Lexington.

Philip J. Carr, Department of Sociology, Anthropology, and Social Work, University of South Alabama.

Carolyn Conklin, Department of Anthropology, Wake Forest University.

D. Randall Cooper, Cultural Resource Analysts, Inc., Lexington.

Jason L. Edmonds, Department of Anthropology, University of California, Davis.

Jay D. Franklin, Department of Sociology and Anthropology, East Tennessee State University.

Albert C. Goodyear III, South Carolina Institute of Archaeology and Anthropology.

Joël Hardison, USDA Forest Service, Uwharrie National Forest.

Maureen A. Hays, Department of Sociology and Anthropology, College of Charleston.

Lucinda M. Langston, Department of Sociology and Anthropology, East Tennessee State University.

D. Shane Miller, Department of Anthropology, University of Arizona.

George H. Odell (deceased), Department of Anthropology, University of Tulsa.

Charlotte D. Pevny, R. C. Goodwin and Associates, New Orleans.

Tara L. Potts, Center for Archaeological Studies, University of South Alabama.

Sarah E. Price, Center for Archaeological Studies, University of South Alabama.

Douglas Sain, Department of Anthropology, University of Tennessee.

Sarah C. Sherwood, Department of Anthropology, Sewanee: The University of the South.

Ashley M. Smallwood, Department of Anthropology, Texas A & M University.

Paul T. Thacker, Department of Anthropology, Wake Forest University.

Index